CONFIGURING PROJECT MANAGEMENT AND ACCOUNTING WITHIN DYNAMICS AX 2012

BY MURRAY FIFE

ISBN-13: 978-1502985262

ISBN-10: 1502985268

Preface

What You Need For This Guide

All the examples shown in this blueprint were done with the Microsoft Dynamics AX 2012 virtual machine image that was downloaded from the Microsoft CustomerSource or PartnerSource site. If you don't have your own installation of Microsoft Dynamics AX 2012, you can also use the images found on the Microsoft Learning Download Center or deployed through Lifecycle Services. The following list of software from the virtual image was leveraged within this guide:

- Microsoft Dynamics AX 2012 R3

Even though all the preceding software was used during the development and testing of the recipes in this book, they may also work on earlier versions of the software with minor tweaks and adjustments, and should also work on later versions without any changes.

Errata

Although we have taken every care to ensure the accuracy of our content, mistakes do happen. If you find a mistake in one of our books—maybe a mistake in the text or the code—we would be grateful if you would report this to us. By doing so, you can save other readers from frustration and help us improve subsequent versions of this book. If you find any errata, please report them by emailing editor@dynamicsaxcompanions.com.

Piracy

Piracy of copyright material on the Internet is an ongoing problem across all media. If you come across any illegal copies of our works, in any form, on the Internet, please provide us with the location address or website name immediately so that we can pursue a remedy.

Please contact us at legal@dynamicsaxcompanions.com with a link to the suspected pirated material.

We appreciate your help in protecting our authors, and our ability to bring you valuable content.

Questions

You can contact us at help@dynamicsaxcompanions.com if you are having a problem with any aspect of the book, and we will do our best to address it.

eBook License Agreement

Murray Fife (the Author) agrees to grant, and the user of the eBook agrees to accept, a nonexclusive license to use the eBook under the terms and conditions of this eBook License Agreement ("Agreement"). Your use of the eBook constitutes your agreement to the terms and conditions set forth in this Agreement. This Agreement, or any part thereof, cannot be changed, waived, or discharged other than by a statement in writing signed by you and Murray Fife. Please read the entire Agreement carefully.

1. **eBook Usage.** The eBook may be used by one user on any device. The user of the eBook shall be subject to all of the terms of this Agreement, whether or not the user was the purchaser.

2. **Printing.** You may occasionally print a few pages of the eBook's text (but not entire sections), which may include sending the printed pages to a third party in the normal course of your business, but you must warn the recipient in writing that copyright law prohibits the recipient from redistributing the eBook content to anyone else. Other than the above, you may not print pages and/or distribute eBook content to others.

3. **Copyright, Use and Resale Prohibitions.** The Author retains all rights not expressly granted to you in this Agreement. The software, content, and related documentation in the eBook are protected by copyright laws and international copyright treaties, as well as other intellectual property laws and treaties. Nothing in this Agreement constitutes a waiver of the authors rights. The Author will not be responsible for performance problems due to circumstances beyond its reasonable control. Other than as stated in this Agreement, you may not copy, print, modify, remove, delete, augment, add to, publish, transmit, sell, resell, license, create derivative works from, or in any way exploit any of the eBook's content, in whole or in part, in print or electronic form, and you may not aid or permit others to do so. The unauthorized use or distribution of copyrighted or other proprietary content is illegal and could subject the purchaser to substantial damages. Purchaser will be liable for any damage resulting from any violation of this Agreement.

4. **No Transfer.** This license is not transferable by the eBook purchaser unless such transfer is approved in advance by the Author.

5. **Disclaimer.** The eBook, or any support given by the Author are in no way substitutes for assistance from legal, tax, accounting, or other qualified professionals. If legal advice or other expert assistance is required, the services of a competent professional person should be sought.

6. **Limitation of Liability.** The eBook is provided "as is" and the Author does not make any warranty or representation, either express or implied, to the eBook, including its quality, accuracy, performance, merchantability, or fitness for a particular purpose. You assume the entire risk as to the results and performance of the eBook. The Author does not warrant, guarantee, or make any representations regarding the use of, or the results obtained with, the eBook in terms of accuracy, correctness or reliability. In no event will the Author be liable for indirect, special, incidental, or consequential damages arising out of delays, errors, omissions, inaccuracies, or the use or inability to use the eBook, or for interruption of the eBook, from whatever cause. This will apply even if the Author has been advised that the possibility of such damage exists. Specifically, the Author is not responsible for any costs, including those incurred as a result of lost profits or revenue, loss of data, the cost of recovering such programs or data, the cost of any substitute program, claims by third parties, or similar costs. Except for the Author's indemnification obligations in Section 7.2, in no case will the Author's liability exceed the amount of license fees paid.

7. **Hold Harmless / Indemnification.**
7.1 You agree to defend, indemnify and hold the Author and any third party provider harmless from and against all third party claims and damages (including reasonable attorneys' fees) regarding your use of the eBook, unless the claims or damages are due to the Author's or any third party provider's gross negligence or willful misconduct or arise out of an allegation for which the Author is obligated to indemnify you.
7.2. The Author shall defend, indemnify and hold you harmless at the Author's expense in any suit, claim or proceeding brought against you alleging that your use of the eBook delivered to you hereunder directly infringes a United States patent, copyright, trademark, trade secret, or other third party proprietary right, provided the Author is (i) promptly notified, (ii) given the assistance required at the Author's expense, and (iii) permitted to retain legal counsel of the Author's choice and to direct the defense. The Author also agrees to pay any damages and costs awarded against you by final judgment of a court of last resort in any such suit or any agreed settlement amount on account of any such alleged infringement, but the Author will have no liability for settlements or costs incurred without its consent. Should your use of any such eBook be enjoined, or in the event that the Author desires to minimize its liability hereunder, the Author will, at its option and expense, (i) substitute a fully equivalent non-infringing eBook for the infringing item; (ii) modify the infringing item so that it no longer infringes but remains substantially equivalent; or (iii) obtain for you the right to continue use of such item. If none of the foregoing is feasible, the Author will terminate your access to the eBook and refund to you the applicable fees paid by you for the infringing item(s). THE FOREGOING STATES THE ENTIRE LIABILITY OF THE AUTHOR AND YOUR SOLE REMEDY FOR INFRINGEMENT OR FOR ANY BREACH OF WARRANTY OF NON-INFRINGEMENT, EXPRESS OR IMPLIED. THIS INDEMNITY WILL NOT APPLY TO ANY ALLEGED INFRINGEMENT BASED UPON A COMBINATION OF OTHER SOFTWARE OR INFORMATION WITH THE EBOOK WHERE THE EBOOK WOULD NOT HAVE OTHERWISE INFRINGED ON ITS OWN.

Table Of Contents

INTRODUCTION

The Project Accounting module within Dynamics AX is a great module for anyone that is trying to track time and costs against projects within the organization. It is especially useful because it is fully integrated with all of the other foundation areas of the product like Payables, Receivables, Inventory, the General Ledger and much more so that as you track costs within them they are automatically applied to the project and as you create transactions within Project Accounting, then they are automatically updated within the foundation modules.

When you add in all of the additional functions that are available within the module like collaboration workspaces, worker assignment and scheduling, integration with MS Project and also Timesheets & Travel and Expense entry through portals, then this is definitely a module that you need to get to know.

In this book we will look at all of the core features within the Project Management and Accounting module of Dynamics AX and show you how to set up and manage simple projects without even breaking a sweat.

CONFIGURING PROJECT MANAGEMENT AND ACCOUNTING CONTROLS

Before we start configuring our Projects we need to configure a few controls within the Project Management and Accounting modules so that everything runs smoothly. These include some new Journals within Dynamics AX for tracking the projects, and also the configuration of the project templates and groupings.

In this chapter we will walk through the core configurations that you need to set up.

Configuring Approval Codes

Project journals within Dynamics AX can have a number of different types of approvals attached to them, so the first configuration that we will start with is to configure a couple of simple **Approval Codes** that we will be able to assign to them.

Configuring Approval Codes

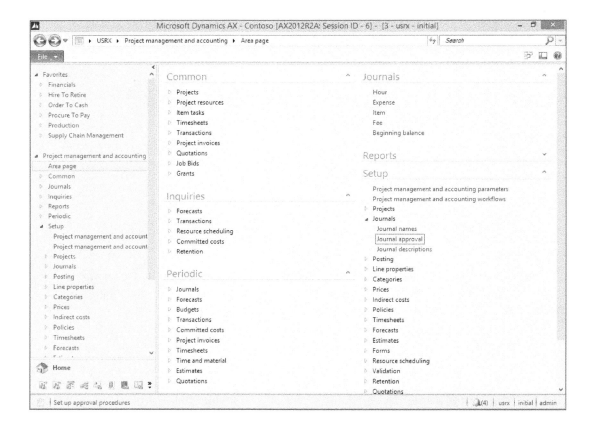

To do this, click on the **Journal Approval** menu item within the **Journals** folder of the **Setup** group of the **Project Management And Accounting** area page.

Configuring Approval Codes

When the **Journal Approval** maintenance form is displayed, click on the **New** button in the menu bar to create a new record.

Configuring Approval Codes

Set the **Approve** field to **APPROVAL** and the **Name** to **Approval Required.**

Configuring Approval Codes

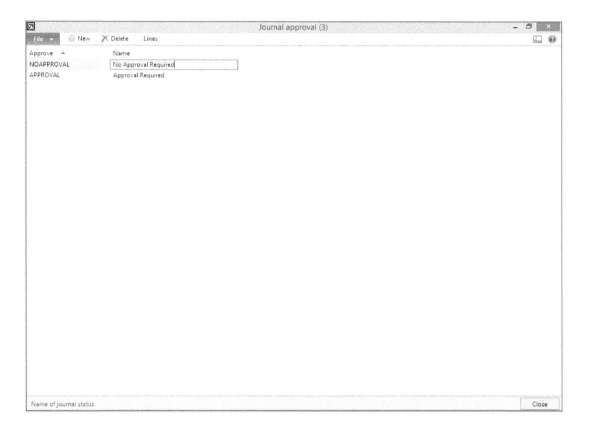

Then click on the **New** button in the menu bar again to create another record and set the **Approve** field to **NOAPPROVAL** and the **Name** to **No Approval Required**.

After you have done that, just click on the **Close** button to exit from the form.

Configuring Default Journal Names

Next we need to configure a few **Journal Names** for the Project Management and Accounting module to use. These will be used to track the Timesheet and Travel & Expense transactions, and also budget transactions later on.

Configuring Default Journal Names

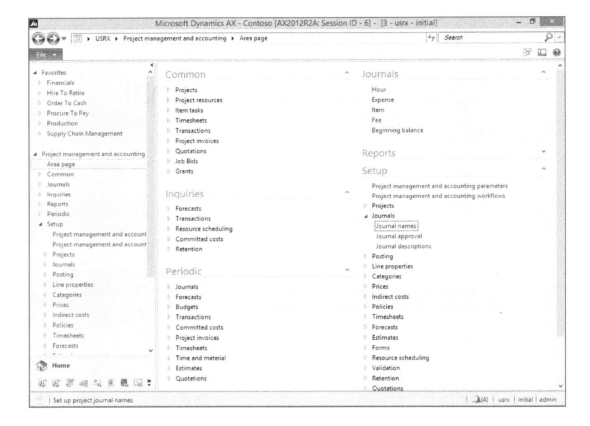

To do this, click on the **Journal Names** menu item within the **Journals** folder of the **Setup** group of the **Project Management And Accounting** area page.

Configuring Default Journal Names

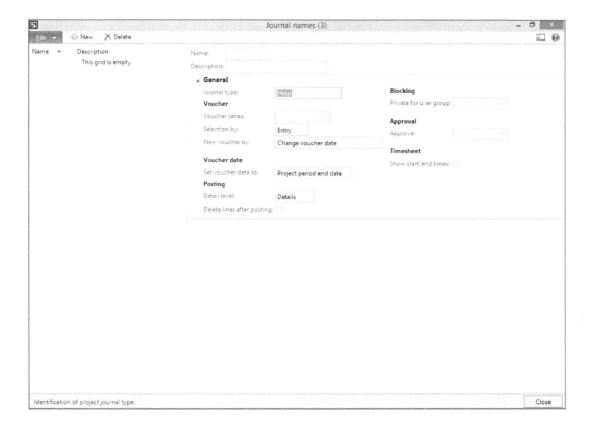

When the **Journal Names** maintenance form is displayed, click on the **New** button in the menu bar to create a new record.

Configuring Default Journal Names

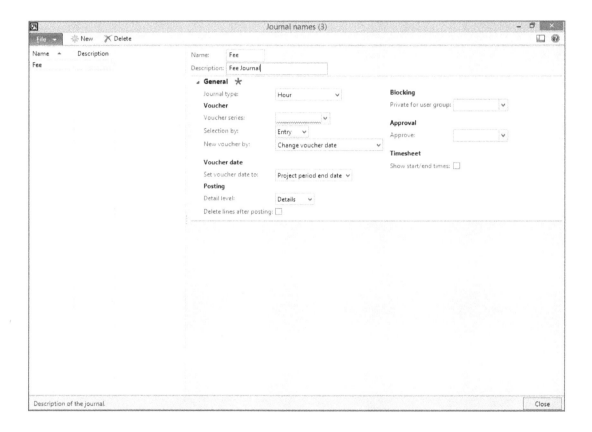

We will start off by creating a journal to track fees and charges, so set the **Name** to *Fee* and the **Description** to *Fee Journal*.

Configuring Default Journal Names

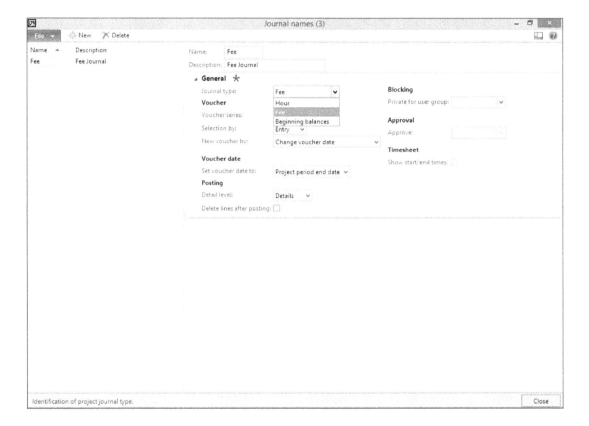

Then click on the **Journal Type** dropdown and select the *Fee* value.

Configuring Default Journal Names

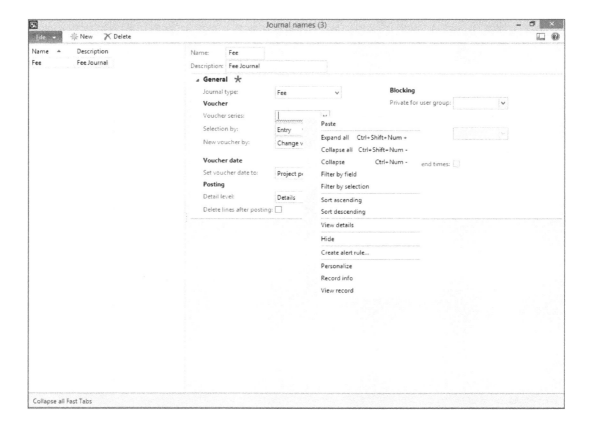

We also need to have a **Voucher Series** associated with the Journal to give it a unique ID. To create one, right-mouse-click on the **Voucher Series** field and select te **View Details** menu item.

Configuring Default Journal Names

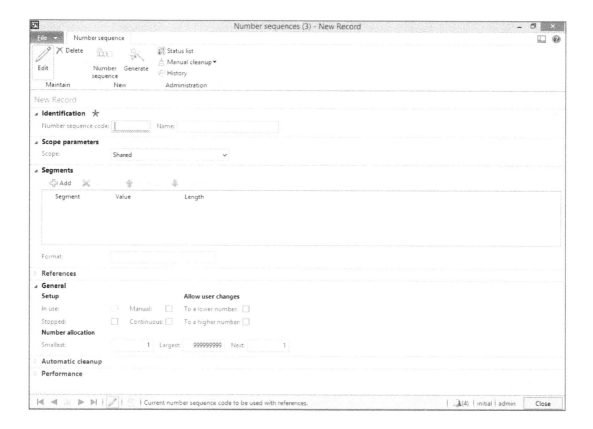

When the **Number Series** maintenance form is displayed, click on the **Number Sequence** button within the **New** group of the **Number Sequences** ribbon bar to create a new number sequence.

Configuring Default Journal Names

Set the Number Sequence Code to ProjFee_01 and the Name to Project Fee Journal.

Configuring Default Journal Names

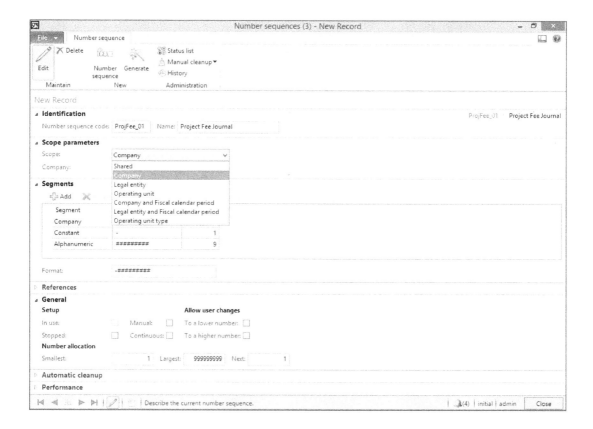

Then click on the **Scope** fields dropdown list and select the **Company** option to tell the system that this number sequence will just apply to the current company.

Configuring Default Journal Names

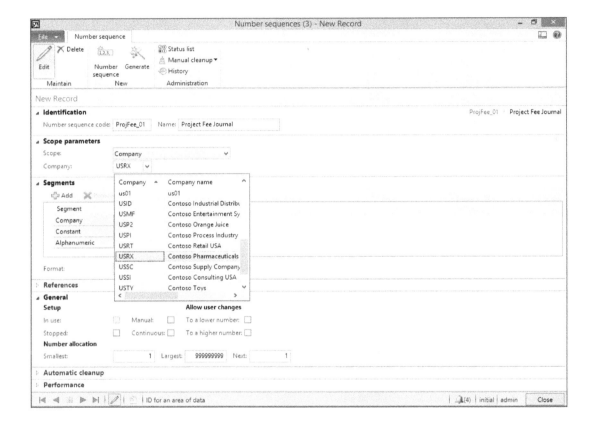

Then select your **Company** from the dropdown list.

Configuring Default Journal Names

Within the **Segments** section of the number sequences, click on the **Company** segment and the company will automatically be populated. Then set the **Constant** segment value to be **–PFJL-** so that the journal will have a unique ID.

Configuring Default Journal Names

Then check the **Continuous** flag on the number sequence.

After you have done that then click the **Close** button to return to the Project Journal.

Configuring Default Journal Names

Now click on the **Voucher Series** dropdown list and select the new number sequence that you just created.

Configuring Default Journal Names

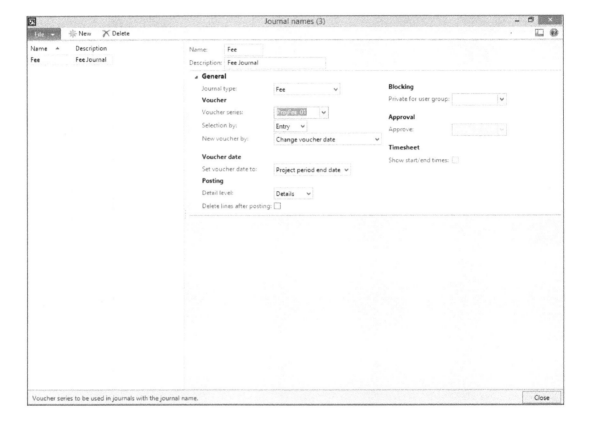

Now you have a **Fee Journal** Journal.

We need to create a few more though, so click on the **New** button within the menu bar to create a new record.

Configuring Default Journal Names

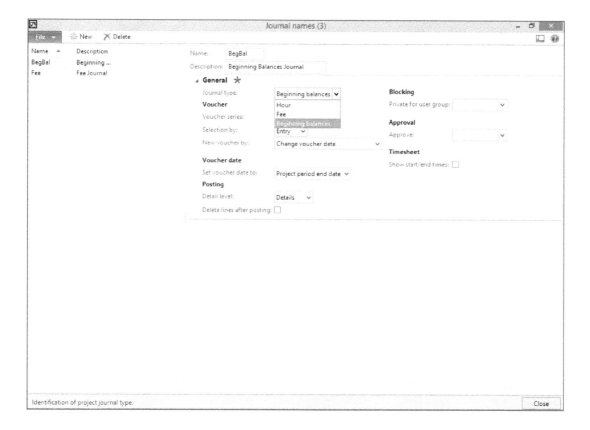

For the next journal, set the **Name** to **BegBal**, the **Name** to **Beginning Balance Journal** and then select the **Beginning Balance** value within the **Journal Type** dropdown list.

Configuring Default Journal Names

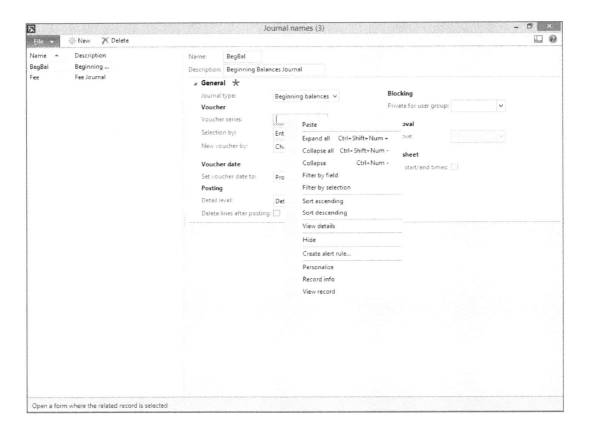

Right-mouse-click on the **Voucher Series** again and select the **View Details** menu item.

Configuring Default Journal Names

When the **Number Sequences** maintenance form is displayed, click on the **Number Sequence** button within the **New** group of the **Number Sequences** ribbon bar to create a new record.

For this number sequence, set the **Number Sequence Code** to **ProjBB_01**, the **Name** to **Project Beginning Balance Journal**, set the **Scope** to your current company, make the **Constant** unique by assigning it a value of **–PBJL-** and set the **Continuous** flag before clicking the **Close** button to exit from the form.

Configuring Default Journal Names

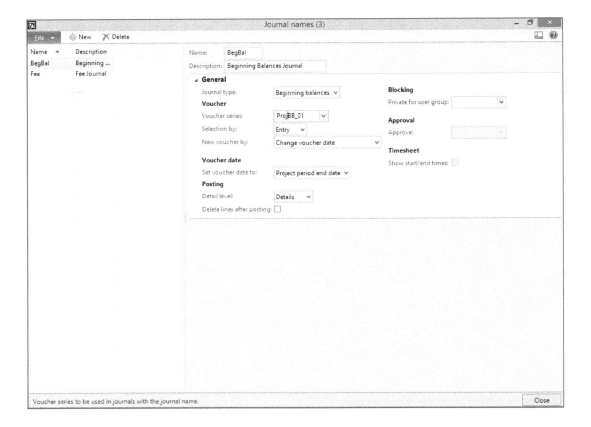

Now you can set the **Voucher Series** to be your newly created number sequence code.

Configuring Default Journal Names

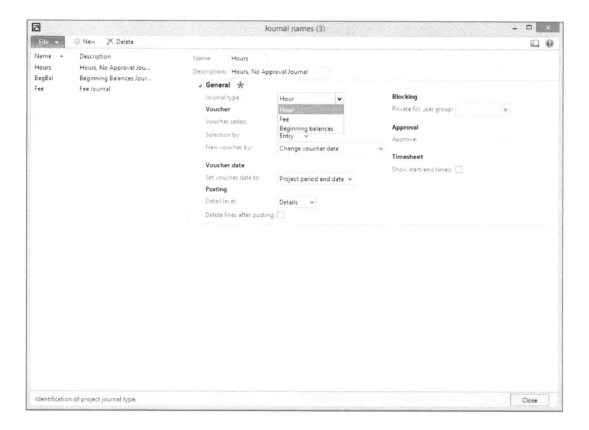

Next we will create some journals for reporting hours. We will create two though — one that does not require approval and another that does.

To start off with the first one, click on the **New** button within the menu bar to create a new record.

Set the **Name** to **Hours**, the **Name** to **Hours, No Approval Journal** and then select the **Hour** value within the **Journal Type** dropdown list.

Configuring Default Journal Names

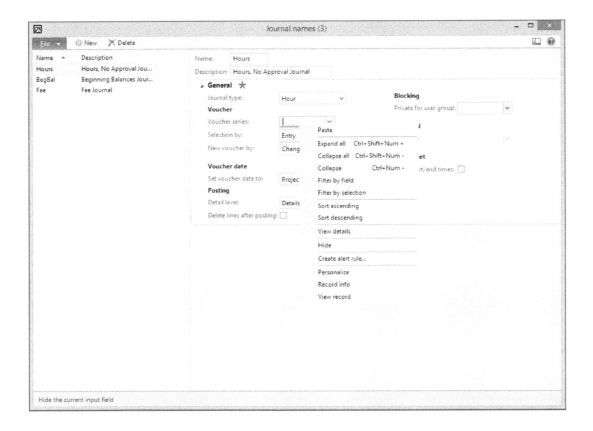

Right-mouse-click on the **Voucher Series** again and select the **View Details** menu item.

Configuring Default Journal Names

When the **Number Sequences** maintenance form is displayed, click on the **Number Sequence** button within the **New** group of the **Number Sequences** ribbon bar to create a new record.

For this number sequence, set the **Number Sequence Code** to **ProjHrs_01**, the **Name** to **Project Hours**, set the **Scope** to your current company, make the **Constant** unique by assigning it a value of **–PHJL-** and set the **Continuous** flag before clicking the **Close** button to exit from the form.

Configuring Default Journal Names

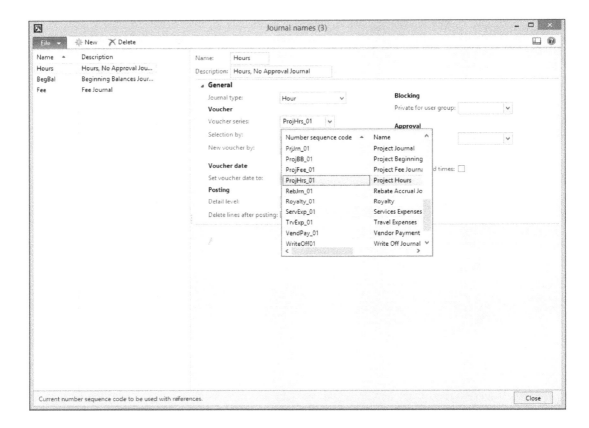

Now you can set the **Voucher Series** to be your newly created number sequence code for the project hours.

Configuring Default Journal Names

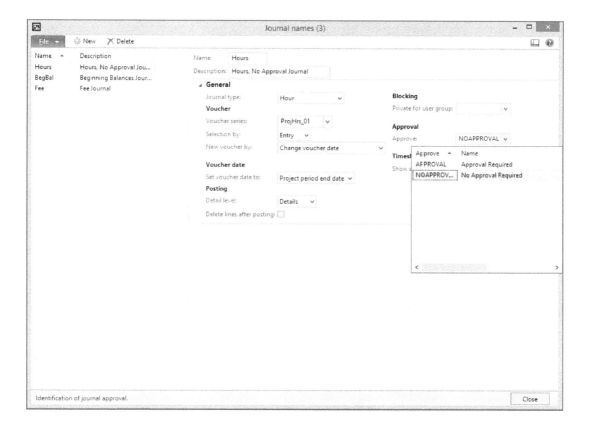

For this journal though set the **Approve** field to be **NOAPPROVAL.**

Configuring Default Journal Names

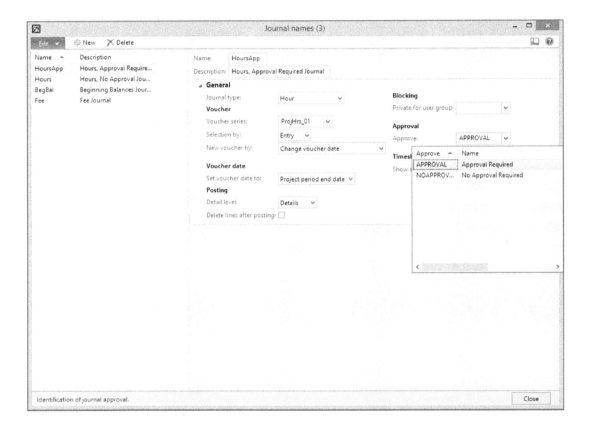

Then click on the **New** button within the menu bar to create a new record again.

This time Set the **Name** to **HoursApp**, the **Name** to **Hours, Approval Required Journal** and then select the **Hour** value within the **Journal Type** dropdown list.

For this journal, reuse the **ProjeHrs_01** number sequence within the **Voucher Series** field to keep the hours journals together.

And then select the **APPROVAL** value from the **Approve** fields dropdown list.

Configuring Default Journal Names

Now that you have all of the basic journals that you need, just click on the **Close** button to exit from the form.

Configuring Line Properties

The next code that we will configure is the **Line Properties** codes. These are use to control how the project lines are tracked and accounted for within the system, and we will configure a couple to track if the project lines are billable or non-billable.

Configuring Line Properties

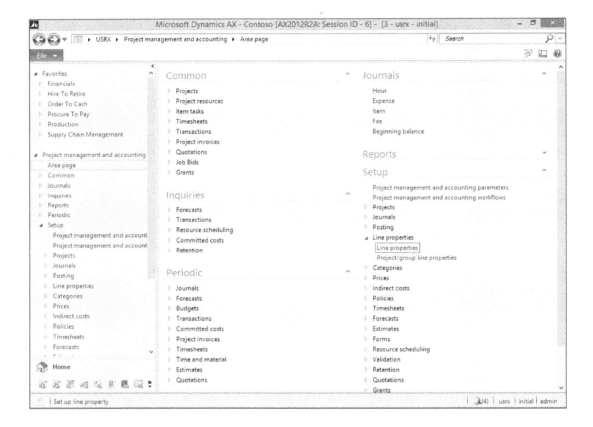

To do this, click on the **Line Properties** menu item within the **Line Properties** folder of the **Setup** group of the **Project Management And Accounting** area page.

Configuring Line Properties

When the **Line Properties** maintenance form is displayed, click on the **New** button in the menu bar to create a new record.

Configuring Line Properties

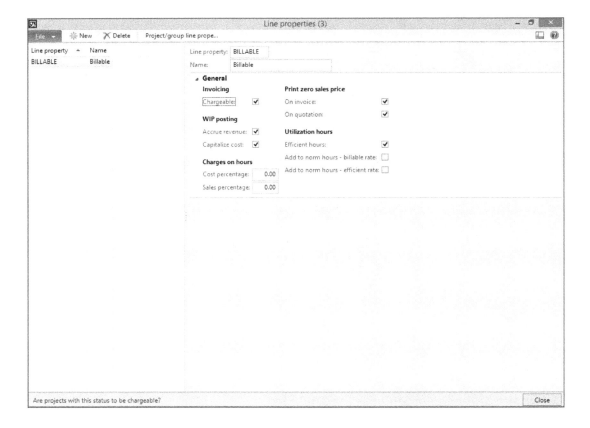

Set the **Line Property** field to **BILLABLE** and the **Name** to **Billable.**

Configuring Line Properties

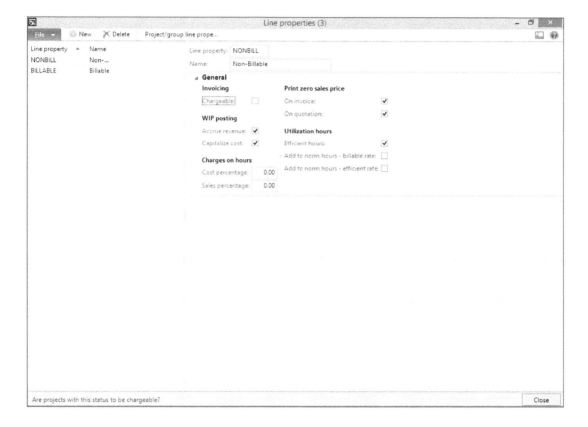

Then create another record by clicking on the **New** button in the menu bar.

Set the **Line Property** for this item to be **NONBILL** and the **Name** to be **Non-Billable**.

For this record though uncheck the **Chargeable** flag within the **Invoicing** group of the **General** fast tab.

Configuring Line Properties

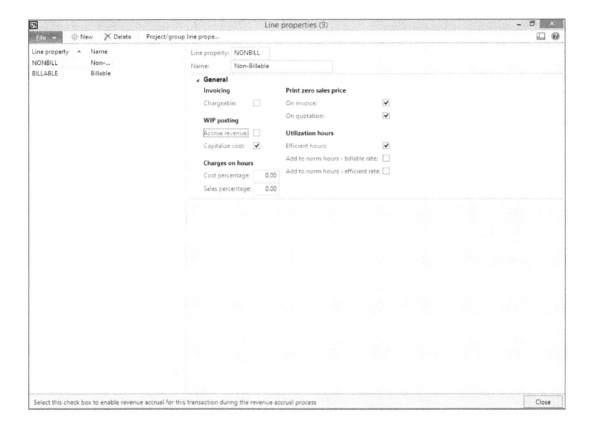

Also uncheck the **Accrue Revenue** flag.

After you have done that you can exit from the form by clicking on the **Close** button.

Configuring Cost Templates

Next we will configure a couple of **Cost Templates** for tracking costs by dollar amount and also by unit.

Configuring Cost Templates

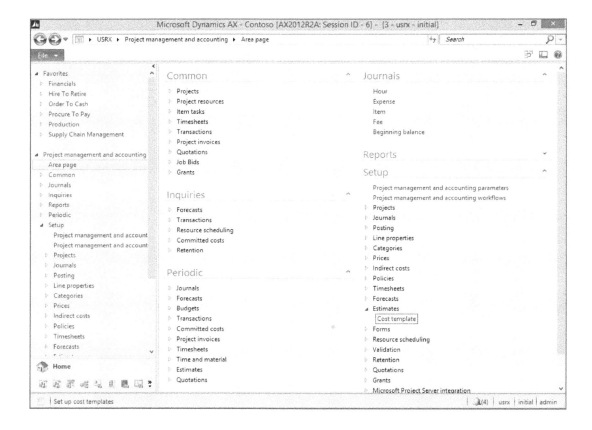

To do this, click on the **Cost Template** menu item within the **Estimates** folder of the **Setup** group within the **Project Management And Accounting** area page.

Configuring Cost Templates

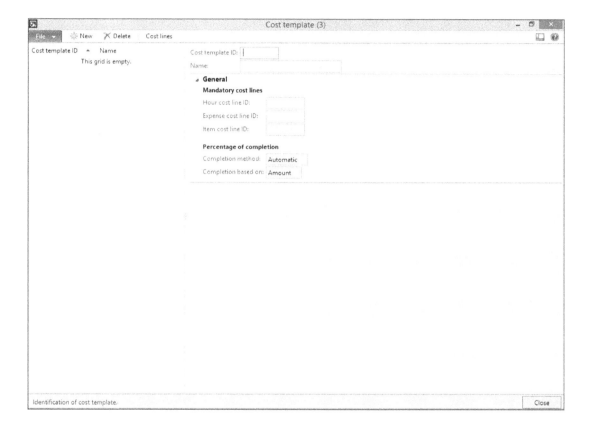

When the **Cost Template** maintenance form is displayed, click on the **New** button in the menu bar to create a new record.

Configuring Cost Templates

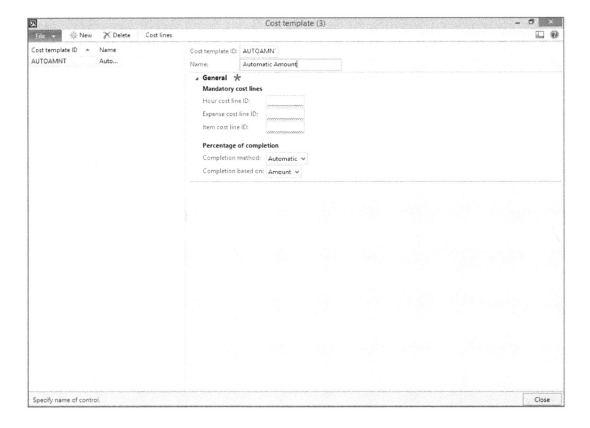

Set the **Cost Template ID** to be **AUTOAMT** and the **Name** to **Automatic Amount**.

Configuring Cost Templates

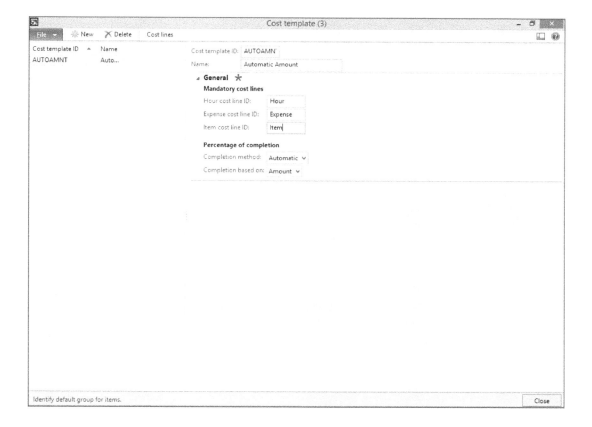

Then set the **Hour Cost Line ID** field to **Hour**, the **Expense Cost Line ID** field to **Expense,** and the **Item Cost Line ID** field to **Item**.

Configuring Cost Templates

Then click on the **New** button within the menu bar to create a new record for a Unit cost template and set the **Cost Template ID** to be **AUTOAMT** and the **Name** to **Automatic Amount**.

Configuring Cost Templates

Set the **Hour Cost Line ID** field to **Hour**, the **Expense Cost Line ID** field to **Expense,** and the **Item Cost Line ID** field to **Item**.

Configuring Cost Templates

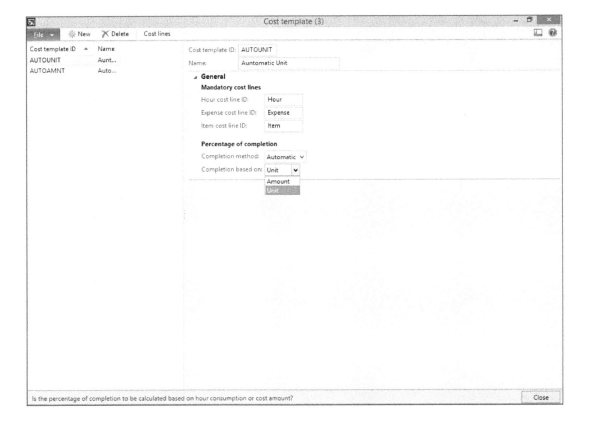

Then set the **Completion Based On** field to be **Unit**.

Configuring Cost Templates

Now you can exit from the form by clicking on the **Close** button.

Configuring Period Types

Next we will configure some period types that we will be able to use within out project estimates and time sheets.

Configuring Period Types

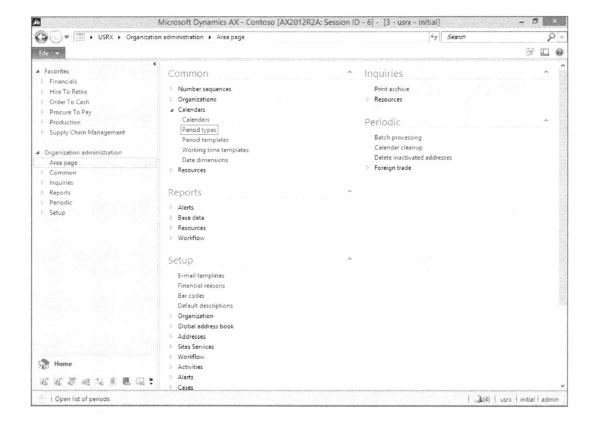

To do this, click on the **Period Types** menu item within the **Calendars** folder of the **Common** group of the **Organization Administration** area page.

Configuring Period Types

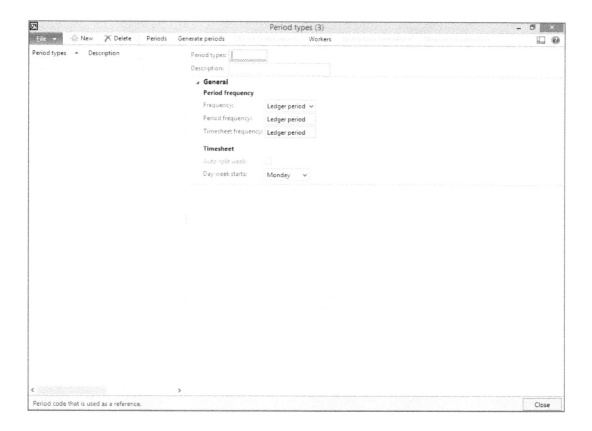

When the **Period Types** maintenance form is displayed, click on the **New** button in the menu bar to create a new record.

Configuring Period Types

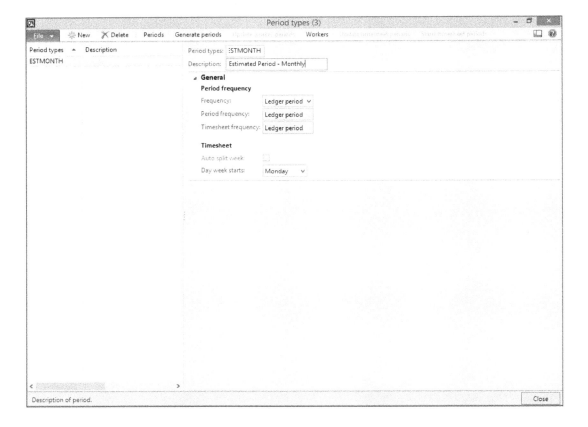

For the first record, set the **Period Type** code top bet **ESTMONTH** an the **Description** to **Estimated Period – Monthly**.

Configuring Period Types

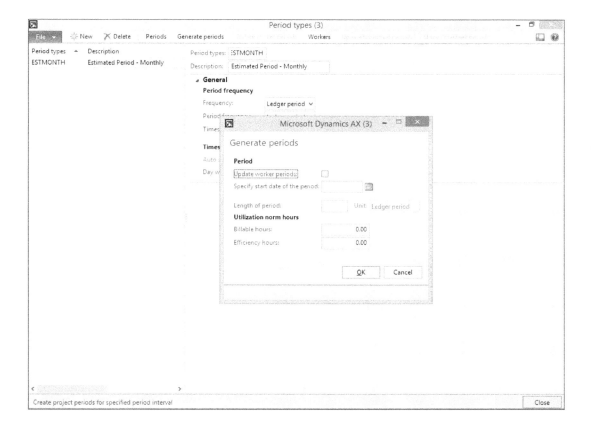

Then click on the **Generate Periods** button within the menu bar to start the period generation wizard.

Configuring Period Types

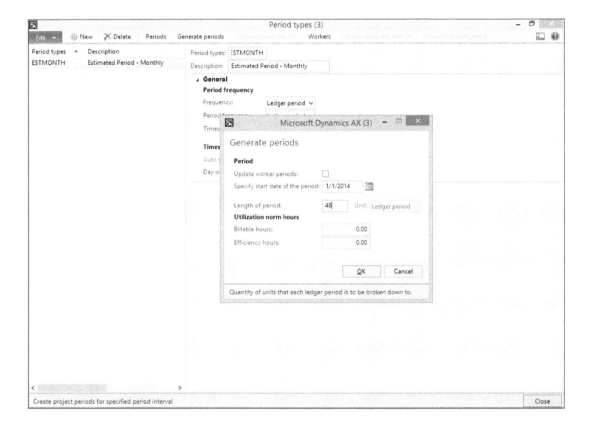

When the **Generate Periods** dialog box is displayed, set the **Start Date Of The Periods** and then set the number of periods that you want to create within the **Length Of Period** field.

When you have done that, click on the **OK** button to generate the periods.

Configuring Period Types

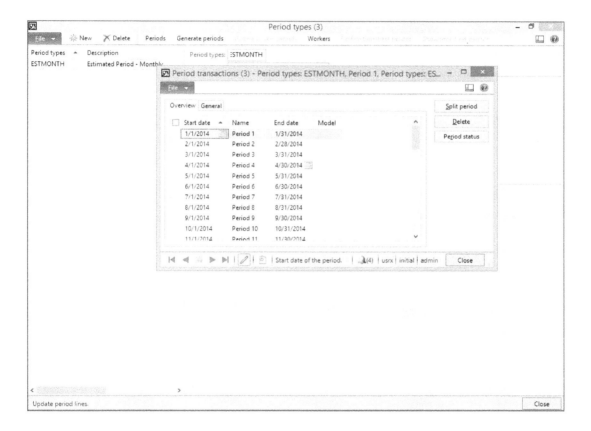

Tip: To see the periods that were generated, just click on the **Periods** button within the menu bar.

Configure Periods Types

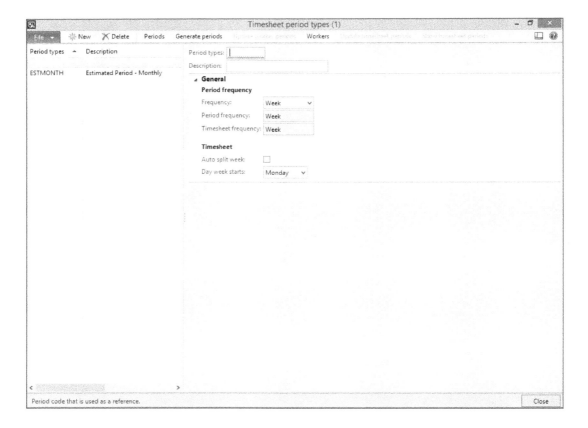

We will create another period code for our timesheets here as well, which is a little different because we want this one to have weekly buckets rather than the ledger periods that we used for the previous one.

To do this, click on the **New** button within the menu bar to create a new record.

Configure Periods Types

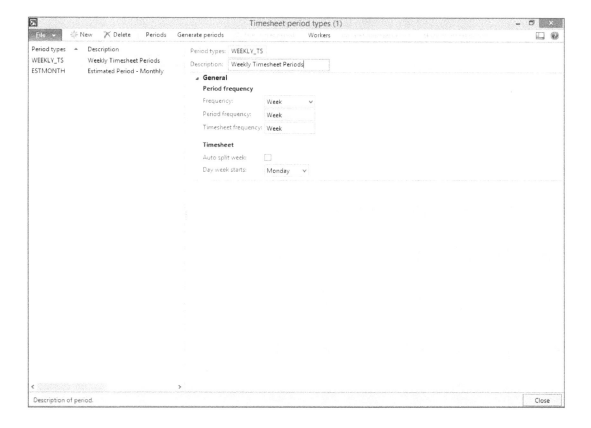

Set the **Period Type** code to **WEEKLY_TS** and the **Description** to be **Weekly Timesheet Periods**. Then set the **Frequency** code to **Week**.

Configure Periods Types

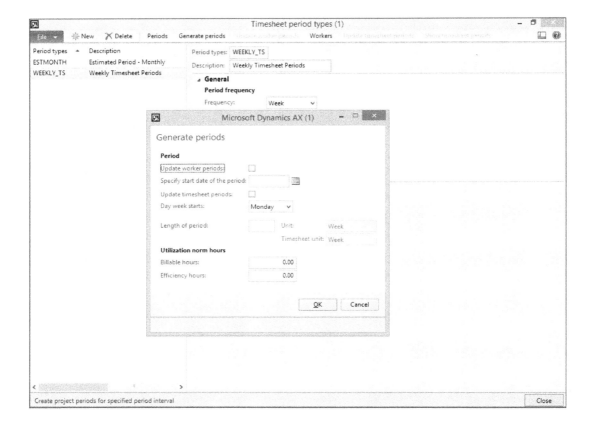

Then click on the **Generate Periods** button in the menu bar to open up the **Generate Periods** dialog box.

Configure Periods Types

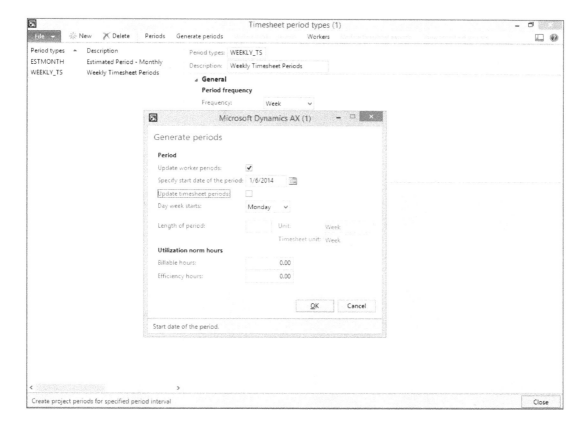

Set the **Start Date Of The Period** to be the first day of the week that you want to start your periods on.

Configure Periods Types

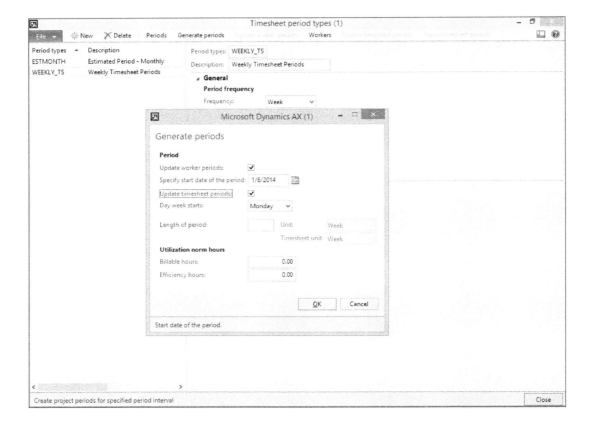

Also check the **Update Timesheet Periods** flag.`

Configure Periods Types

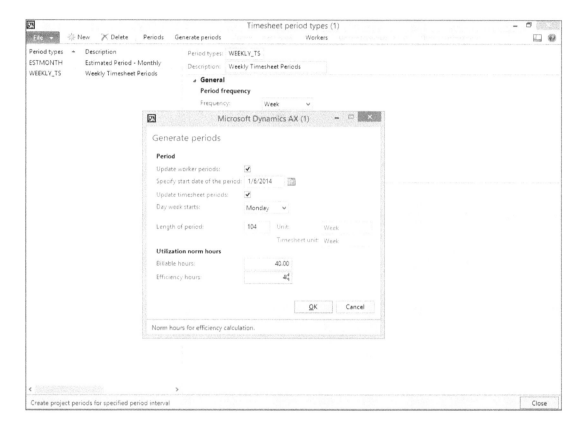

Then specify the number of periods that you want to create within the **Length Of Period** field.

Finally, set the number of **Billable Hours** that are to be used within the period, and also set the **Efficiency Hours** to the same value.

When you have done that, just click on the **OK** button to create the periods.

Configure Periods Types

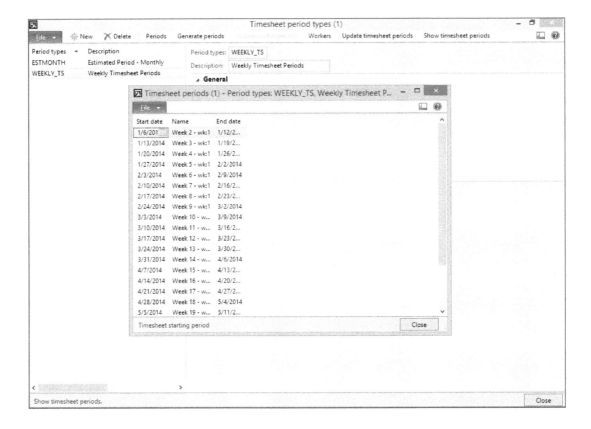

Tip: To see the periods that were generated, just click on the **Periods** button within the menu bar.

Configure Periods Types

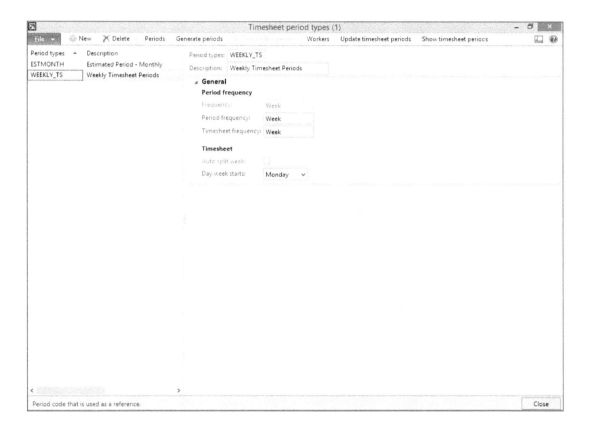

After you have set up your Period Types, just click on the **Close** button to exit from the form.

Configuring Shared Categories

Next we need to configure some **Shared Categories** that will be used as the basis for our **Project Categories** later on. These will be used to identify all of the different types of project categories that we will use within our project itself.

Configuring Shared Categories

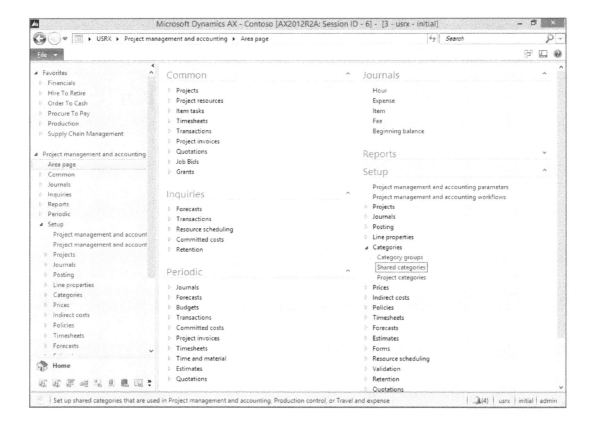

To do this, click on the **Shared Categories** menu item within the **Categories** folder of the **Setup** group within the **Project Management And Accounting** area page.

Configuring Shared Categories

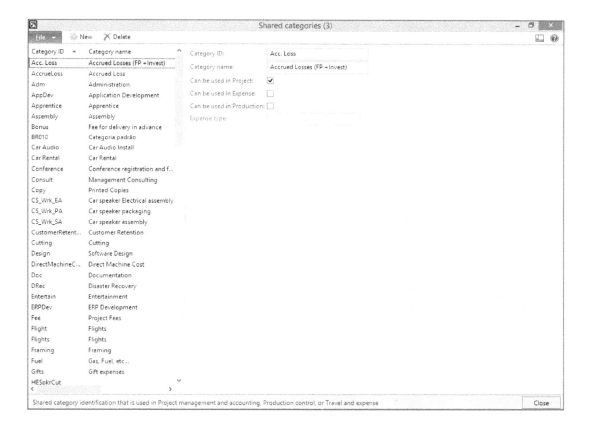

When the **Shared Categories** maintenance form is displayed, you can add additional categories to the existing list just by clicking on the **New** button within the menu bar and then specifying a **Category ID** code and a **Category Name**.

Note: To make these available within Projects you need to make sure that you check the **Can Be Used In Project** flag.

When you are done, just click the **Close** button to exit from the form.

Configuring Category Groups

Next we need to define the **Category** groups that we will use within our projects. The **Category Groups** store all of the default posting profiles for our Categories.

Configuring Category Groups

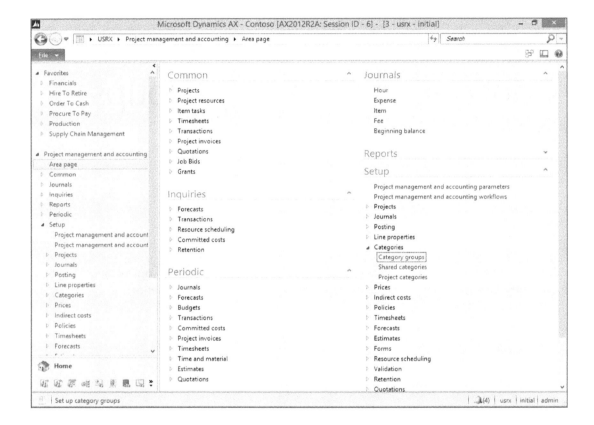

To do this, click on the **Category Groups** menu item within the **Categories** folder of the **Setup** group of the **Project Management And Accounting** area page.

Configuring Category Groups

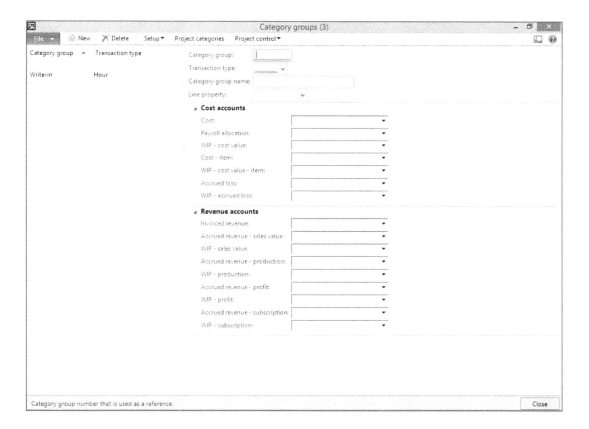

When the **Category Groups** maintenance form is displayed, click on the **New** button within the menu bar to create a new record.

Configuring Category Groups

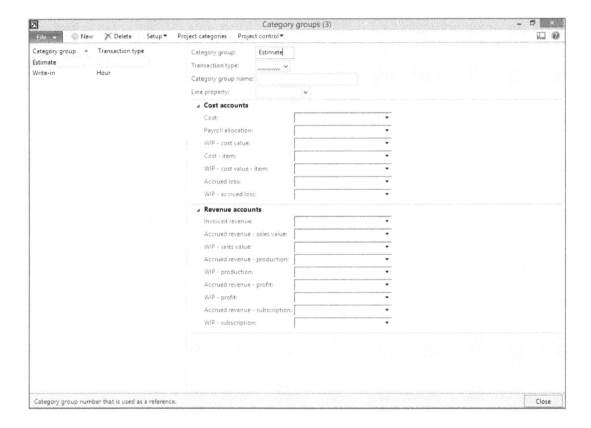

Set the **Category Group** for the first record to be **Estimate**.

Configuring Category Groups

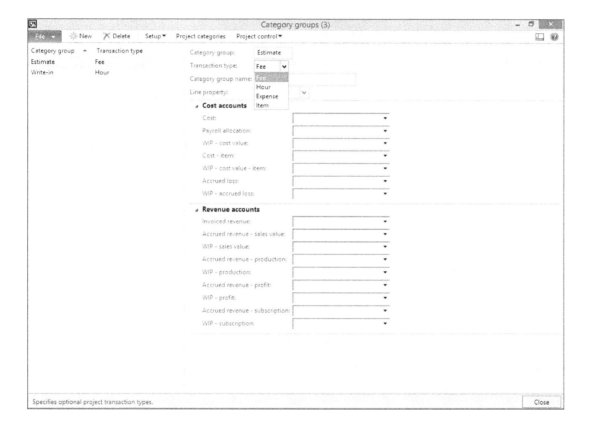

And then select the **Fee** item from the **Transaction Type** dropdown list.

Configuring Category Groups

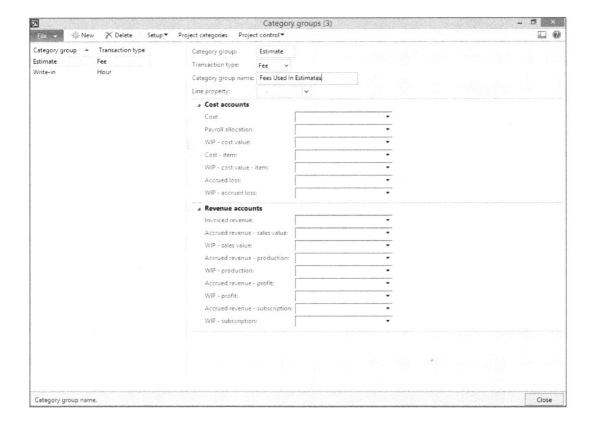

Then set the **Category Group Name** to be **Fee Used In Estimates**.

Configuring Category Groups

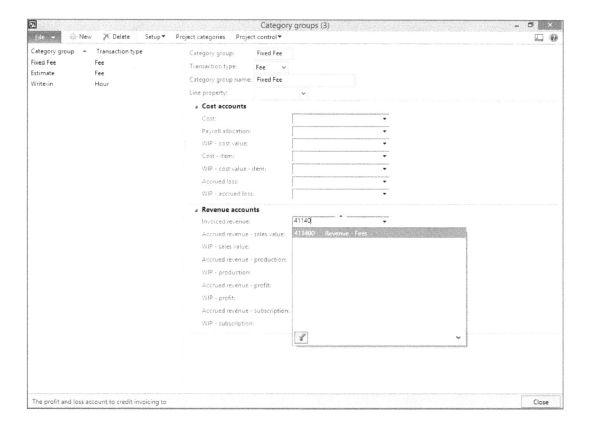

For this Category Group we will need to specify a default Main Account for the **Invoiced Revenue** field.

Configuring Category Groups

And also a main account for the **WIP – Sales Update**.

Configuring Category Groups

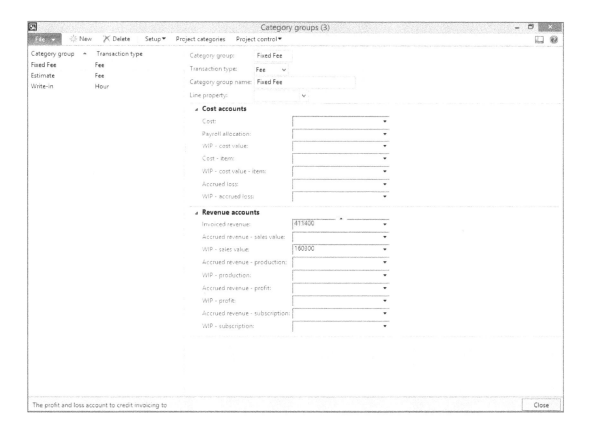

Click on the **New** button in the menu bar and repeat the process setting the **Category Group** field to **Fixed Fee** the **Transaction Type** to **Fee** and the **Category Group Name** to **Fixed Fee.**

Configuring Category Groups

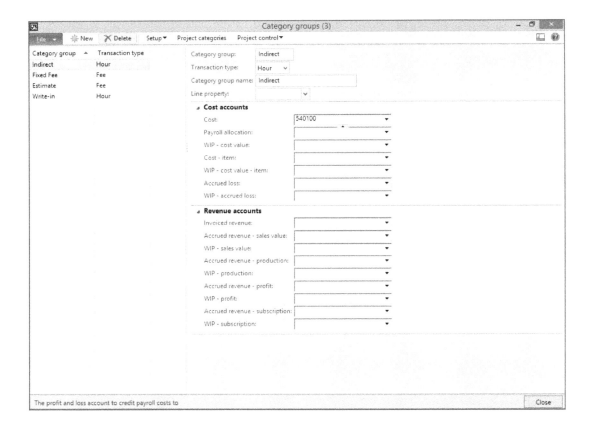

Click on the **New** button in the menu bar and create a new record for the posting of indirect hours.

Set the **Category Group** field to **Indirect** the **Transaction Type** to **Hour** and the **Category Group Name** to **Indirect**.

For this record you will need to set the main account for the **Cost** field.

Configuring Category Groups

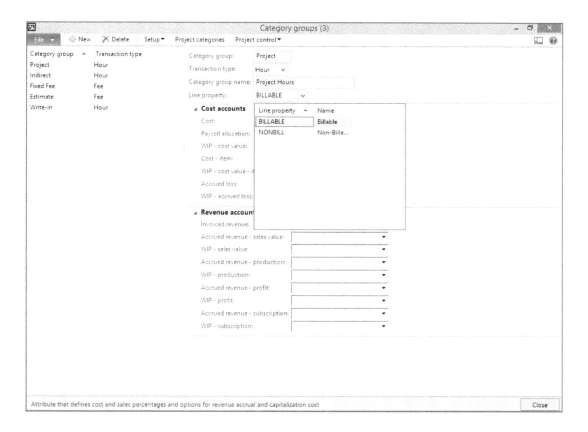

Click on the **New** button in the menu bar and create a new record for the posting of billable project hours.

Set the **Category Group** field to **Project**, the **Transaction Type** to **Hour** and the **Category Group Name** to **Project Hours.**

For this record set the default **Line Property** to be **BILLABLE**.

Configuring Category Groups

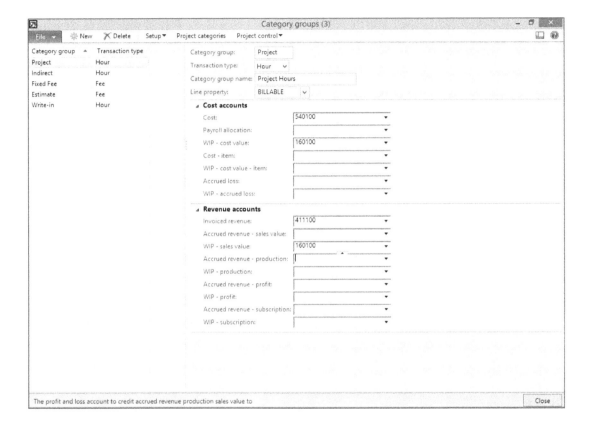

For this Category Group to post correctly you will need to set the main account for the **Cost**, **WIP – Cost Value**, **Invoiced Revenue** and also **WIP – Sales Value** fields.

Configuring Category Groups

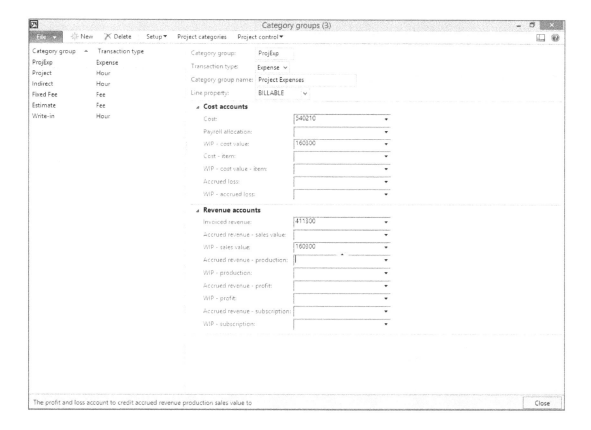

Click on the **New** button in the menu bar and create a new record for the posting of billable project expenses.

Set the **Category Group** field to **ProjExp**, the **Transaction Type** to **Expenses** and the **Category Group Name** to **Project Expenses.**

Set the default **Line Property** to be **BILLABLE**.

And set the main account for the **Cost, WIP – Cost Value, Invoiced Revenue** and also **WIP – Sales Value** fields.

Configuring Category Groups

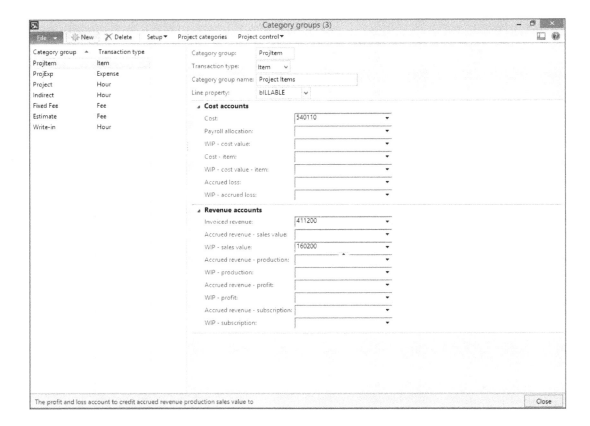

Click on the **New** button in the menu bar and create a new record for the posting of billable project items.

Set the **Category Group** field to **ProjItem**, the **Transaction Type** to **Item** and the **Category Group Name** to **Project Items.**

Set the default **Line Property** to be **BILLABLE**.

And set the main account for the **Cost**, **Invoiced Revenue** and also **WIP – Sales Value** fields.

Configuring Category Groups

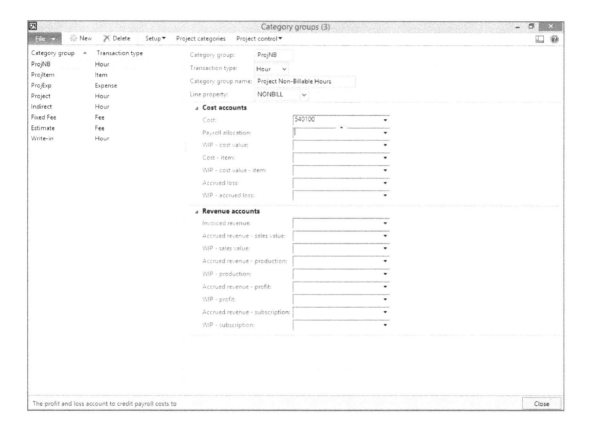

Click on the **New** button in the menu bar and create a new record for the posting of non-billable project hours.

Set the **Category Group** field to **ProjNB**, the **Transaction Type** to **Hour** and the **Category Group Name** to **Project Non-Billable Hours.**

Set the default **Line Property** to be **NONBILL**.

And set the main account for the **Cost** field.

Configuring Category Groups

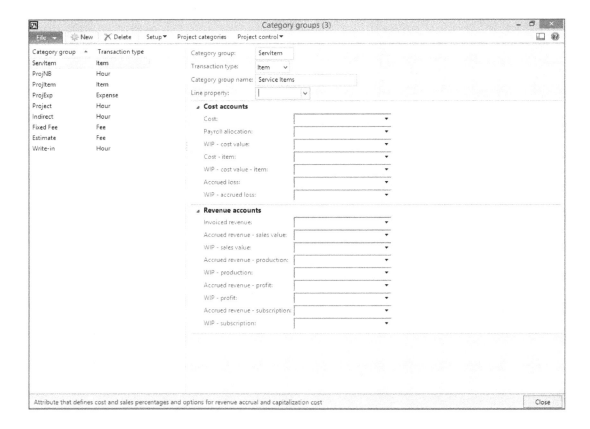

Click on the **New** button in the menu bar and create a new record for the posting of service items.

Set the **Category Group** field to **ServItem**, the **Transaction Type** to **Item** and the **Category Group Name** to **Service Items**.

Configuring Category Groups

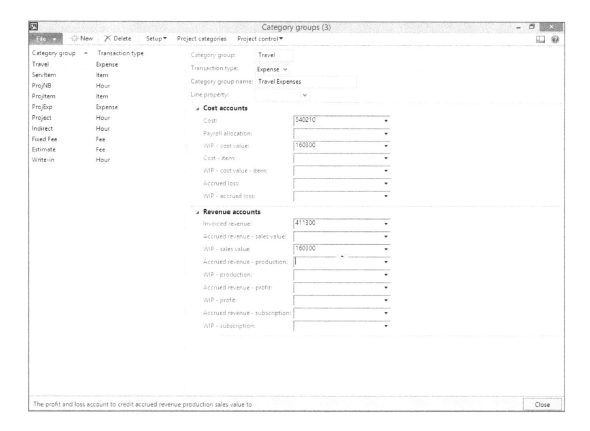

Finally click on the **New** button in the menu bar one last time and create a new record for the posting of travel expenses.

Set the **Category Group** field to **Travel**, the **Transaction Type** to **Expense** and the **Category Group Name** to **Travel Expenses.**

And set the main account for the **Cost**, **WIP – Cost Value**, **Invoiced Revenue** and also **WIP – Sales Value** fields.

When you are done, click on the **Close** button to exit from the form.

Configuring Project Categories

Next we will start to configure the Project Categories that we will be able to post to within our projects.

Configuring Project Categories

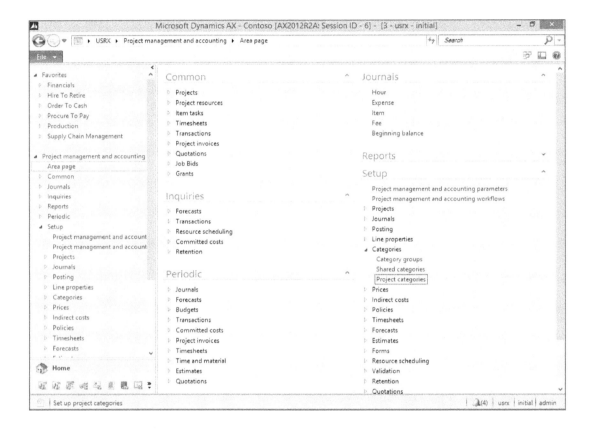

To do this, click on the **Project Categories** menu item within the **Categories** folder of the **Setup** group witan the **Project Management And Accounting** area page.,

Configuring Project Categories

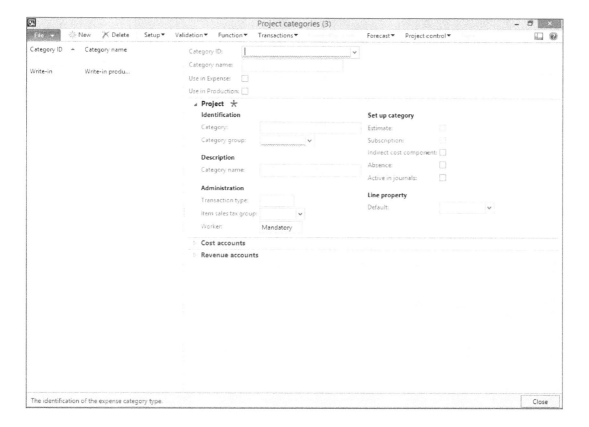

When the **Project Categories** maintenance form is displayed, click on the **New** button in the menu bar to add a new record.

Configuring Project Categories

From the **Category ID** dropdown list, choose the **Shared Category** that you want to create a **Project Category** based off.

Configuring Project Categories

Then select the **Category Group** that you want to assign the **Project Category** to.

Configuring Project Categories

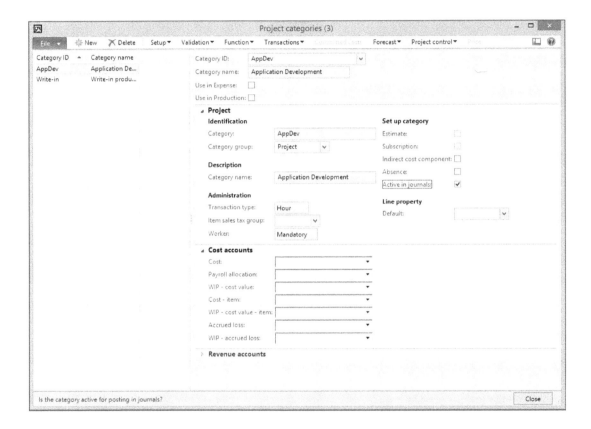

Then check the **Activate In Journals** flag on the Project Category to show that you want to be able to create Project Journals against it.

Configuring Project Categories

If you create a **Project Category** that is associated with a **Category Group** of **Estimate** don't check the **Activate In Journals** flag, but check the **Estimates** flag instead.

Configuring Project Categories

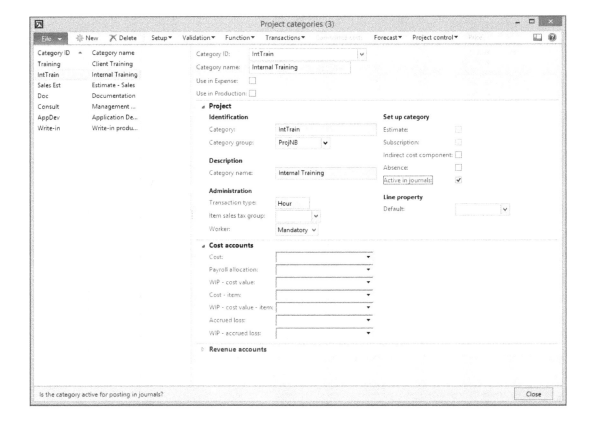

If you create a **Project Category** that is associated with a **Category Group** of **ProjectNB** then check the **Activate In Journals** flag.

Configuring Project Categories

If you create a **Project Category** that is associated with a **Category Group** of **ProjectExp** then check the **Activate In Journals** flag.

Configuring Project Categories

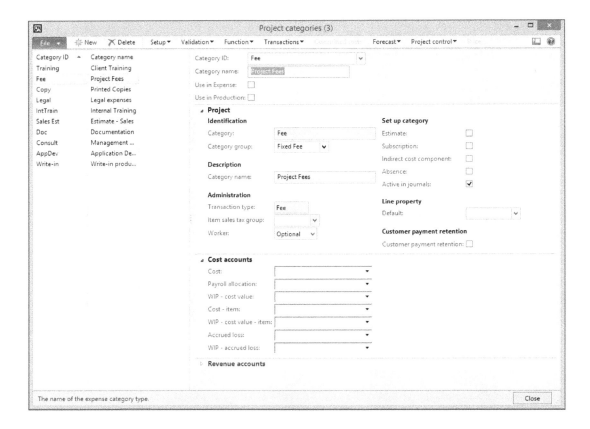

If you create a **Project Category** that is associated with a **Category Group** of **Fixed Fee** then check the **Activate In Journals** flag.

Configuring Project Categories

If you create a **Project Category** that is associated with a **Category Group** of **ProjectItem** then check the **Activate In Journals** flag.

Configuring Project Categories

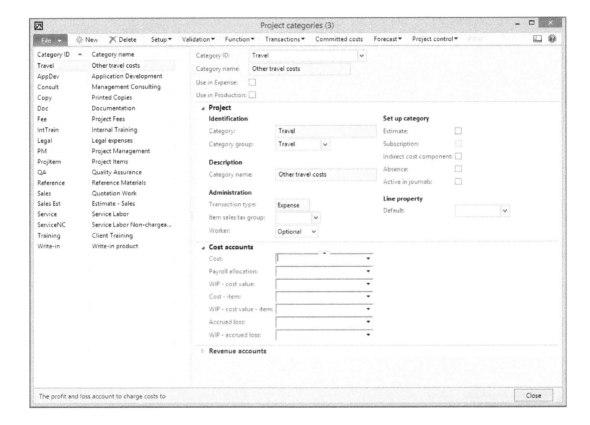

If you create a **Project Category** that is associated with a **Category Group** of **Travel** then there is no need to check any of the flags.

Configuring Project Groups

Next we will configure the **Project Groups**. These control how your Projects act and what rules are used for billing, and revenue recognition. In this section we will show how to configure the typical **Project Groups** that you might need.

Configuring Project Groups

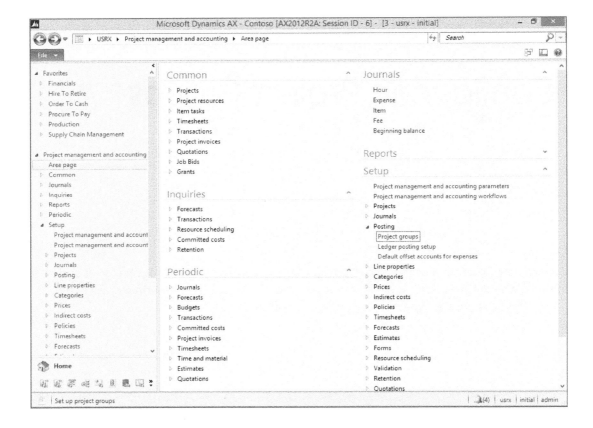

To do this, click on the **Project Groups** menu item within the **Posting** folder of the **Setup** group within the **Project Management And Accounting** area page.

Configuring Project Groups

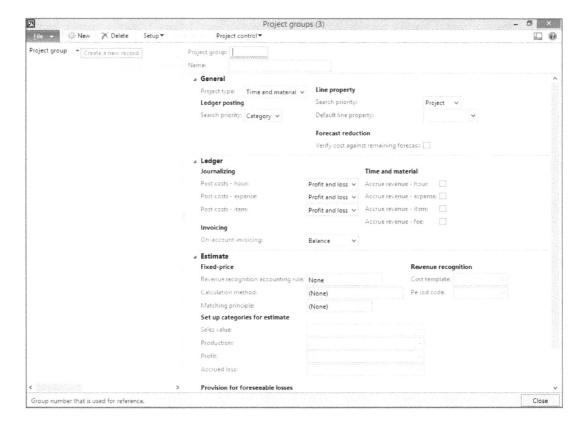

When the **Project Groups** maintenance form is displayed, click on the **New** button within the menu bar to create a new record.

Configuring Project Groups

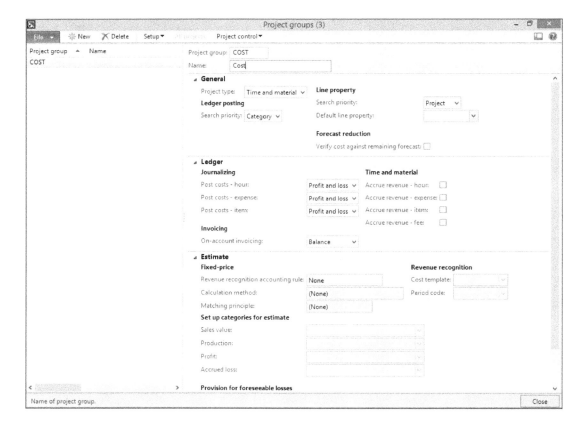

For the first **Project Group** we will configure a Cost Only project group. Set the **Project Group** code to **COST** and the **Name** to **Cost**.

Configuring Project Groups

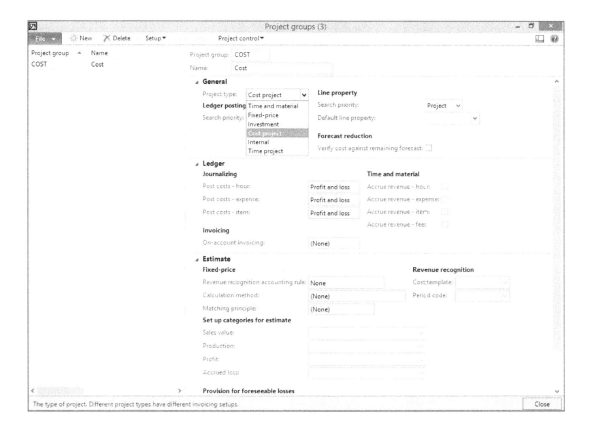

Then from the **Project Type** dropdown list, select the **Cost Project** type.

Configuring Project Groups

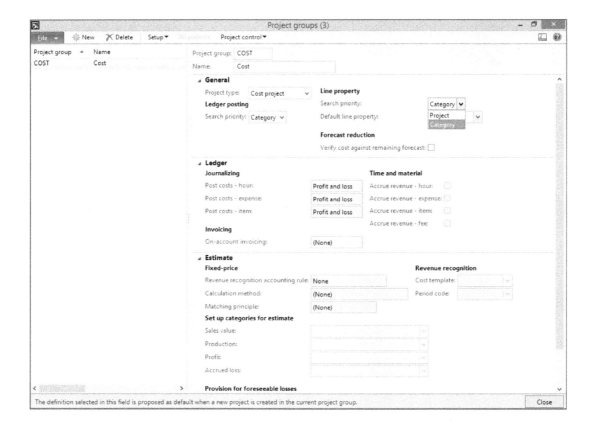

And set the **Search Priority** field to **Category**.

Configuring Project Groups

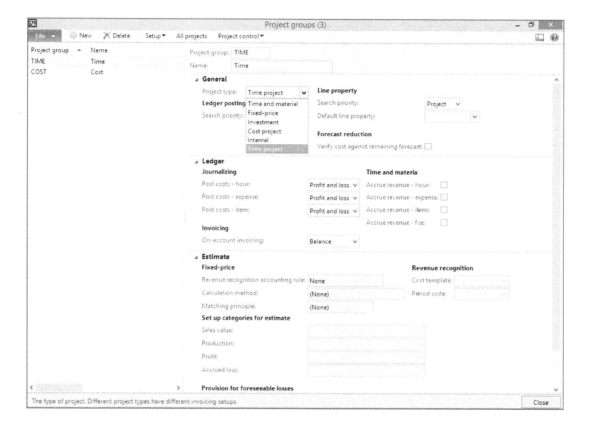

Next we will create a time based project group. To do this click on the **New** button within the menu bar to create a new record.

Set the **Project Group** code to **TIME**, the **Name** to **Time** and from the **Project Type** dropdown select the **Time Project** value.

Configuring Project Groups

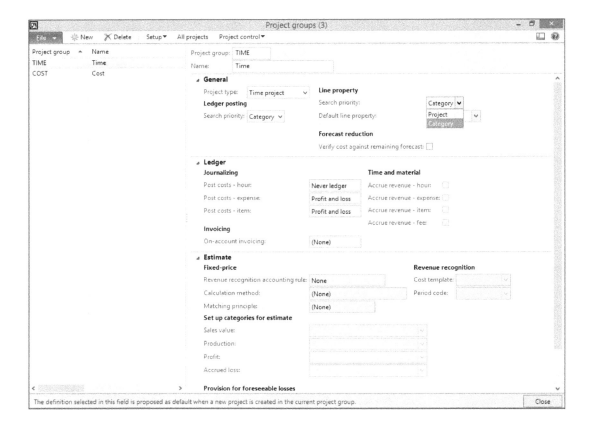

And set the **Search Priority** field to **Category**.

Configuring Project Groups

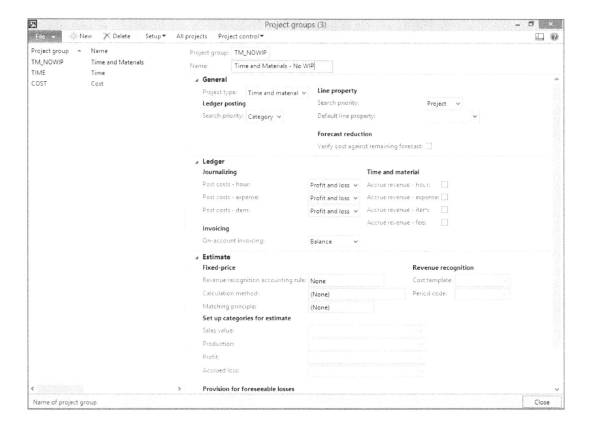

Next we will create a time and material based project group. These can either track WIP, or not track the WIP. This first one will not track the WIP. To do this click on the **New** button within the menu bar to create a new record.

Set the **Project Group** code to **TM_NOWIP**, the **Name** to **Time and Materials – No WIP** and from the **Project Type** dropdown select the **Time And Material** value.

Configuring Project Groups

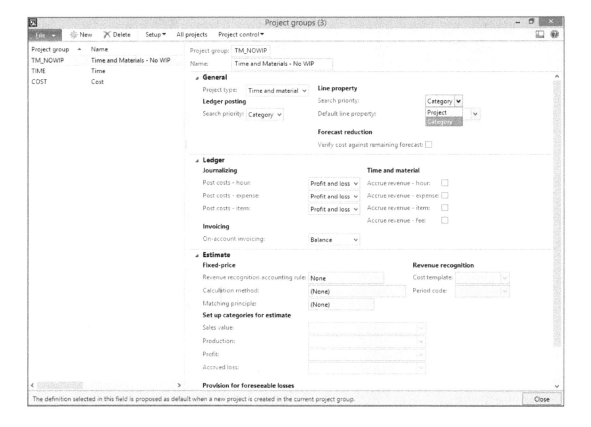

And set the **Search Priority** field to **Category**.

Configuring Project Groups

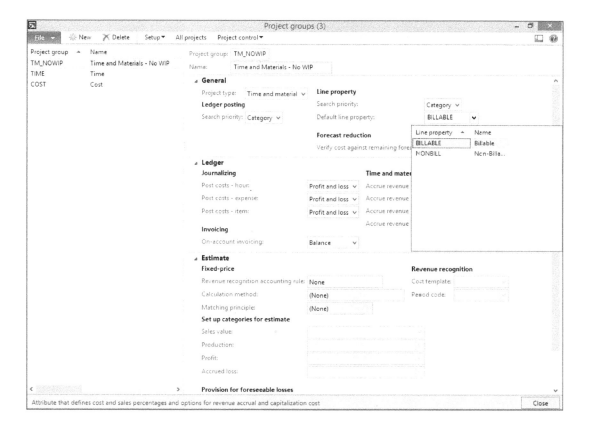

Because this is a billable **Project Group** set the **Default Line Property** to **BILLABLE**.

Configuring Project Groups

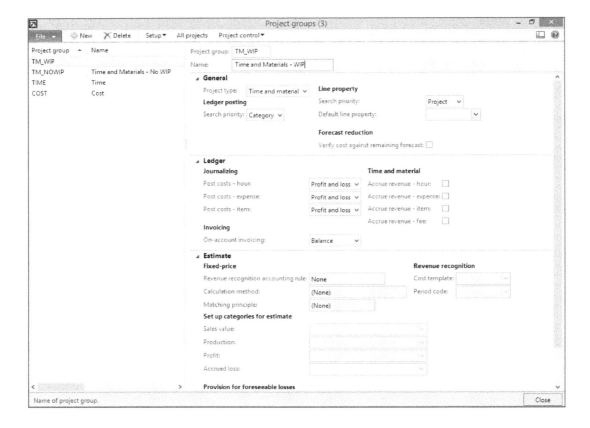

Now we will create the other time and material based project group that does track WIP. To do this click on the **New** button within the menu bar to create a new record.

Set the **Project Group** code to **TM_WIP**, the **Name** to **Time and Materials – WIP** and from the **Project Type** dropdown select the **Time And Material** value.

Configuring Project Groups

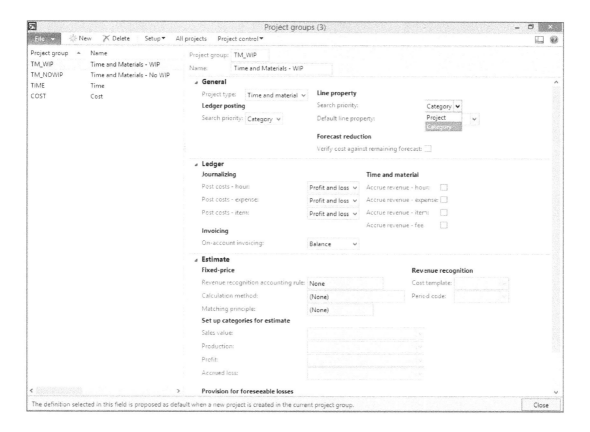

And set the **Search Priority** field to **Category**.

Configuring Project Groups

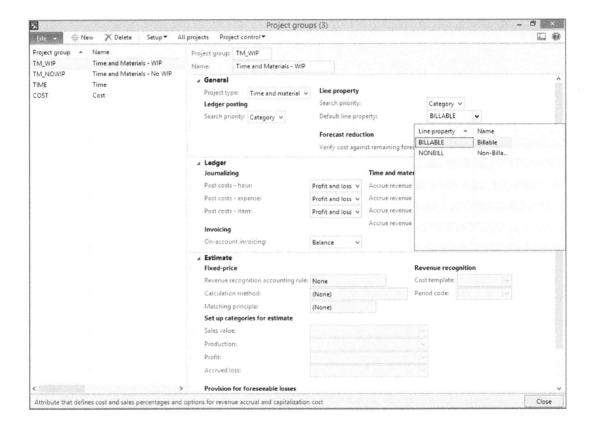

Because this is a billable **Project Group** set the **Default Line Property** to **BILLABLE**.

Configuring Project Groups

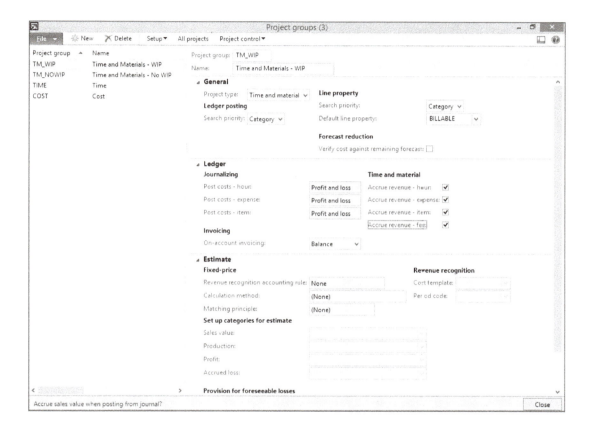

Within the **Ledger** fast tab, check the **Accrue revenue – hour**, **Accrue revenue – expense**, **Accrue revenue – item** and **Accrue revenue – fee** flags to tell the system to accrue all of the costs – which is what makes it a WIP project group.

Configuring Project Groups

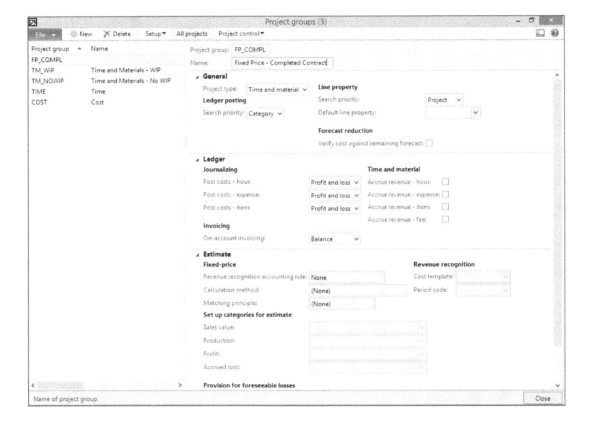

Next we will create a **Project Group** for fixed price projects. The can have a couple of variations. The ones that we will use are payment due based on completion, and based on milestones. To create the first one click on the **New** button within the menu bar to create a new record.

Set the **Project Group** code to **FP_COMPL**, the **Name** to **Fixed Price – Completed Contract**.

Configuring Project Groups

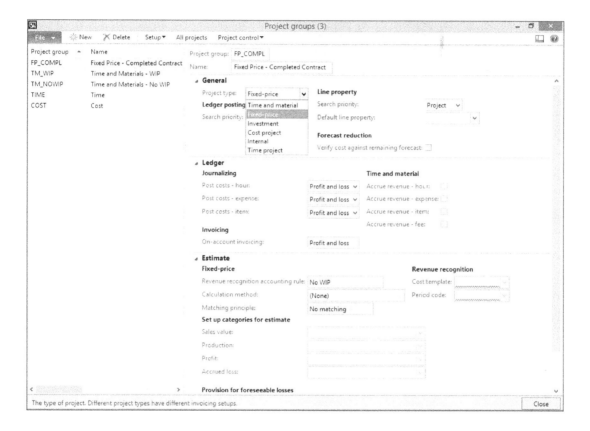

Then from the **Project Type** dropdown select the **Fixed Price** value.

Configuring Project Groups

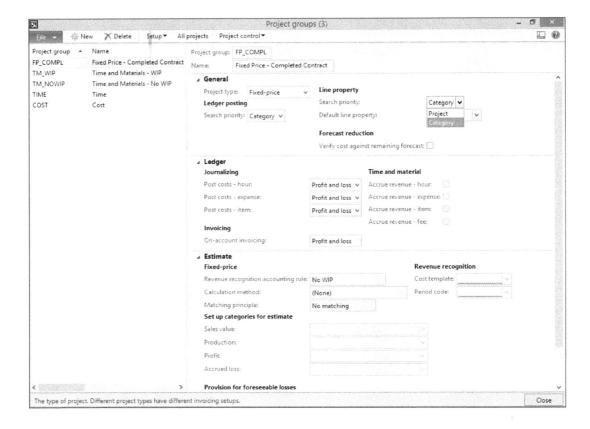

And set the **Search Priority** field to **Category**.

Configuring Project Groups

Because this is a billable **Project Group** set the **Default Line Property** to **BILLABLE**.

Configuring Project Groups

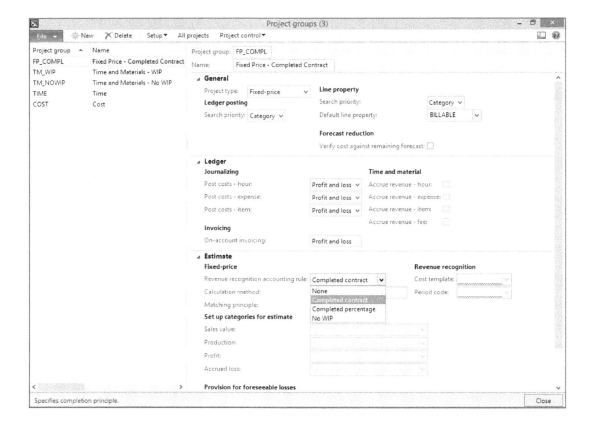

Within the **Estimate** fast tab, click on the **Revenue Recognition Accounting Rule** dropdown list and select the **Completed Project** option.

Configuring Project Groups

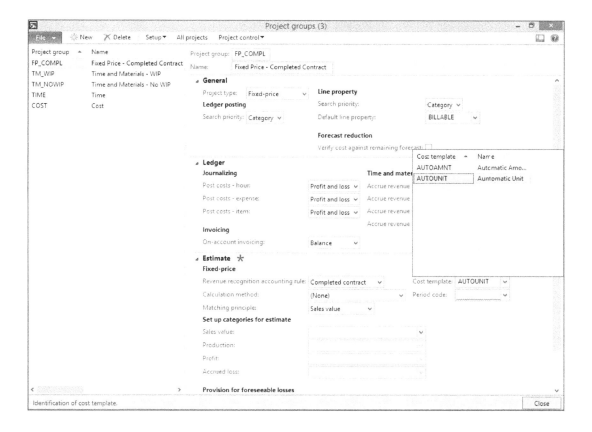

Then click on the **Cost Template** dropdown and select the **AUTOUNIT** option to bill by unit.

Configuring Project Groups

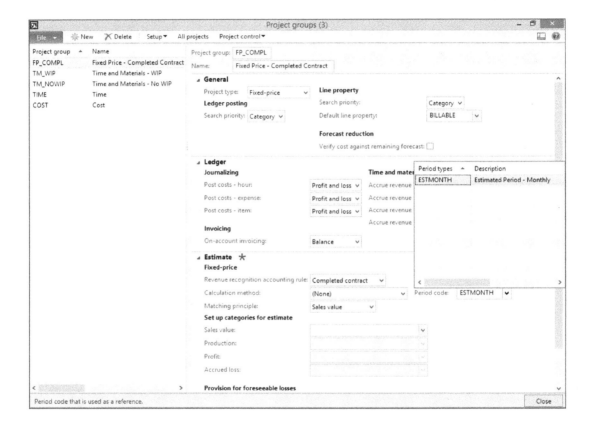

And then select the **ESTMONTH** value from the **Period Code** dropdown.

Configuring Project Groups

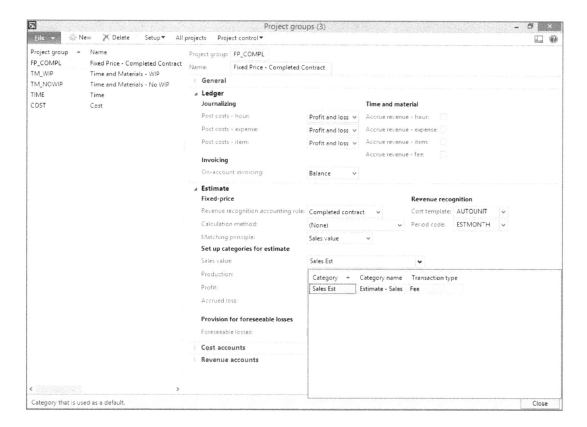

Then select the **Sales Est** value from the **Sales Value** to identify that the amount billed will be fixed to the estimate from sales.

Configuring Project Groups

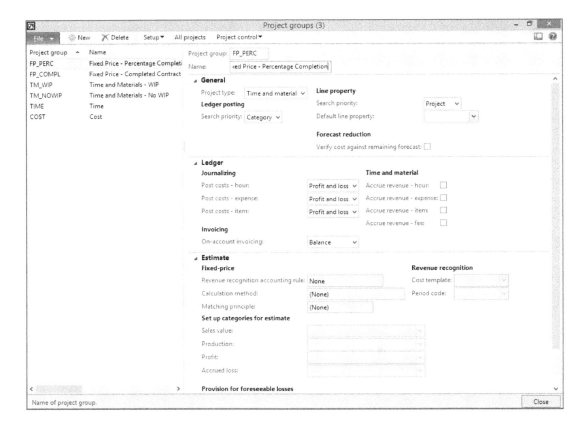

Now we will create the other fixed price **Project Group** which will be based on milestones. To create the first one click on the **New** button within the menu bar to create a new record.

Set the **Project Group** code to **FP_PERC**, the **Name** to **Fixed Price – Percentage Completed**.

Configuring Project Groups

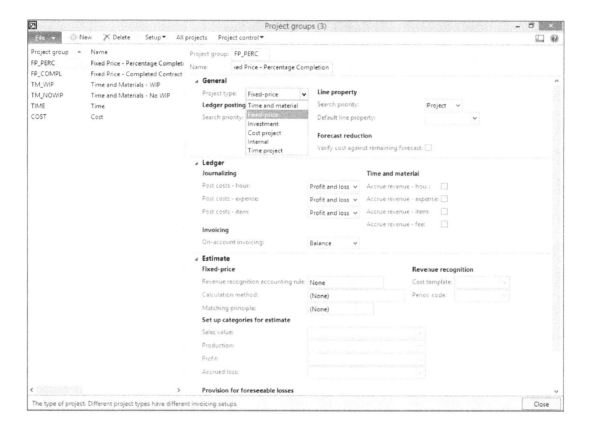

Then from the **Project Type** dropdown select the **Fixed Price** value.

Configuring Project Groups

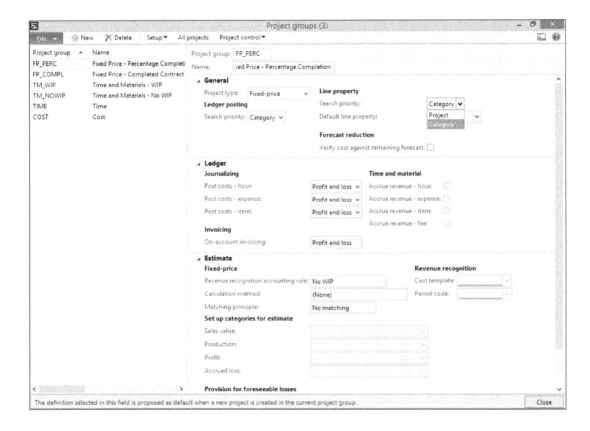

And set the **Search Priority** field to **Category**.

Configuring Project Groups

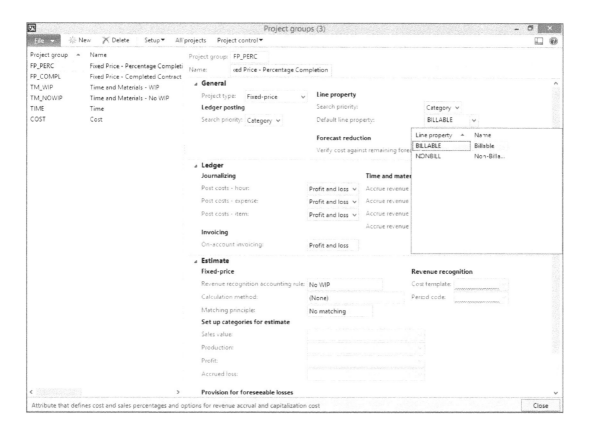

Because this is a billable **Project Group** set the **Default Line Property** to **BILLABLE**.

Configuring Project Groups

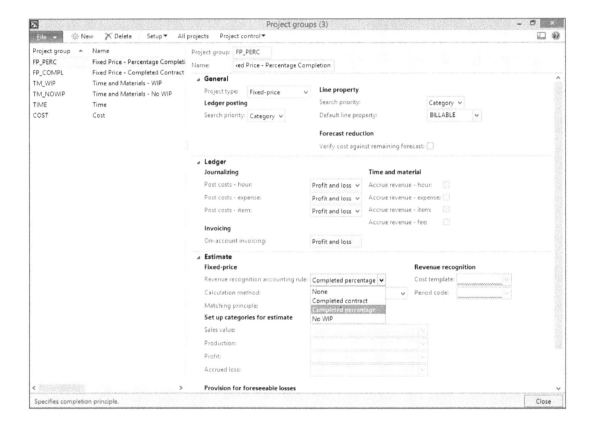

Within the **Estimate** fast tab, click on the **Revenue Recognition Accounting Rule** dropdown list and select the **Completed Percentage** option.

Configuring Project Groups

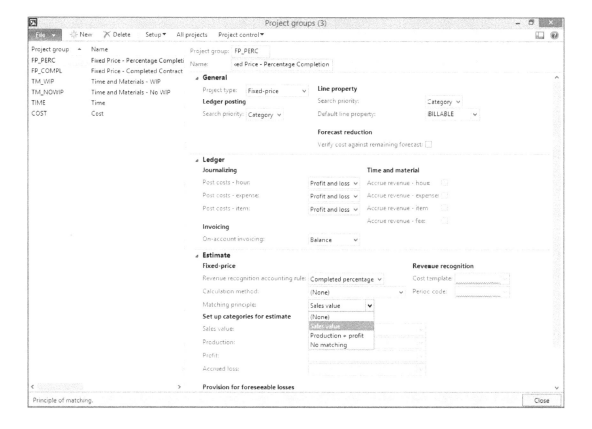

Click on the dropdown list for the **Matching Principle** and select the **Sales Value** option.

Configuring Project Groups

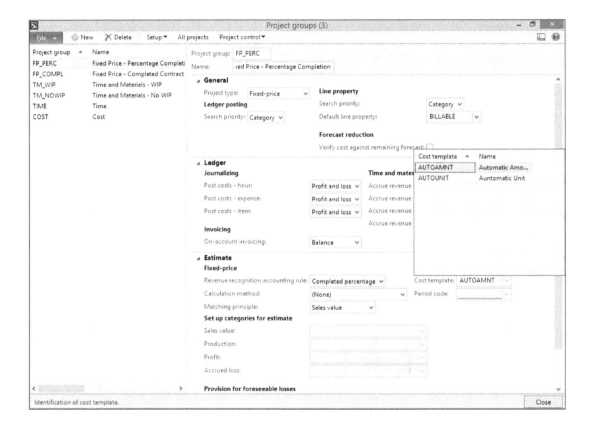

Then click on the **Cost Template** dropdown and select the **AUTOAMNT** option to bill by dollar value of the project.

Configuring Project Groups

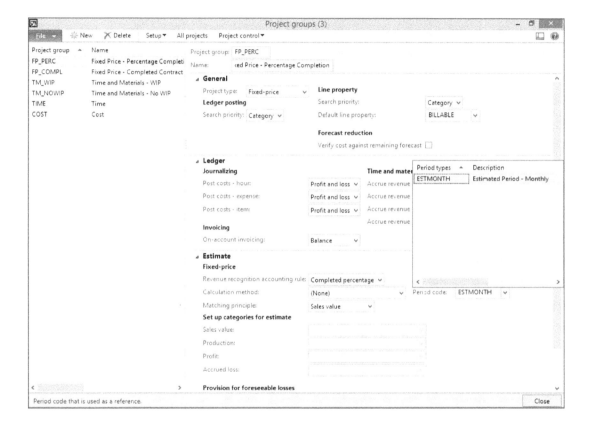

And then select the **ESTMONTH** value from the **Period Code** dropdown.

Configuring Project Groups

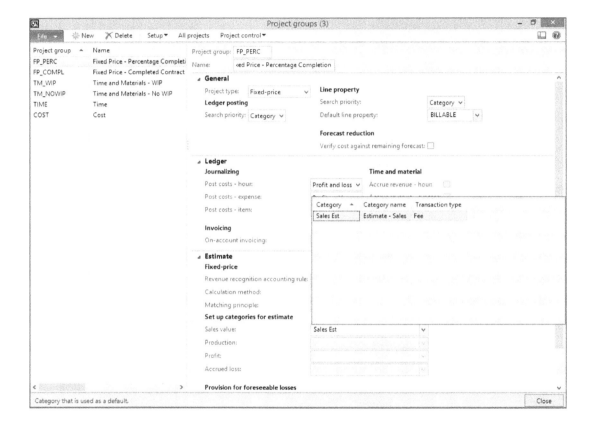

Then select the **Sales Est** value from the **Sales Value** to identify that the amount billed will be fixed to the estimate from sales.

Configuring Project Groups

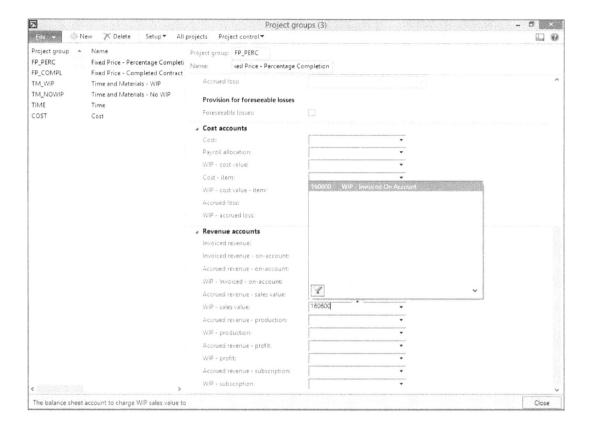

Because this project will have WIP tracked against it. Then also set the **WIP – Sales Value** main account within the **Revenue Accounts** fast tab/

Configuring Project Groups

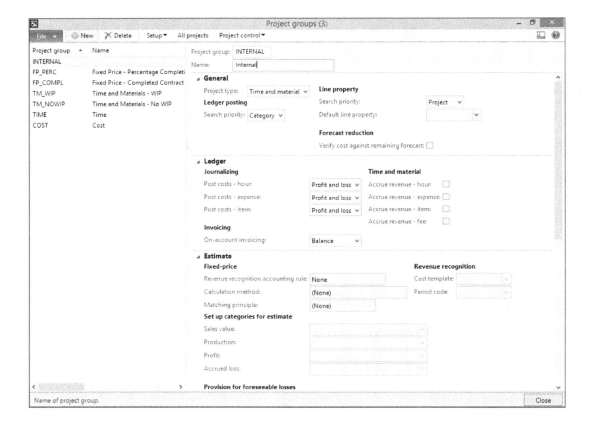

Finally, we will create an internal **Project Group** to track non-revenue related projects. To create the first one click on the **New** button within the menu bar to create a new record.

Set the **Project Group** code to **INTERNAL**, the **Name** to **Internal**.

Configuring Project Groups

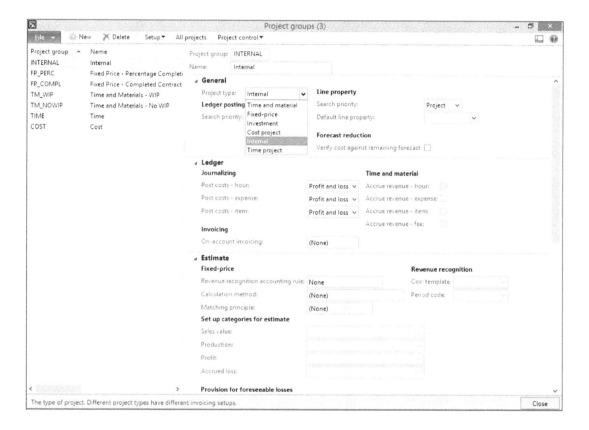

Then from the **Project Type** dropdown select the **Internal** value.

Configuring Project Groups

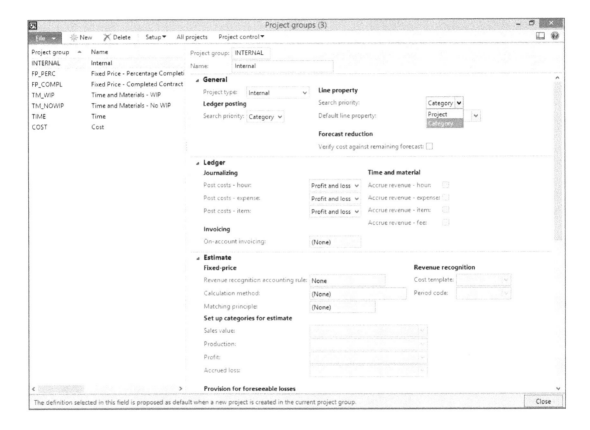

And set the **Search Priority** field to **Category**.

Configuring Project Groups

Because this is a non-billable **Project Group** set the **Default Line Property** to **NONBILL**.

Configuring Project Groups

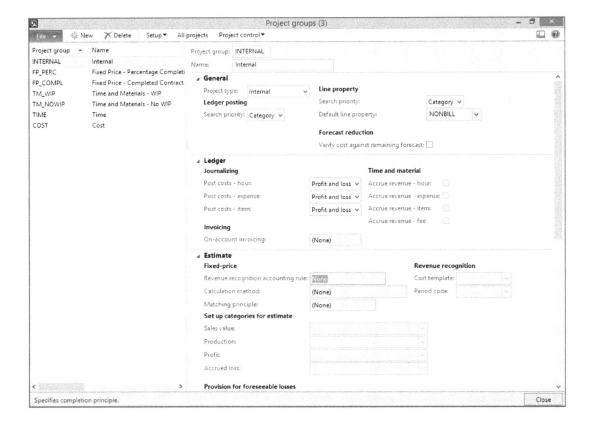

Now you have all of the typical **Project Groups** configured. Just click on the **Close** button to exit from the form.

Creating A Working Time Template

Later on we will show you how to configure workers and schedule them against projects. In order to do this though they need to have a working time calendar, and in order to create one of those we need to create a simple **Working Time Template**.

Creating A Working Time Template

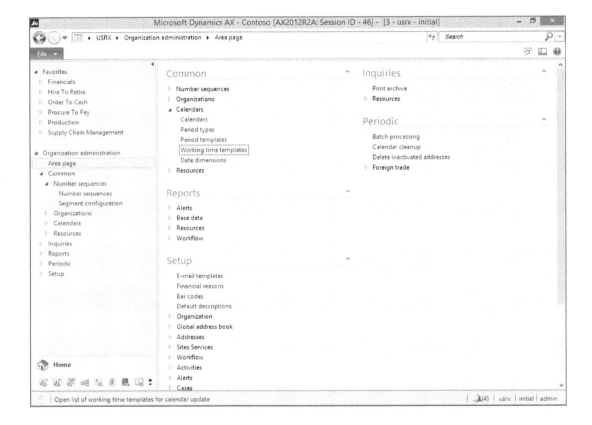

To do this, click on the **Working Time Templates** menu item within the **Calendars** folder of the **Common** group of the **Organization Administration** area page.

Creating A Working Time Template

When the **Working Time Template** maintenance form is displayed, click on the **New** button to add a new record.

Creating A Working Time Template

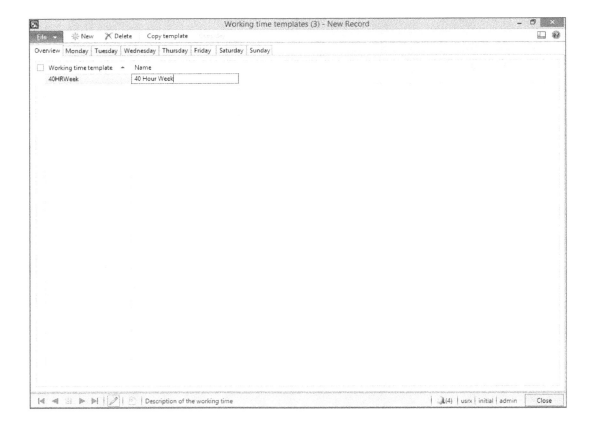

We will create a simple 40 hour work week template, so set the **Working Time Template** code to **40HRWeek** and the **Name** to **40 Hour Week**.

Creating A Working Time Template

Then switch to the **Monday** tab.

Creating A Working Time Template

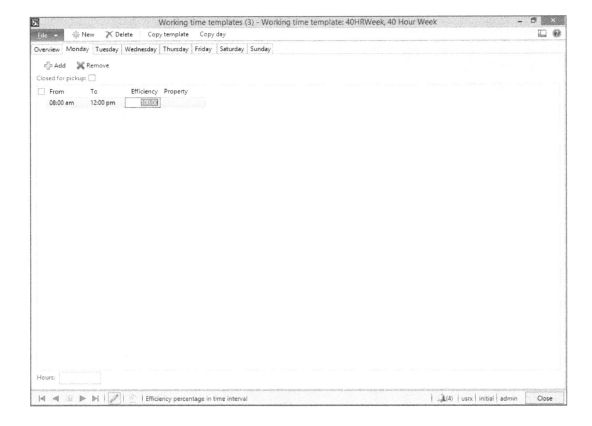

Click on the **Add** button within the **Monday** tab and set the **From** time to **08:00 AM**, the **To** time to **12:00 PM** and the **Efficiency** percentage to **100**.

Creating A Working Time Template

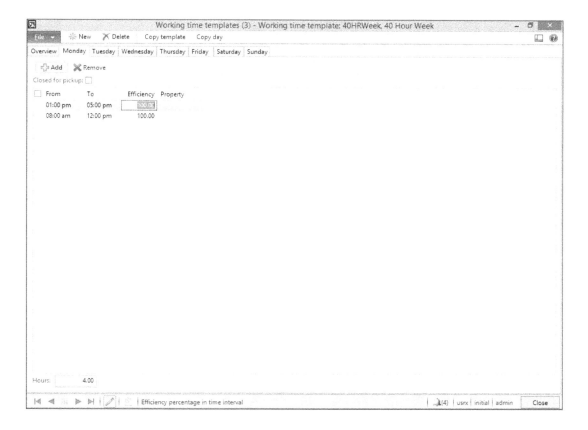

Click on the **Add** button again and set the **From** time to **01:00 PM**, the **To** time to **05:00 PM** and the **Efficiency** percentage to **100**.

Creating A Working Time Template

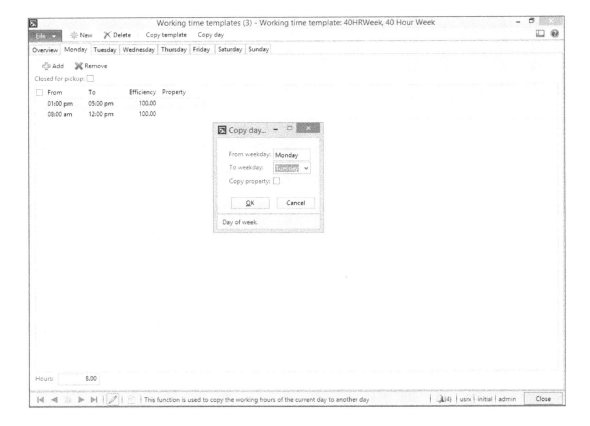

Rather than repeat those steps for all of the other days, you can just click on the **Copy Day** button in the menu bar. This will open up a dialog box allowing you to copy the times from Monday to Tuesday. Just click **OK**.

Creating A Working Time Template

Repeat the copy function so that you set up **Wednesday**, **Thursday**, and **Friday**, and then click the **Close** button to exit from the form.

Creating A Project Scheduling Calendar

Now that we have a Work Time Template, we can use it to create the **Project Calendar**.

Creating A Project Scheduling Calendar

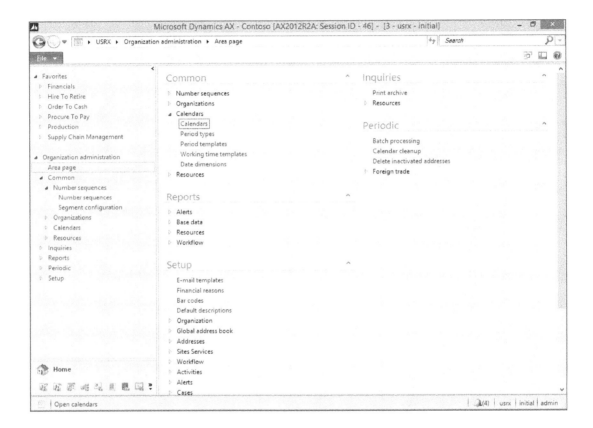

To do this, click on the **Calendars** menu item within the **Calendars** folder of the **Common** group within the **Organization Administration** area page.

Creating A Project Scheduling Calendar

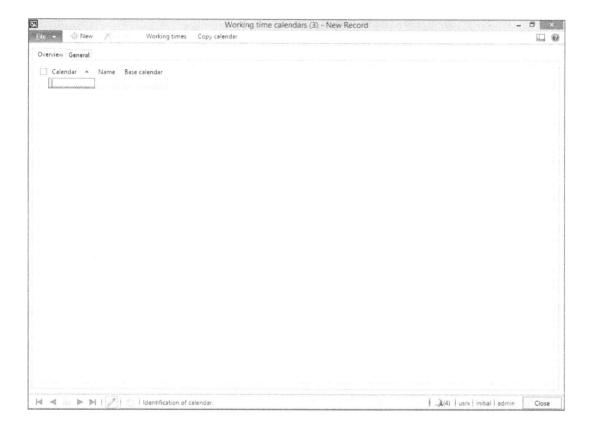

When the **Working Time Calendars** maintenance form is displayed, click on the **New** button to create a new record.

Creating A Project Scheduling Calendar

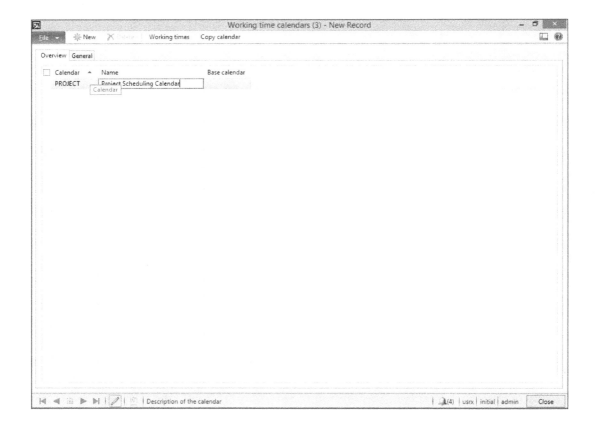

Set the **Calendar** code to **Project** and the **Name** to **Project Scheduling Calendar**.

Creating A Project Scheduling Calendar

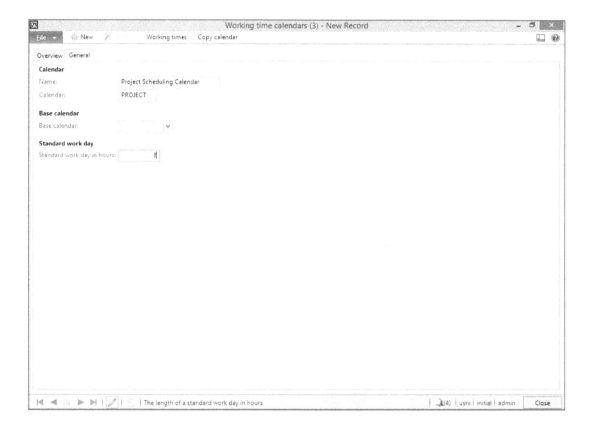

Then switch to the **General** tab and set the **Standard Work Day In Hours** to **8**.

Note: This is a small but critical field. If you don't set this then no scheduling will occur.

Creating A Project Scheduling Calendar

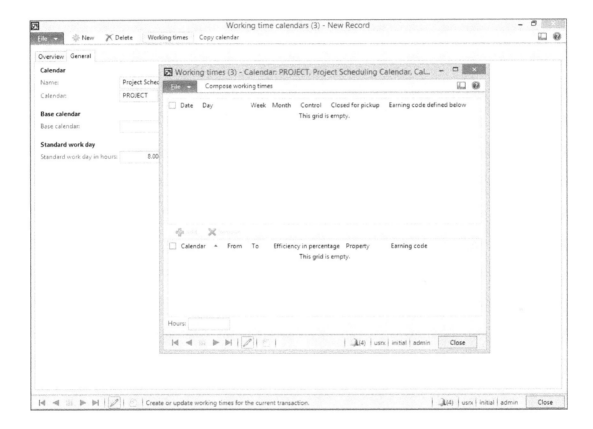

No we want to set up the working times for the calendar. To do that click on the **Working Times** button within the menu bar. Then when the **Working Times** maintenance form is displayed, click on the **Compose Working Times** button in that forms menu bar.

Creating A Project Scheduling Calendar

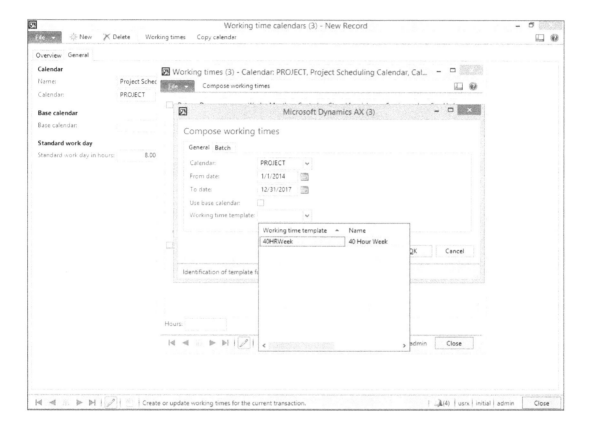

When the **Compose Working Times** dialog box is displayed, set the **From Date** and **To Date** to be wise enough to allow you to crack all of your projects, and then set the **Working Time Template** to be the **40HRWeek** template that you just created.

Creating A Project Scheduling Calendar

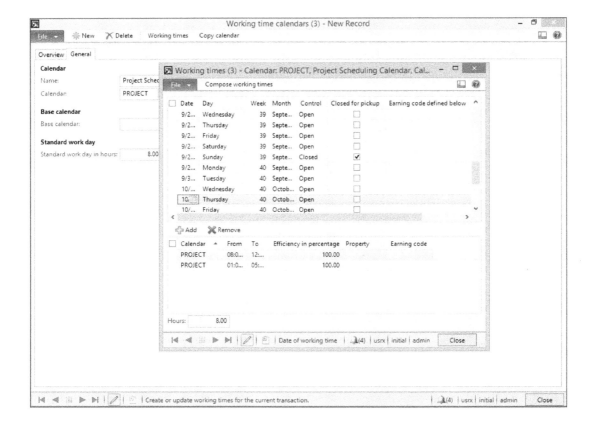

When you return to the **Working Times** form you will see that your calendar is populated with working times and dates.

Now you can click the **Close** button to exit out of all the forms.

Configuring Inventory Journals

Since we will probably want to consume inventory through our projects then we need to remember to configure some Inventory Journals just for Projects to track these.

Configuring Inventory Journals

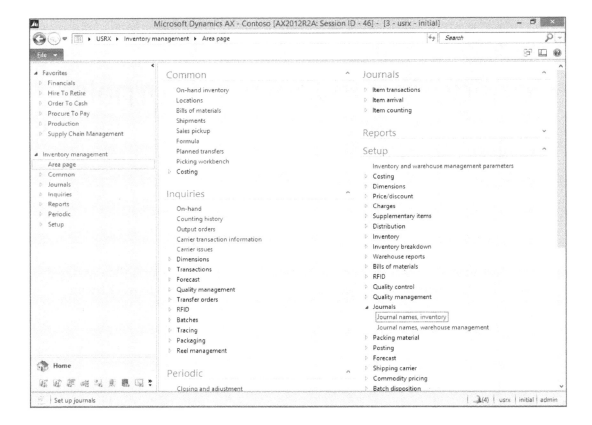

To do this, click on the **Journal Names, Inventory** menu link within the **Journals** folder of the **Setup** group within the **Inventory Management** area page.

Configuring Inventory Journals

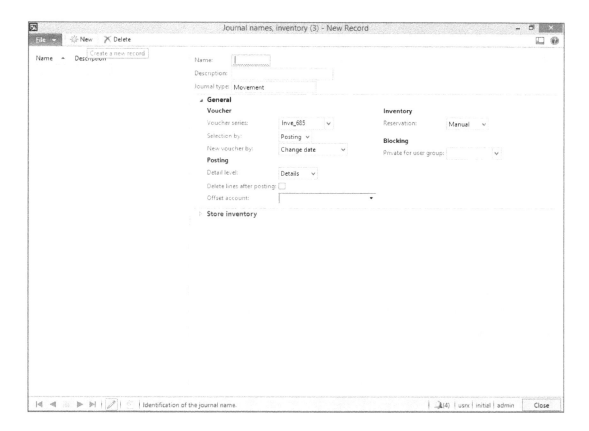

When the **Journal Names** maintenance form is displayed, click on the **New** button within the menu bar to create a new record.

Configuring Inventory Journals

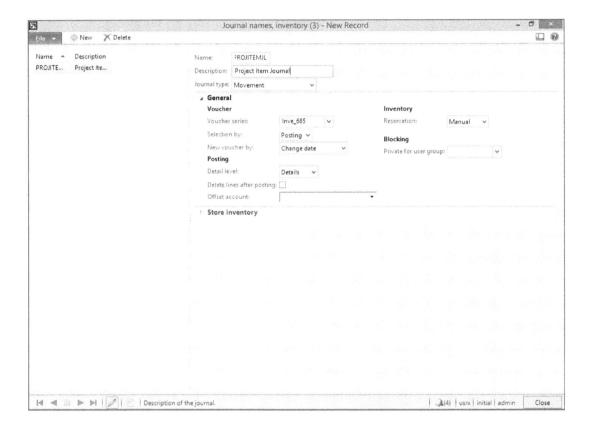

Then set the **Name** code to **PROJITEMJL** and the **Description** to **Project Item Journal**.

Configuring Inventory Journals

From the **Journal Type** dropdown list, select the **Project** option.

Configuring Inventory Journals

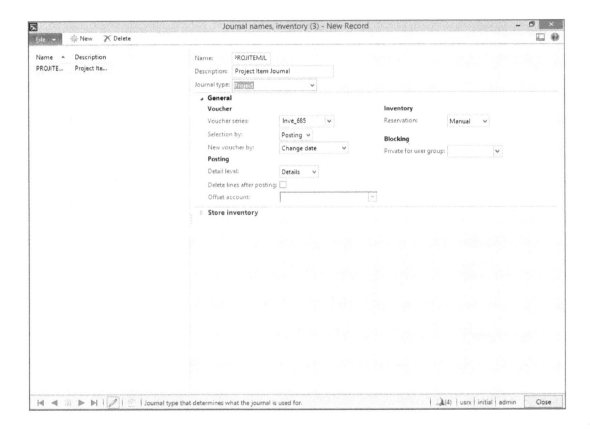

After you have done that, just click on the **Close** button to exit from the form.

Configuring Project Forecast Models

One final code setup that we need to do is to create a **Forecast Model** for our projects so that we can use it for forecasting budgeted amnounts.

Configuring Project Forecast Models

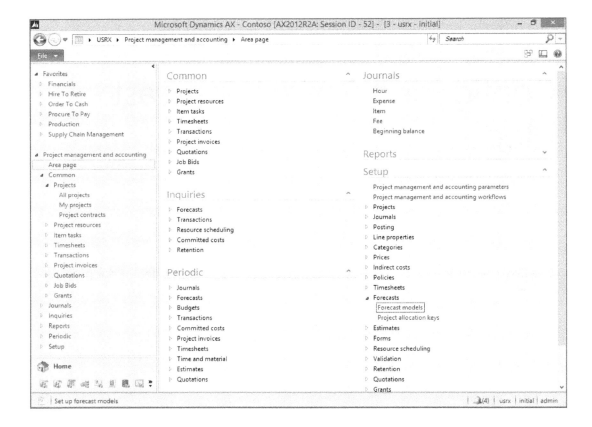

To do this, click on the **Forecast Models** menu item within the **Forecasts** folder fo the **Setup** group within the **Project Management And Accounting** area page.

Configuring Project Forecast Models

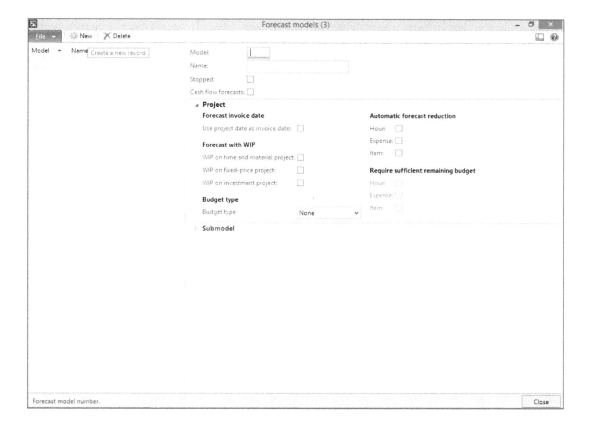

When the **Forecast Models** maintenance form is displayed, click on the **New** button in the menu bar to create a new record.

Configuring Project Forecast Models

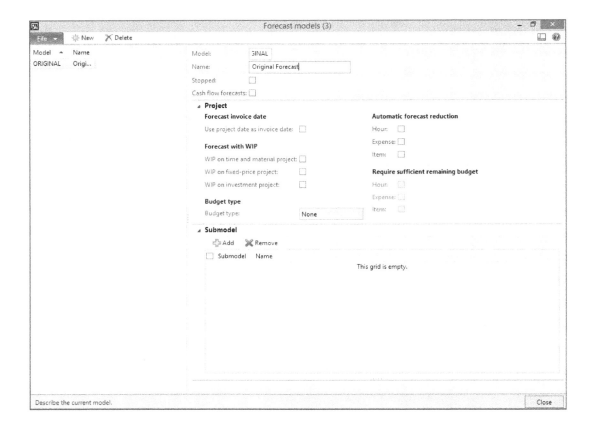

Set the **Model** code to be **ORIGINAL** and the **Name** to **Original Forecast**.

Configuring Project Forecast Models

Click on the **New** button in the menu bar to create another forecast model, and set the **Model** code to be **REMAINING** and the **Name** to be **Remaining Forecast**.

Configuring Project Forecast Models

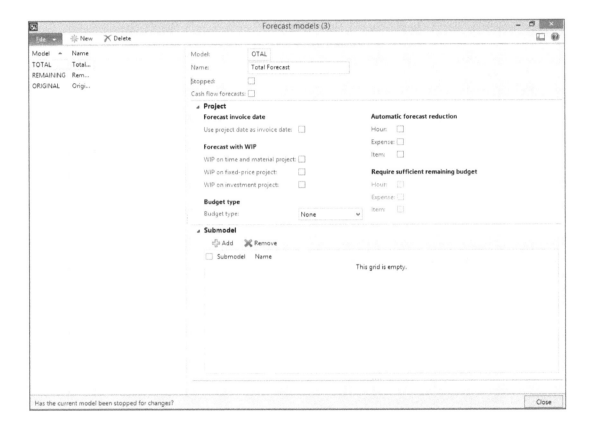

Click on the **New** button in the menu bar one last time to create another forecast model, and set the **Model** code to be **TOTAL** and the **Name** to be **Total Forecast**.

After creating these three forecast models, click on the **Close** button to exit from the form.

Configuring The Project Management Controls

Now all that is left is to configure the Project Management And Accounting controls to default in as much of this setup information as we can.

Configuring The Project Management Controls

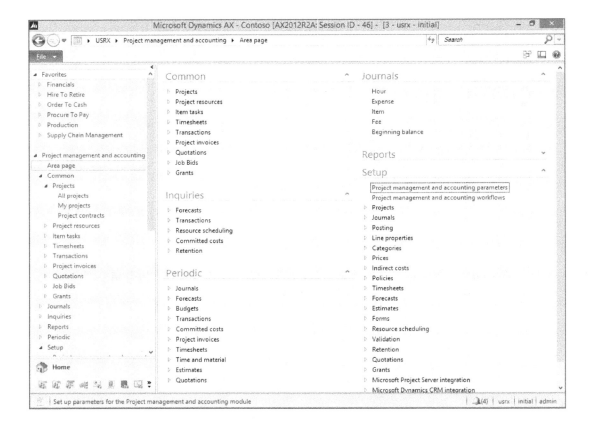

To do this, click on the **Project Management And Accounting Properties** menu button within the **Setup** group of the **Project Management And Accounting** area page.

Configuring The Project Management Controls

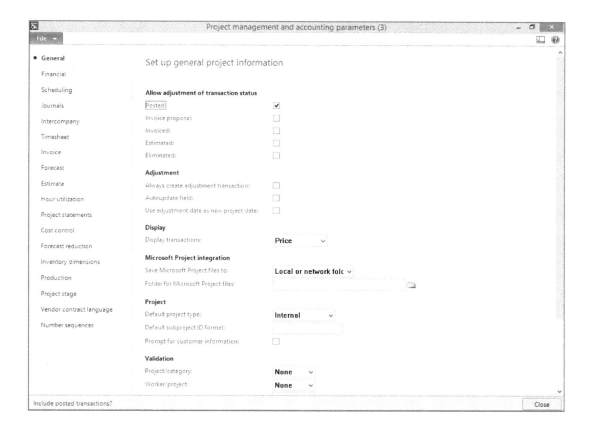

When the **Project Management And Accounting Parameters** maintenance form is displayed, start off on the **General** tab and check the **Posted** flag.

Configuring The Project Management Controls

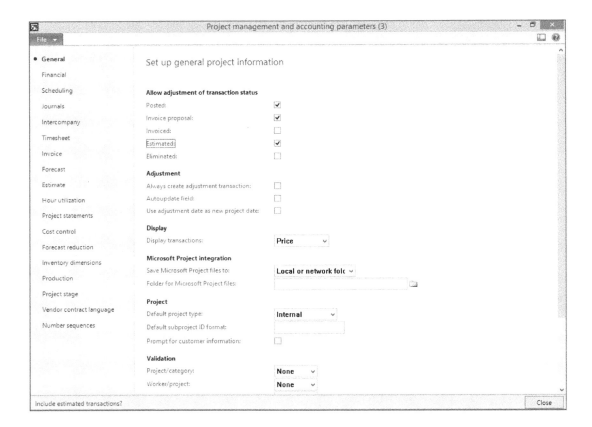

Also make sure that the **Invoice Proposal** and the **Estimated** flags are set within the **Allow Adjustments of Transactions Status** field group.

Configuring The Project Management Controls

To enable the integration with the Microsoft Project client, we need to set a default working directory that will store all of the projects. To do that, click on the **Folder** icon to the right of the **Folder For Microsoft Project Files** field and use the folder browser to point to a working directory that everyone is able to access.

Configuring The Project Management Controls

Also, if you want to create subprojects, then you can save time by setting the **Default Subproject ID Format** field to have a valid mask - **-##** works great.

Configuring The Project Management Controls

Then check the **Set the Cost Price As The Sales Price By Default** flag to save time with the pricing and quoting.

Configuring The Project Management Controls

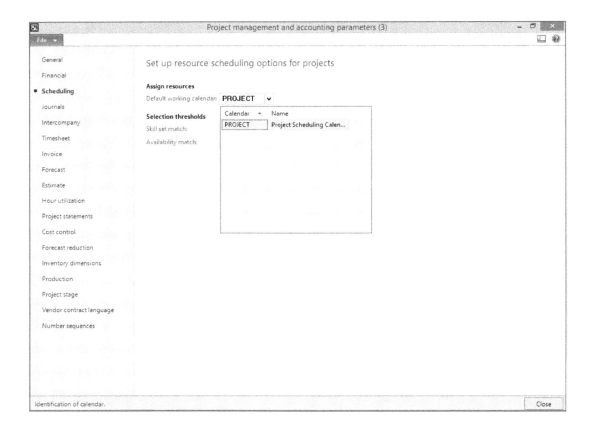

Now switch to the **Scheduling** tab and set the **Default Working Calendar** to the **PROJECT** calendar that you just configured.

Configuring The Project Management Controls

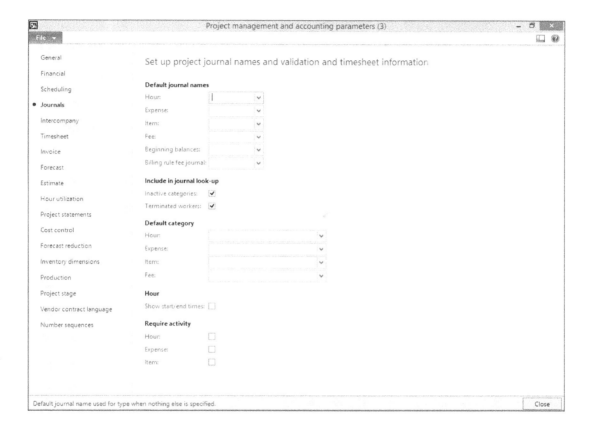

Now switch to the **Journals** tab. This contains all of the default journals that will be used by the Projects.

Configuring The Project Management Controls

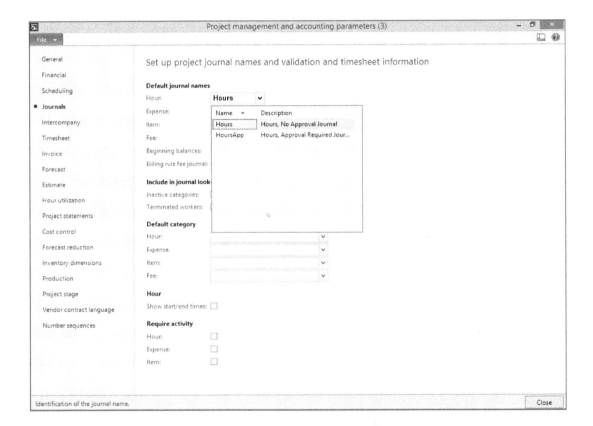

Click on eth **Hour Default Journal Name** dropdown and select the **Hours** journal.

Configuring The Project Management Controls

Repeat this by setting the **Expense** Journal to be **PROJJRN**, the **Item** Journal to be **PROJITEMJL**, the **Fee** Journal to be **Fee**, the **Beginning Balance** Journal to be **BegBal**, and the **Billing Rule Fee Category** to be **Fee**.

Configuring The Project Management Controls

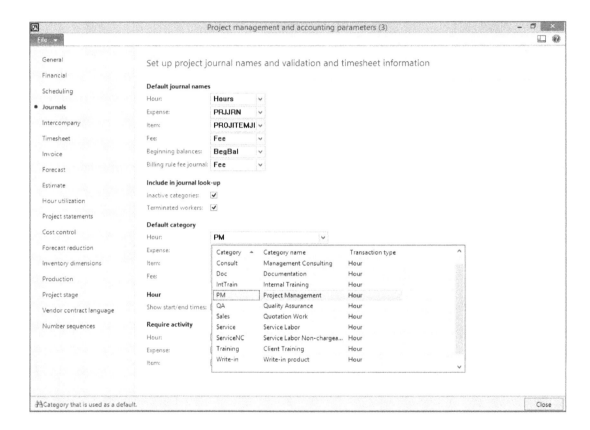

Within the **Default Category** field group set the **Hour** field to one of your default Hour Categories.

Configuring The Project Management Controls

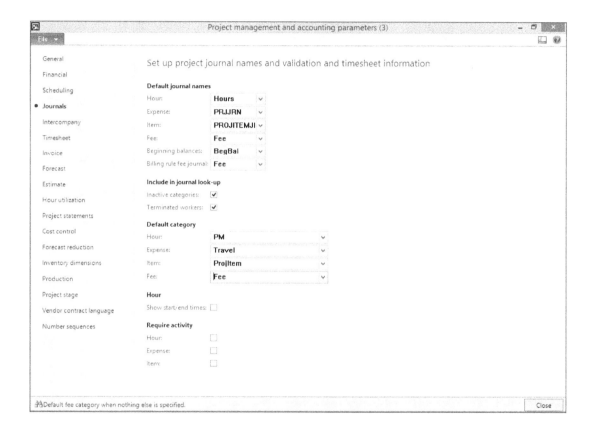

And repeat the process for the **Expense**, **Item**, and **Fee** Default Categories.

Configuring The Project Management Controls

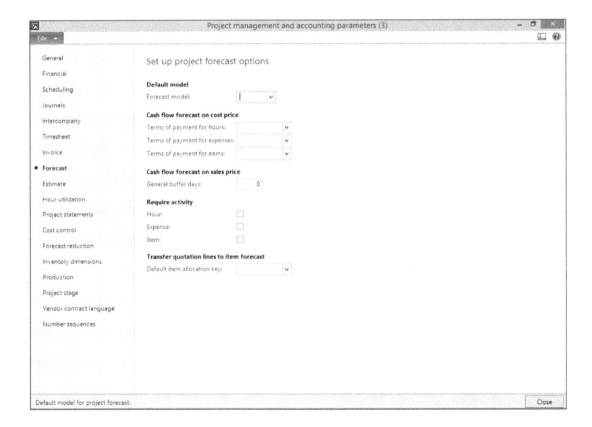

Now switch to the **Forecast** tab.

Configuring The Project Management Controls

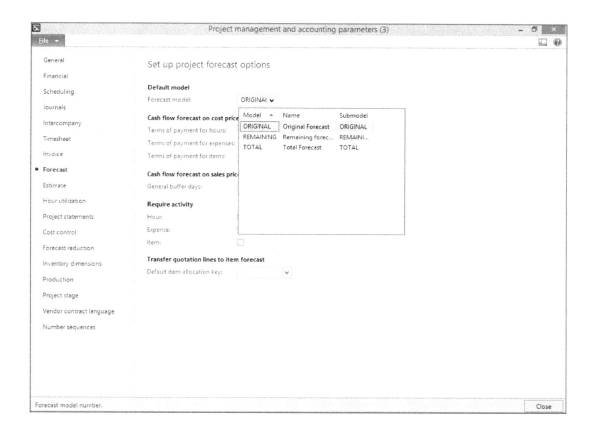

Click on the **Forecast Model** dropdown list and set it to be your **ORIGINAL** forecast model that you created.

Configuring The Project Management Controls

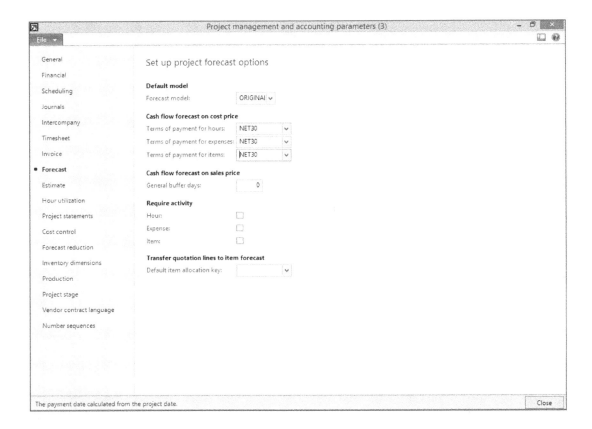

You can also set the **Terms Of Payment For Hours, Terms Of Payment For Expenses**, and **Terms Of Payment For Items** to be your typical payment terms.

Configuring The Project Management Controls

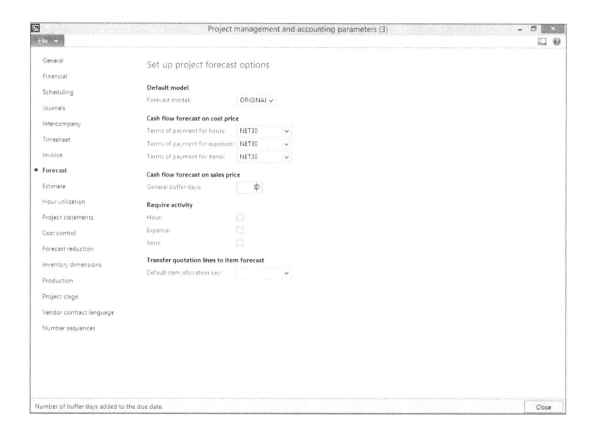

Also update the **General Buffer Days** to **30** to add a little bit of wiggle room to your forcasts.

Configuring The Project Managemnt Controls

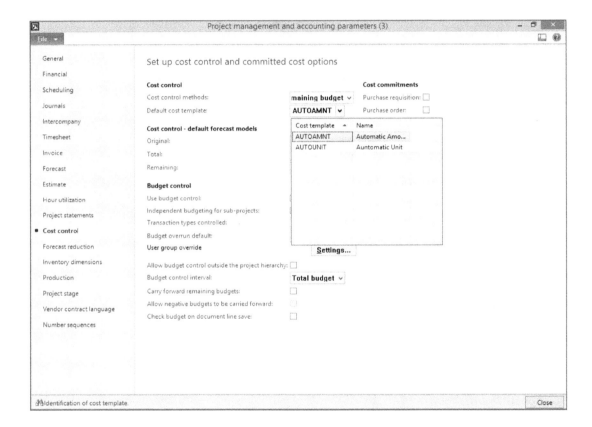

Now switch to the **Cost Control** tab.

Set the **Default Cost Template** code to be **AUTOAMNT**.

Configuring The Project Management Controls

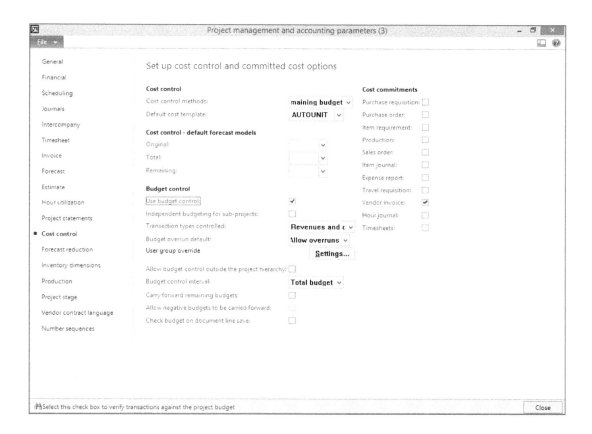

And if you want to control your projects so that the budgets warn them about over spending then you can check the **Use Budget Control** flag.

Configuring The Project Management Controls

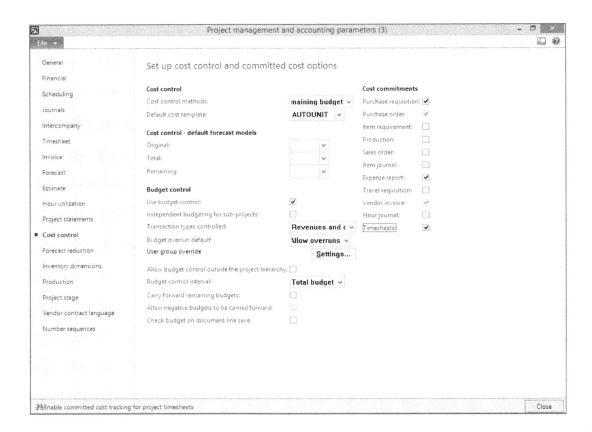

Within the **Cost Containment** field group, check the **Purchase Requisition, Purchase Order, Expense Report,** and **Timesheet** flags to enable budget checks on those documents.

Configuring The Project Management Controls

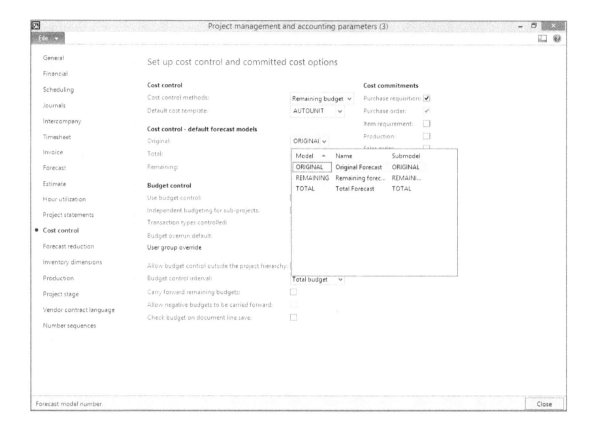

Within the **Cost Control – Default Forecast Models** field group, click on the **Original** fields dropdown list and select the **ORIGINAL** model.

Configuring The Project Management Controls

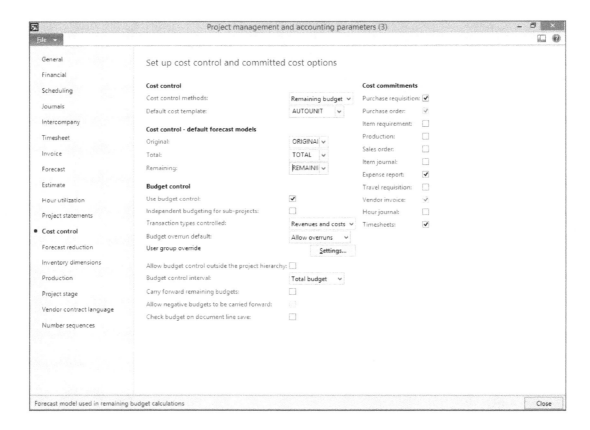

The click on the **Total** fields dropdown list and select the **TOTAL** model and click on the **Remaining** fields dropdown list and select the **REMAINING** model.

Configuring The Project Management Controls

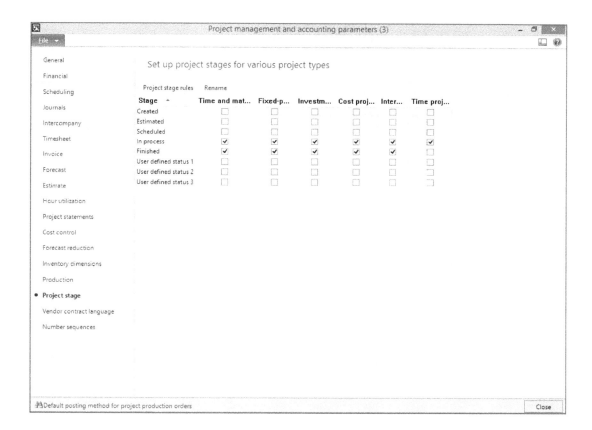

The final step is to click on the **Project Stage** tab.

Configuring The Project Management Controls

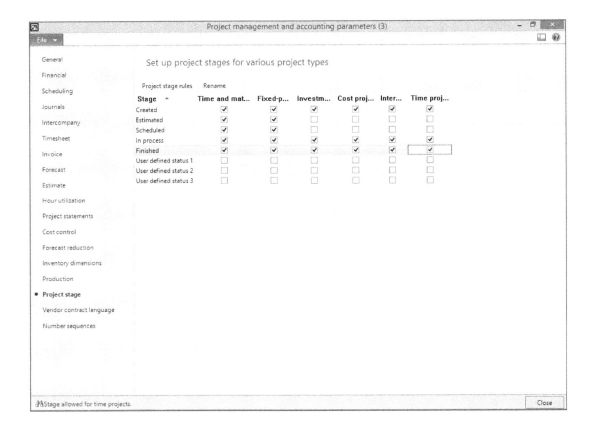

This form allows you to enable the different stages that a project may be placed in by Project Type. You can update these so that you can have additional stages if you like.

After you have done that, just click on the **Close** button and exit from the form.

All the main setup is now done.

CONFIGURING PROJECTS

Once you have all of the codes and controls set up for your projects you can start building your projects within Dynamics AX. You can start by creating your work breakdown structures, then create estimates and budgets, and also track workers and resources against the projects. Additionally, once you have created your projects you can save them as templates and reuse them for other similar projects as well making you even more productive.

In this chapter we will walk through the main components of **Projects** and show you how to set up and manage all of these project components.

Creating Projects

The first step is just to create a project.

Creating Projects

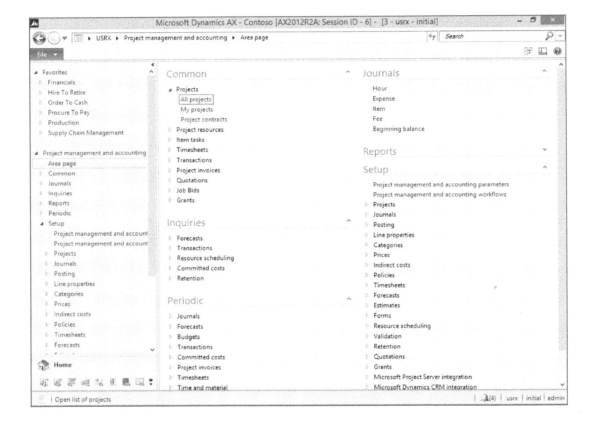

To do this, click on the **All Projects** menu item within the **Projects** folder of the **Common** group within the **Project Management And Accounting** area page.

Creating Projects

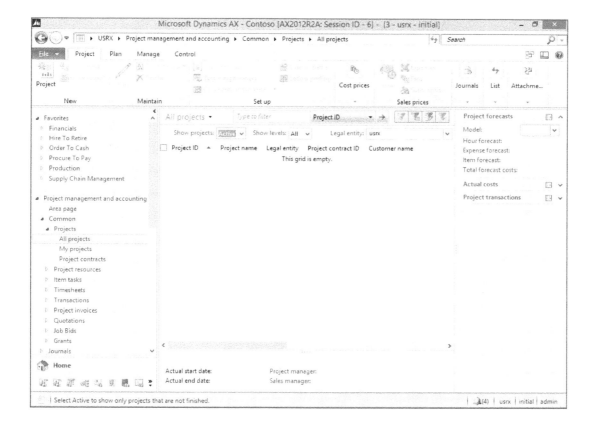

This will take you to the **Projects** list page. To create a new project just click on the **Project** button within the **New** group of the **Project** ribbon bar.

Creating Projects

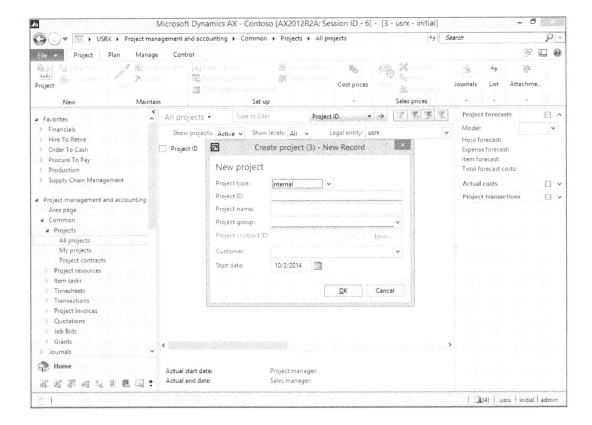

This will open up the **New Project** dialog box.

Creating Projects

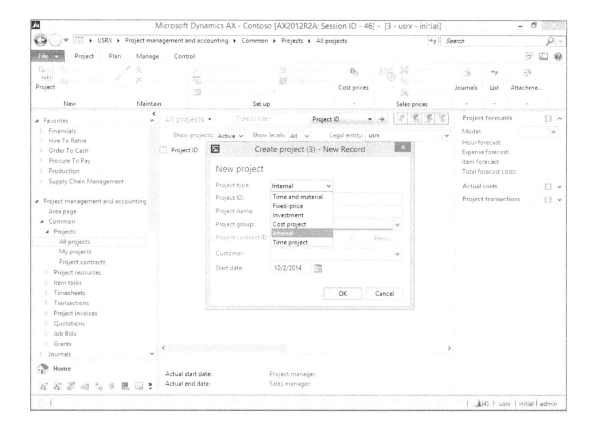

From the **Project Type** dropdown box, select the type of project that you want to create. This will filter out the **Project Group** to just the groups that match.

Creating Projects

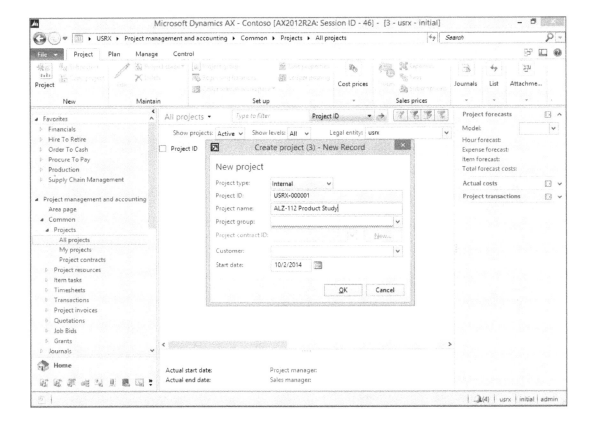

Then assign your project and **Project Name**.

Creating Projects

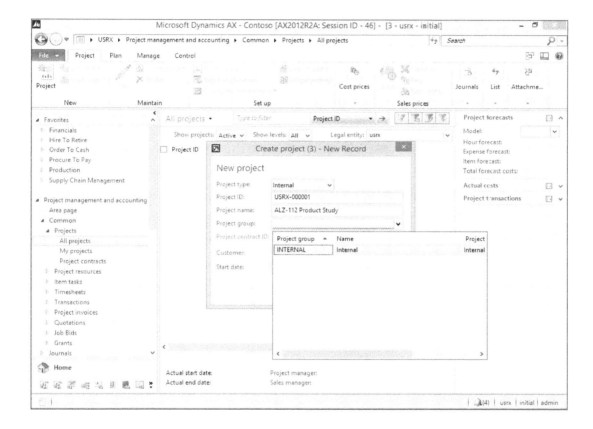

Then click on the **Project Group** dropdown list and select the **Project Group** that you want to assign to this project.

Creating Projects

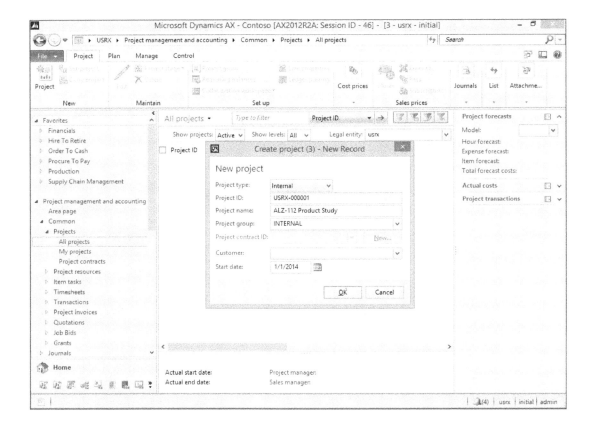

Finally, adjust the **Start Date** for the project and then click on the **OK** button to create the project.

Creating Projects

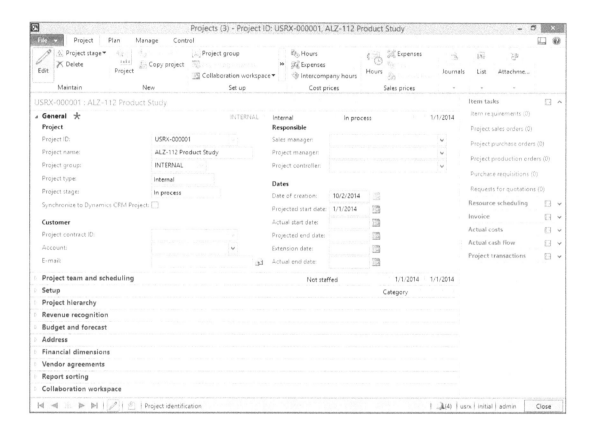

Dynamics AX will then create a new **Project** for you and take you to the detail page where you can start refining your project setup.

Assigning Scheduling Calendars To Projects

If you are going to be assigning resources to your project then you need to make sure that you assign a **Scheduling Calendar** to your project for the project to work off. A benefit of this is that projects can have different calendars associated with them, allowing you to schedule them differently within the system.

Assigning Scheduling Calendars To Projects

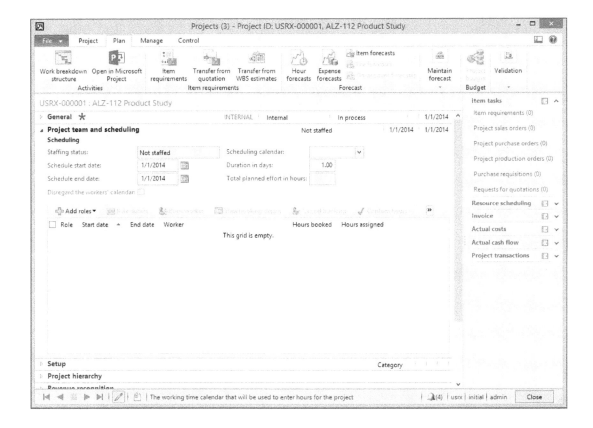

To do this, open up your **Project** and expand our the **Project Team And Scheduling** tab group.

Assigning Scheduling Calendars To Projects

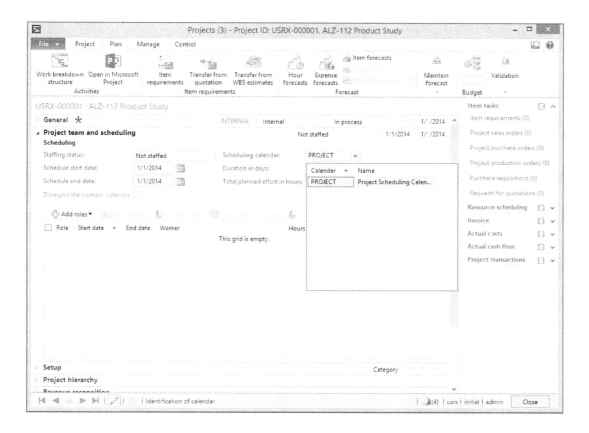

Click on the **Scheduling Calendar** dropdown list and select the **Calendar** that you want to use for your project.

Assigning Scheduling Calendars To Projects

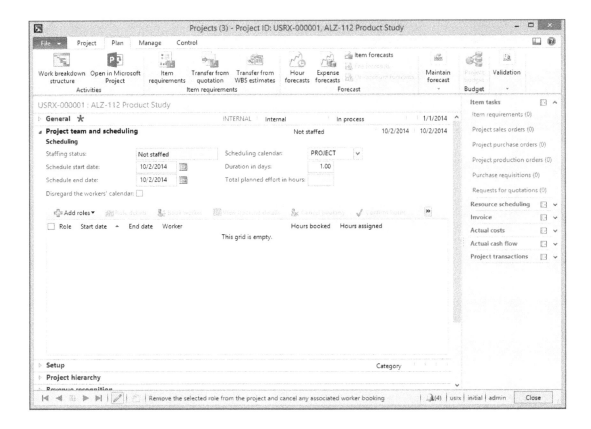

This will default in your initial project dates and durations for the project and you are done.

Creating A Project Work Breakdown Structure

Once you have your base project set up, you can start adding structure to your project by creating a more detailed **Work Breakdown Structure** to detail all of the project steps and milestones.

Creating A Project Work Breakdown Structure

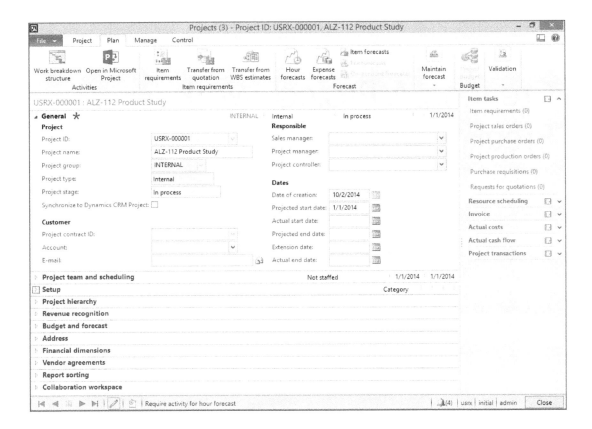

To do this, open up your **Project** and switch to the **Plan** ribbon bar. You will notice that this contains all of the options for setting up and estimating your project activities, requirements, and forecasts. For this step though, click on the **Work Breakdown Structure** button within the **Activities** group of the **Plan** ribbon bar.

Creating A Project Work Breakdown Structure

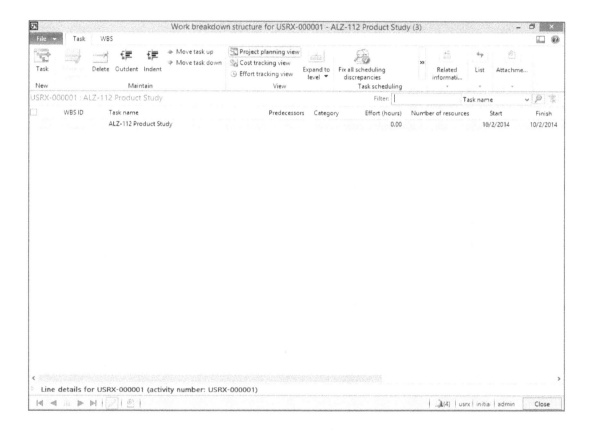

This will open up the **Work Breakdown Structure** maintenance form for the project with the parent level already attached to it.

Creating A Project Work Breakdown Structure

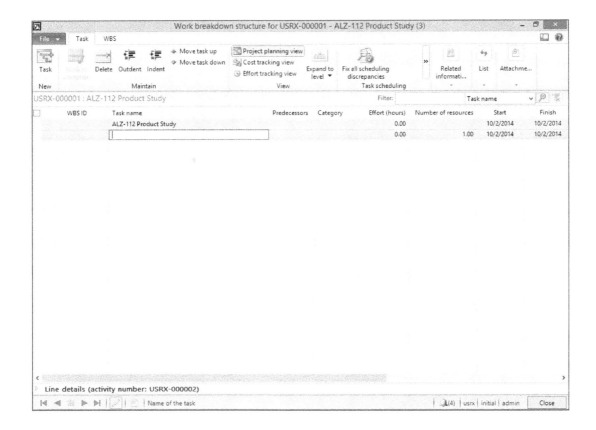

To create a new level to the work breakdown structure, click on the **Task** button within the **New** group of the **Task** ribbon bar.

Creating A Project Work Breakdown Structure

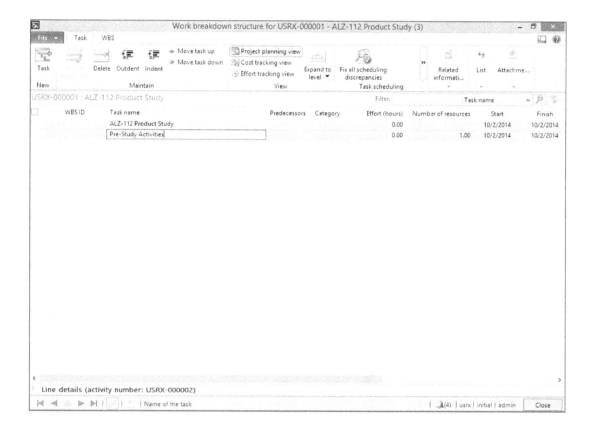

Then enter in a **Task Name**.

Creating A Project Work Breakdown Structure

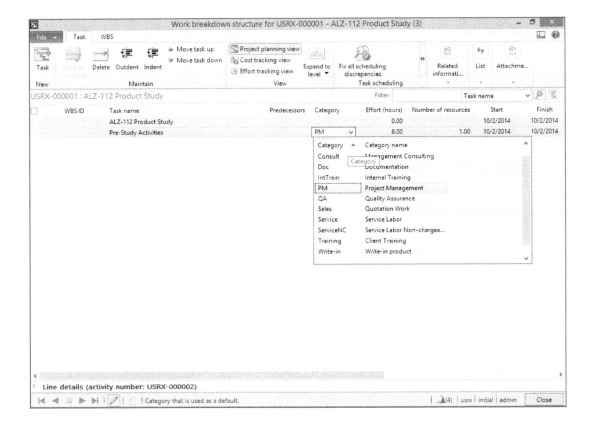

From the **Category** dropdown list, select the type of activity that this will be assigned.

Creating A Project Work Breakdown Structure

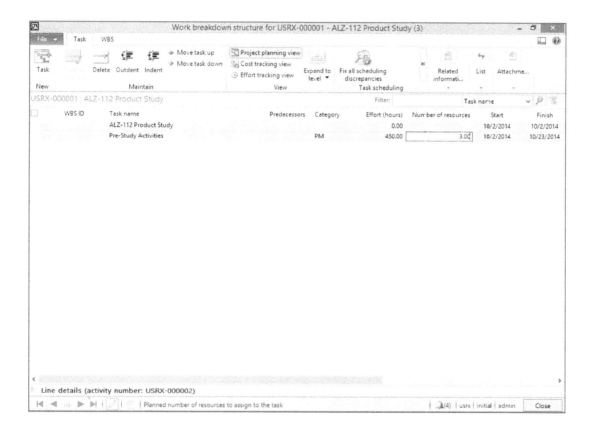

And then enter in the number of hours that this task will take within the **Effort** field and also the **Number Of Resources** that will be required for this task.

Notice that the **Start** and **Finish** dates will start to update themselves based on the man hours that you start defining here.

Creating A Project Work Breakdown Structure

You can click on the **Task** button within the **New** group of the **Task** ribbon bar to create the next task in the work breakdown structure and configure it just the same way.

Creating A Project Work Breakdown Structure

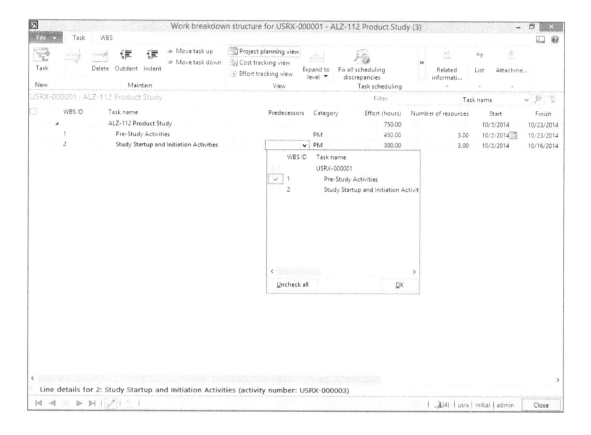

If a task is dependent on a prior task to be completed then you can click on the **Predecessors** dropdown list and select any tasks that need to be completed before moving on to this task, and then click the **OK** button.

Creating A Project Work Breakdown Structure

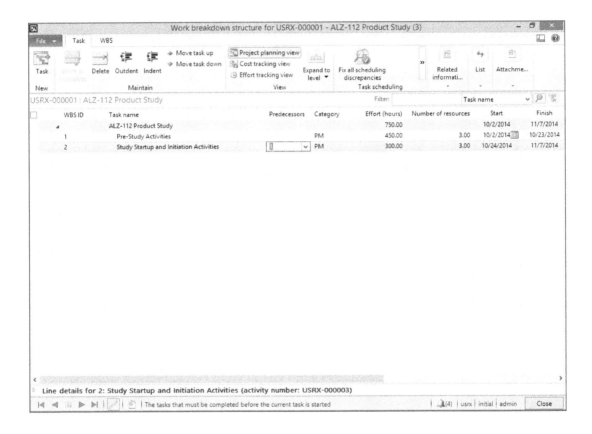

You will notice that the **Start** and **Finish** dates will start to cascade based on these dependancies.

Creating A Project Work Breakdown Structure

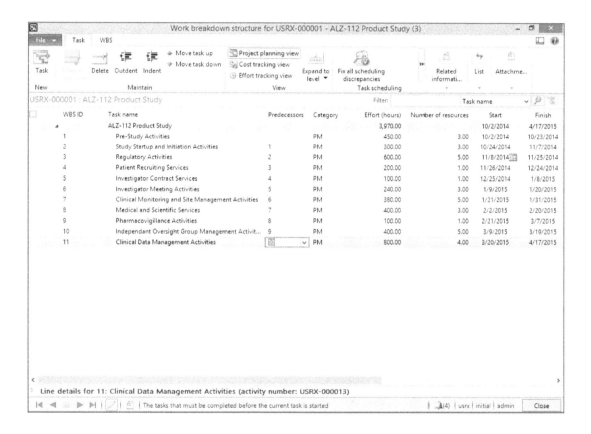

You can keep on adding as many of the tasks that you have defined all of the work breakdown structure.

Editing Work Breakdown Structures Through Microsoft Project

Although editing your work breakdown structure through Dynamics AX is great, if you have a copy of Microsoft Project on your desktop then you can make it even easier by using that as your editing and maintenance tool.

Editing Work Breakdown Structures Through Microsoft Project

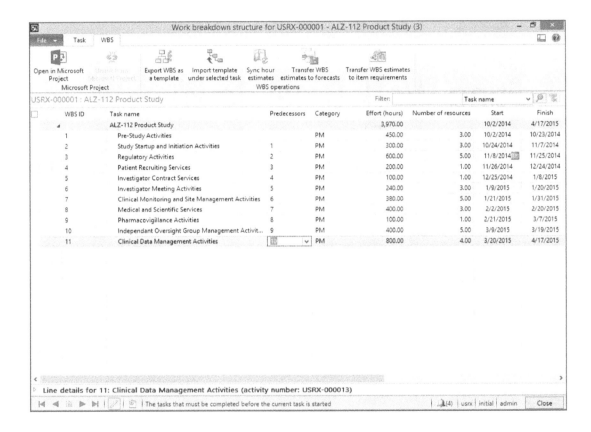

To use Microsoft Project, all you need to do is click on the **Open In Microsoft Project** menu button within the **Microsoft Project** group of the **WBS** ribbon bar.

Editing Work Breakdown Structures Through Microsoft Project

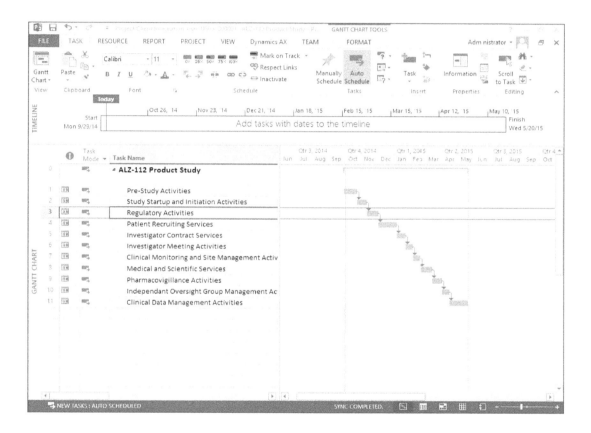

That will open up Microsoft Project for you and copy all of the work breakdown structure tasks over to it preserving all of the links and relationships that you had built in the original clients version.

Editing Work Breakdown Structures Through Microsoft Project

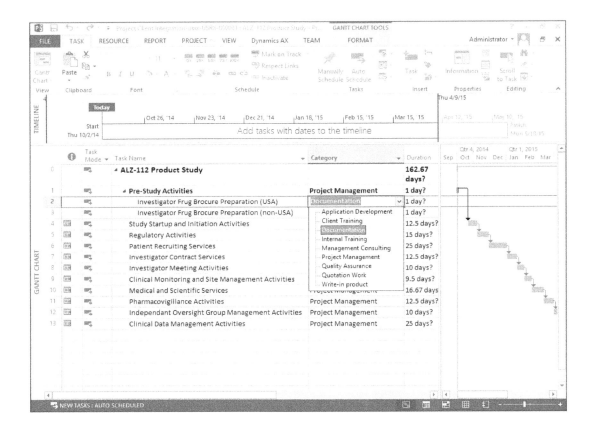

You can then add any additional tasks that you like into the project, and also all of the categories that you have configured within Dynamics AX show up as **Categories** within Microsoft Project.

Editing Work Breakdown Structures Through Microsoft Project

Once you have made all of the changes that you need to the project tasks you can update Dynamics AX by clicking on the **Publish** button within the Update group of the **Dynamics AX** ribbon bar of Microsoft Project.

Editing Work Breakdown Structures Through Microsoft Project

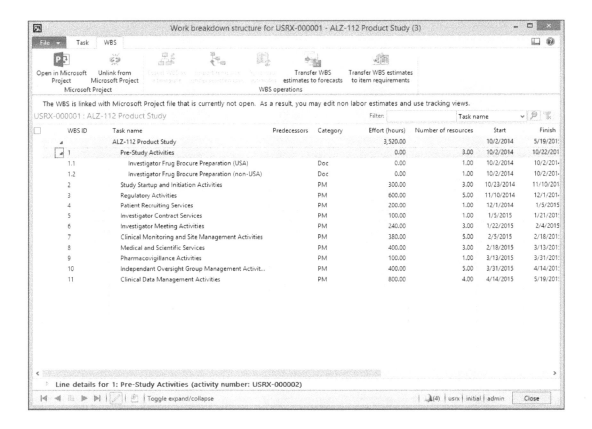

When you return to Dynamics AX you will see that all of the tasks that you updated within Microsoft Project have been updated within the original **Work Breakdown Structure**.

Editing Work Breakdown Structures Through Microsoft Project

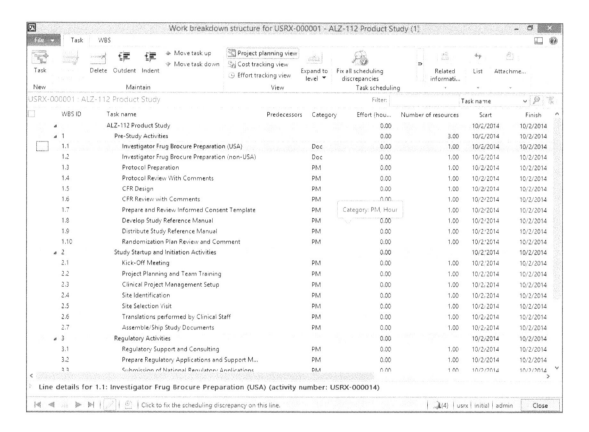

This is a great way to easily manage and update large project plans.

Using The Cost Tracking View To Estimate Costs

Once you have set up your projects **Work Breakdown Structure** you can start estimating the costs of the project. A quick way to don this is to just enter in your estimated costs through the **Cost Tracking View**.

Using The Cost Tracking View To Estimate Costs

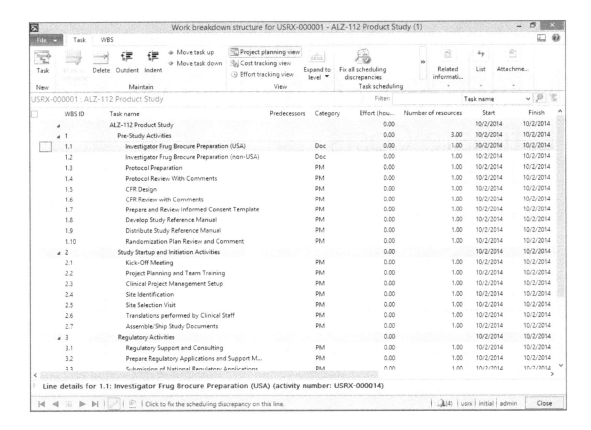

The default view is the **Project Planning View** which shows you all the dates, and resource requirements for your project.

Using The Cost Tracking View To Estimate Costs

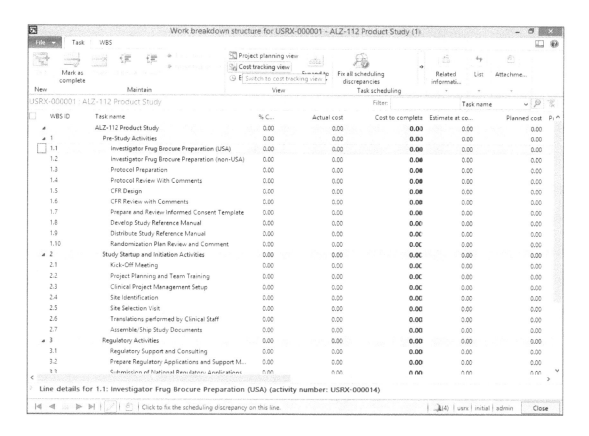

To view this a better way for cost management, click on the **Cost Tracking View** menu button within the **View** group of the **Task** ribbon bar. This will switch you to a view that is more tailored to estimating costs.

Using The Cost Tracking View To Estimate Costs

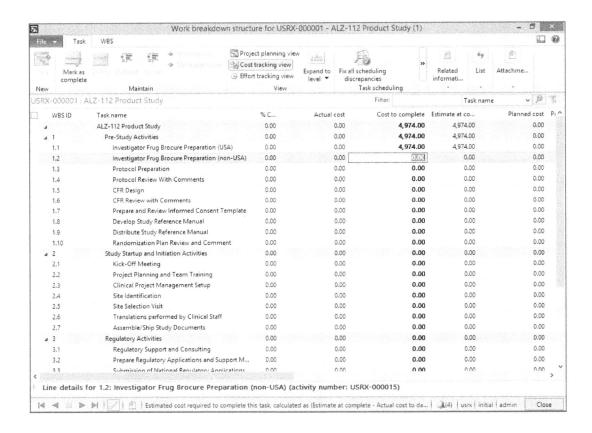

All you need to do is fill in the **Cost To Complete** field within the work breakdown structure and the costs will roll up to the parent levels.

Using The Cost Tracking View To Estimate Costs

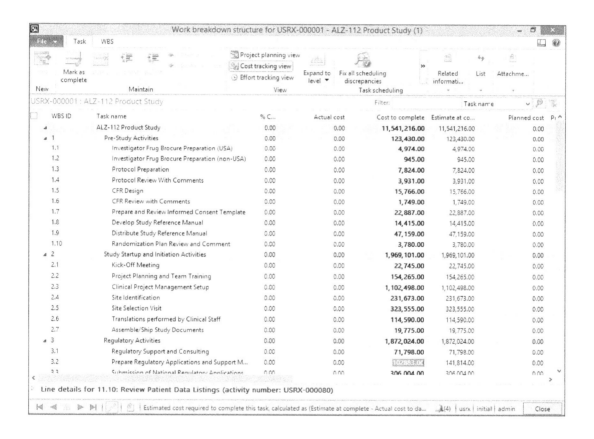

After estimating all of the costs you will be able to see an estimate of the true costs and every level of the project.

Using The Cost Tracking View To Estimate Costs

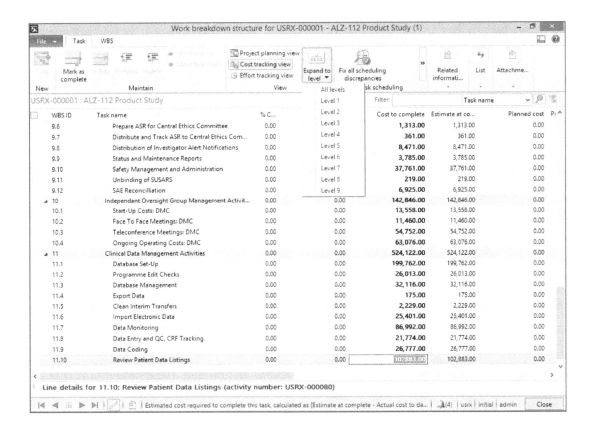

If you click on the **Expand To Level** button within the **Task Scheduling** group of the **Task** ribbon bar then you will be able to select which levels within the work breakdown structure you want to see.

Using The Cost Tracking View To Estimate Costs

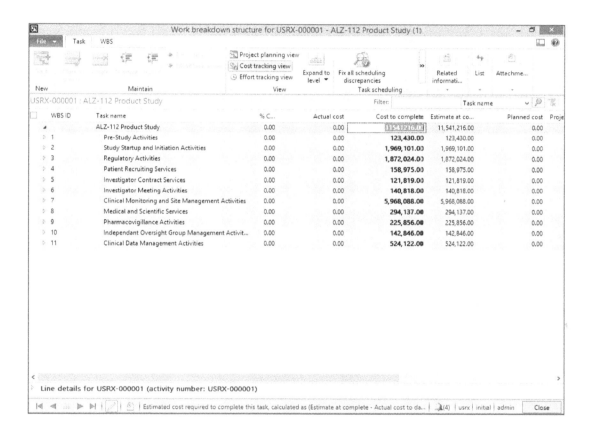

By Selecting the **Level 2** option you will see just the costs for eash of the individual project phases.

Adding Estimated Costs To WBS Lines

If you want to get even more granular during your project estimation phase then you can definitely do that by adding detailed estimates to the work breakdown structure lines. This allows you to itemize your project costs and then have those costs roll up to the task lines.

Adding Estimated Costs To WBS Lines

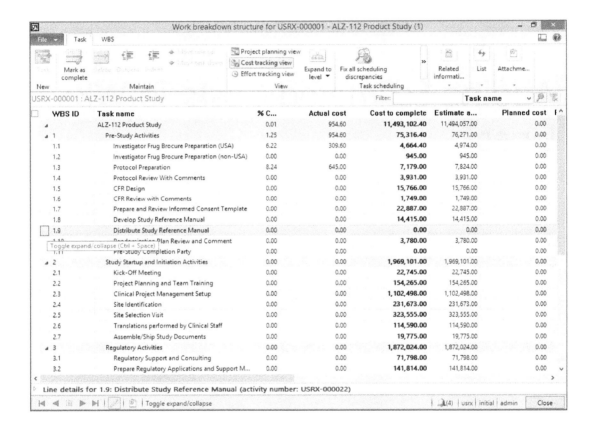

To do this, select the line that you want to itemize the cost estimates for.

Adding Estimated Costs To WBS Lines

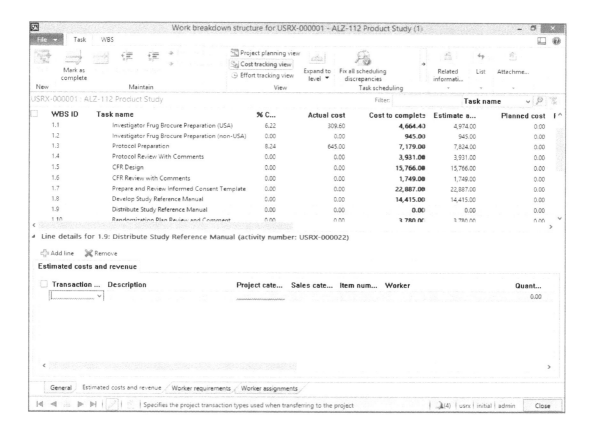

Then expand the **Line Details** tab at the bottom of the form. This will show you a new section where you can enter in the **Estimated Costs And Revenue**.

Adding Estimated Costs To WBS Lines

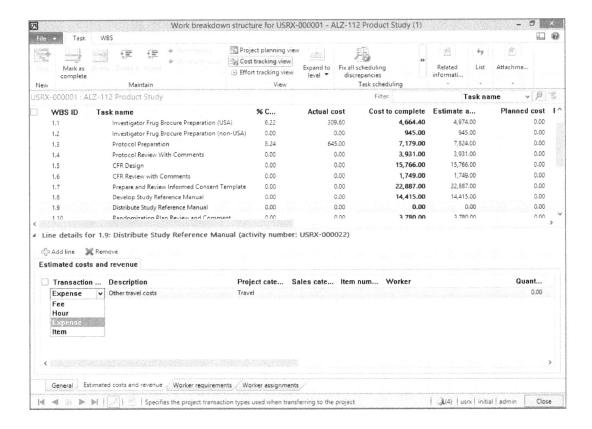

To add a new cost estimate, click on the **Add Line** button within the tabs header to create a new line.

Then from the **Transaction Type** dropdown list, select the type of project element this will be.

Adding Estimated Costs To WBS Lines

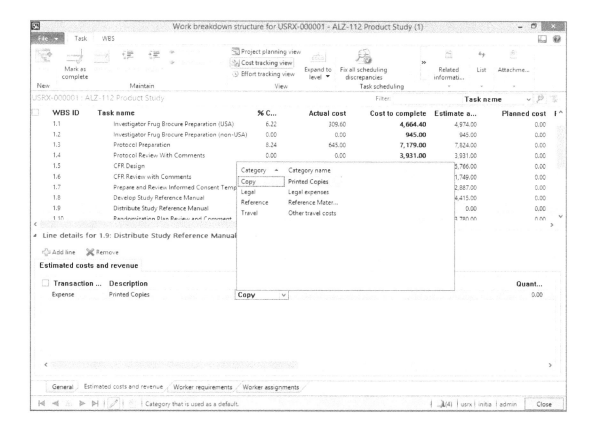

Then enter in a **Description** and also a **Project Category** from the dropdown list.

Adding Estimated Costs To WBS Lines

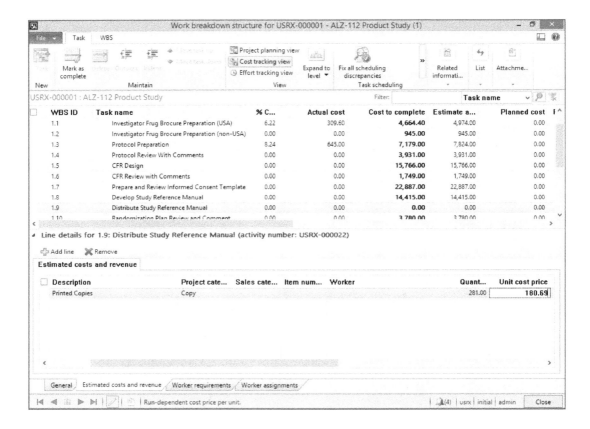

Then enter in a **Quantity** and also a **Unit Cost Price** for the line item.

Adding Estimated Costs To WBS Lines

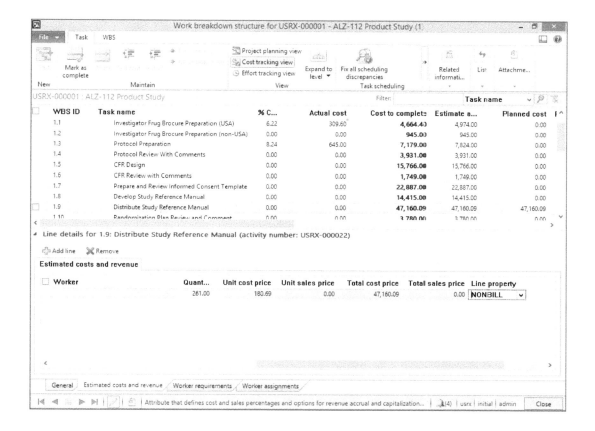

Finally scroll over to the far end of the table and set the **Line Property** to either Billable or Non-Billable.

After you save the line you will notice that the **Cost To Complete** for the line will be updated to include these estimated costs, and also the **Planned Cost** will be updated with these estimates as well so that you can see which lines have actual detail behind them.

Transferring WBS Estimates To Project Forecasts

Once you have configured your Work Breakdown Structures estimate details, you can use them to populate the **Project Forecasts** rather than entering them in yourself.

Transferring WBS Estimates To Project Forecasts

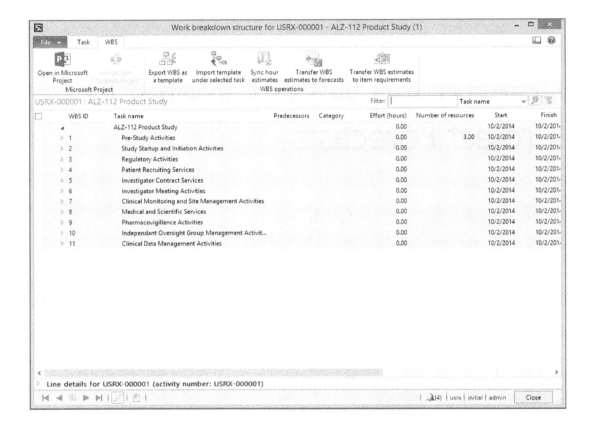

To do this all you need to do is click on the **Transfer WBS Estimates To Forecasts** button within the **WBS Operations** group od the **WBS** ribbon bar.

Transferring WBS Estimates To Project Forecasts

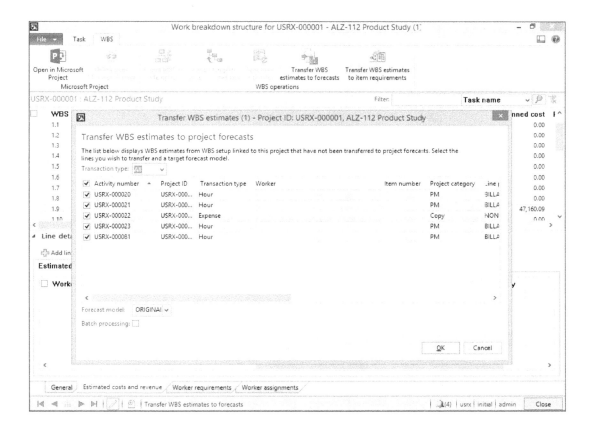

This will open up a dialog box that shows you all of the line estimates that you have configured within you project. All you need to do is mark the ones that you want to be transferred to the forecast a then click on the **OK** button.

Transferring WBS Estimates To Project Forecasts

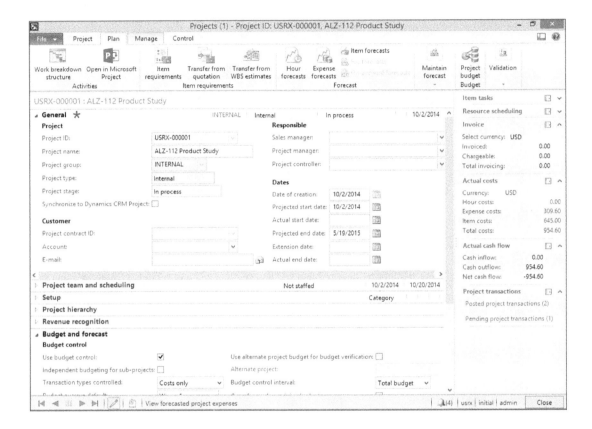

To view them, simply open up the **Project** and click on the **Expense Forecasts** button within the **Forecast** group of the **Plan** ribbon bar.

Transferring WBS Estimates To Project Forecasts

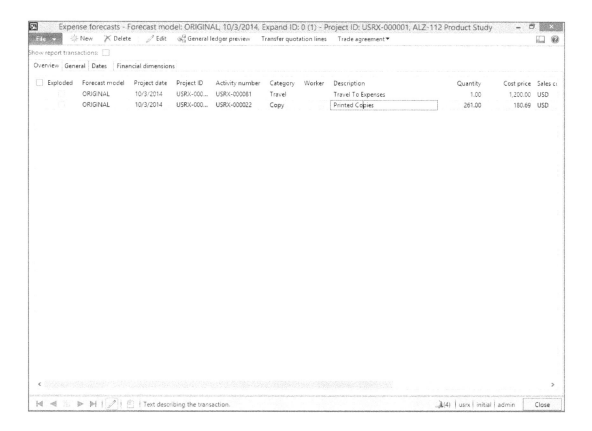

This will open up a new maintenance form that shows you all of the line items expenses from the work breakdown structure as forecasted costs.

Posting AP Invoices Against Project Activities

Now that we have a project structure and some estimates and forecasts, we can start posting actual expenses against it and then start to track our project costs. This is done a number of different ways, but the simplest is through is just to enter in an AP Invoice and then associate it with a project.

Posting AP Invoices Against Project Activities

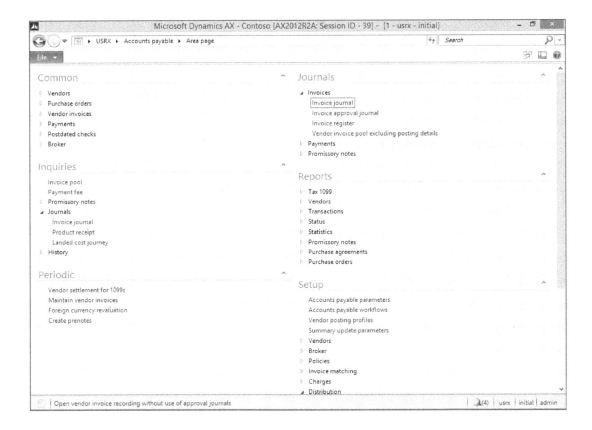

To do this, click on the **Invoice Journal** menu item within the **Invoices** folder of the **Journals** group within the **Accounts Payable** area page.

Posting AP Invoices Against Project Activities

When the **Invoice Journal** list form is displayed, click on the **New** button within the menu bar to create a new journal.

Posting AP Invoices Against Project Activities

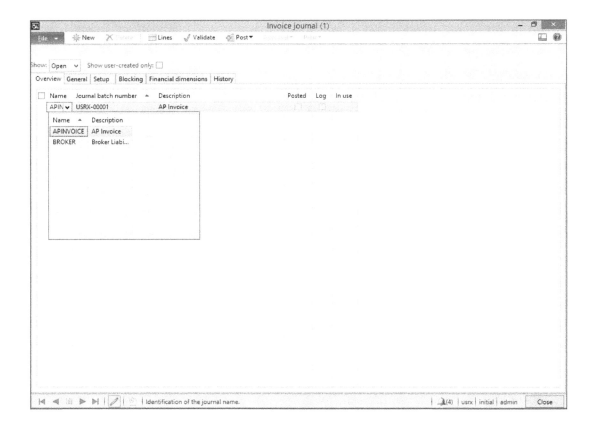

Then select the **Journal Name** that you want to use for the invoice journal.

Posting AP Invoices Against Project Activities

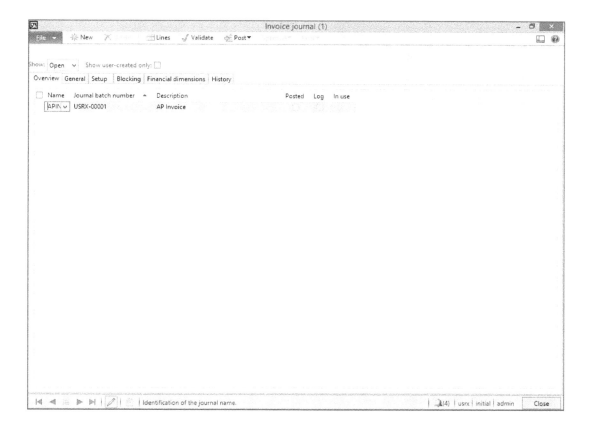

And then click on the **Lines** button in the menu bar to start entering in the AP Invoice Journal lines.

Posting AP Invoices Against Project Activities

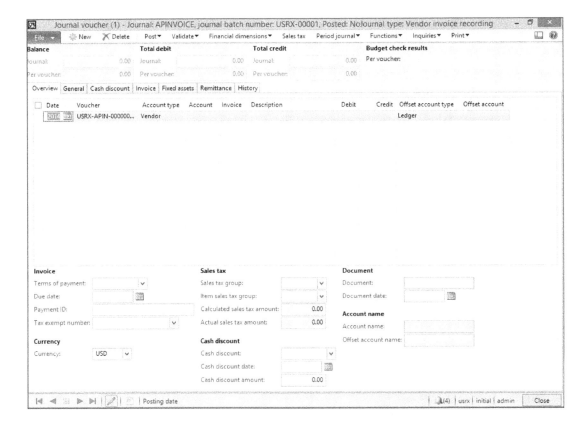

When the **Journal Voucher** form is displayed, click on the **New** button in the menu bar to create a new line.

Posting AP Invoices Against Project Activities

Fill in all of the details for your Invoice Voucher and then change the **Offset Account Type** to **Project**.

Posting AP Invoices Against Project Activities

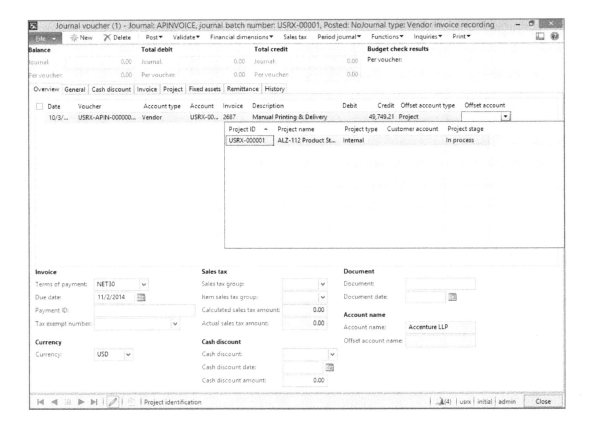

This will allow you to select the **Project ID** that you want to associate this voucher with.

Posting AP Invoices Against Project Activities

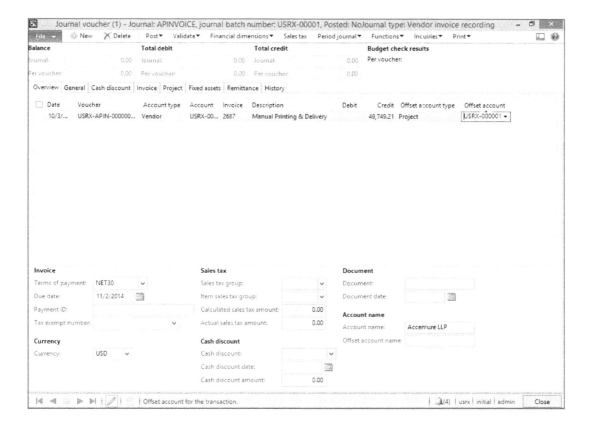

After you have done that notice that there is now a new tab within the voucher line form for **Project**.

Posting AP Invoices Against Project Activities

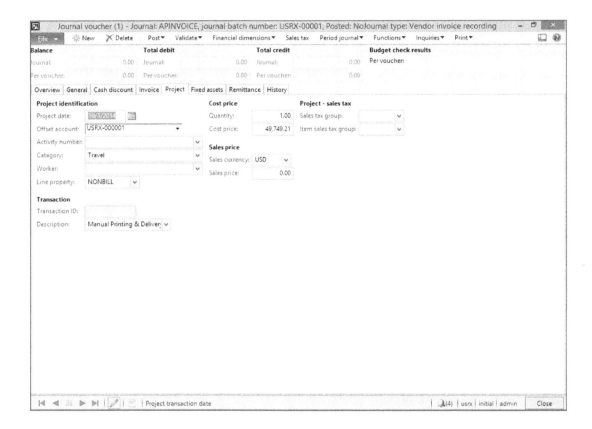

If you click on that tab you will see that there is a lot more detail that you can add for the voucher line.

Posting AP Invoices Against Project Activities

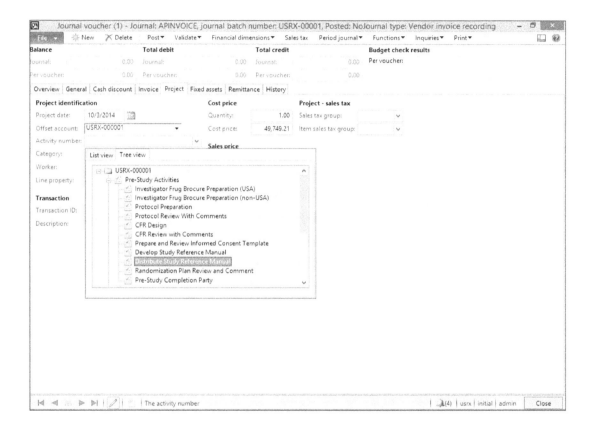

If you click on the **Activity Number** dropdown list you will be able to associate these costs to an activity within the work breakdown structure.

Posting AP Invoices Against Project Activities

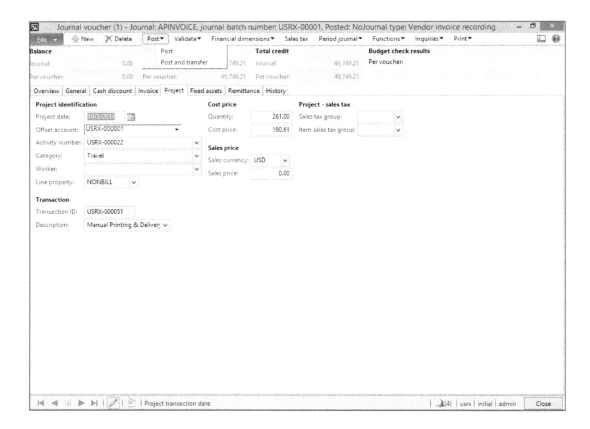

After you have updated the project details within the AP Voucher, click on the **Post** menu item within the **Post** menu in the menu bar.

Posting AP Invoices Against Project Activities

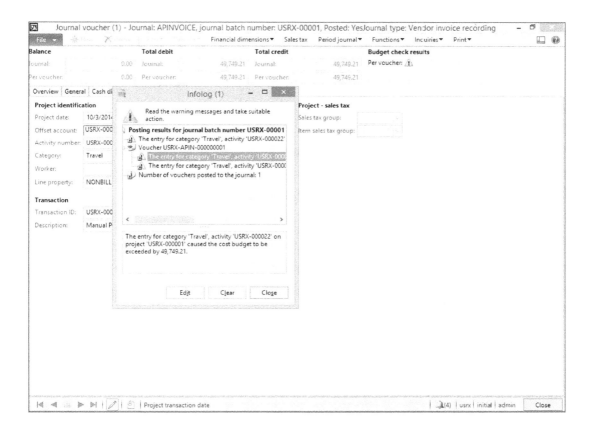

After posting, your costs will be associated with the project task and if there are any budget constraints then it will notify you right away.

Monitoring Costs Using The Cost Tracking View

As people start posting to your projects through the other modules you will want to start monitoring them and making sure that your project doesn't start running out of control.

Monitoring Costs Using The Cost Tracking View

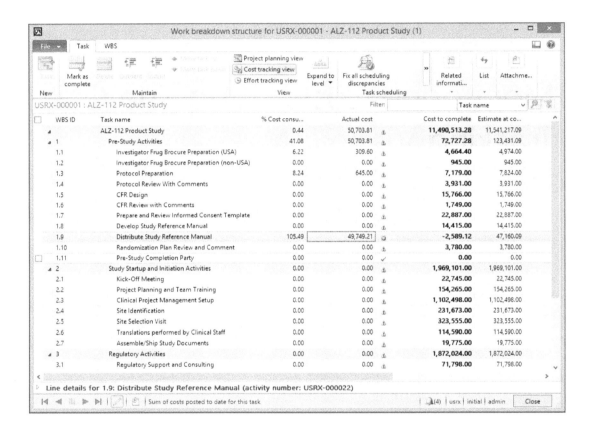

To do this, just return to your projects work breakdown structure and switch to the **Cost Tracking View** so that you can see all of the estimated and posted costs. You will be able to see any lines that have actual costs that are close to or exceeding the planned costs.

Monitoring Costs Using The Cost Tracking View

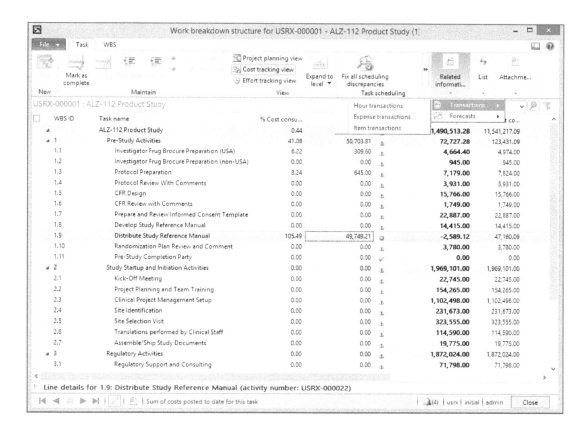

To see the detail below the costs, just select the line within the work breakdown structure and click on the **Transactions** button within the **Related Information** group of the **Task** ribbon bar. That will allow you to select the type of transaction that you want to view.

Monitoring Costs Using The Cost Tracking View

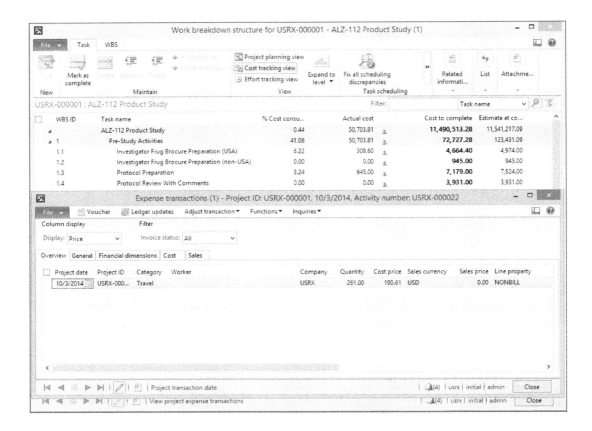

When you select the transaction type you will be taken into a detailed list of the transactions including the ones that were posted from the other modules.

Creating Project Statements To Analyze Project Performance

As projects run through their lifecycle you may want a to create **Project Statements** that allow you to see all of the costs and how the project is performing against the planned costs.

Creating Project Statements To Analyze Project Performance

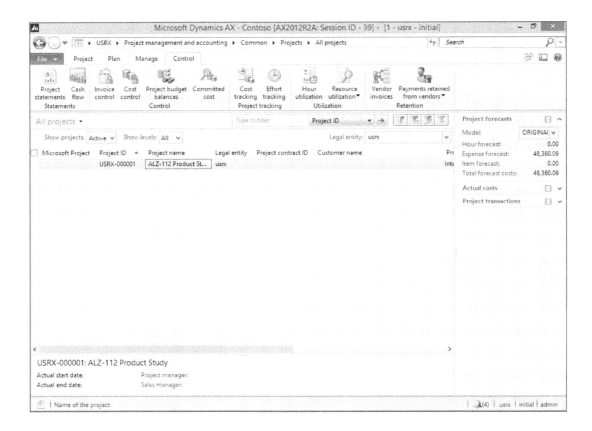

To do this, click on the **Project Statements** button within the **Statements** group of the **Control** ribbon bar.

Creating Project Statements To Analyze Project Performance

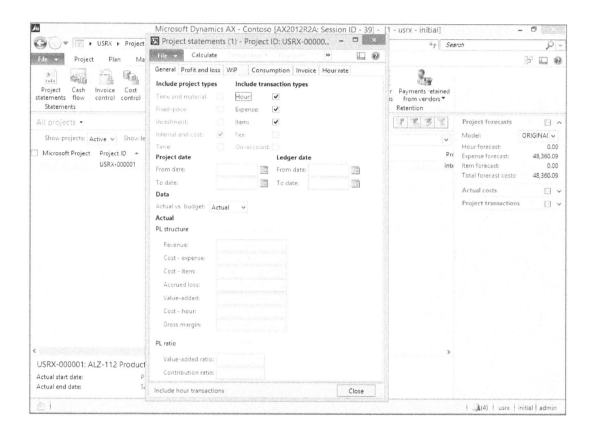

This will open up the **Project Statements** summary form. You can check or uncheck any of the transactions types that you want to include or remove from the statement.

Creating Project Statements To Analyze Project Performance

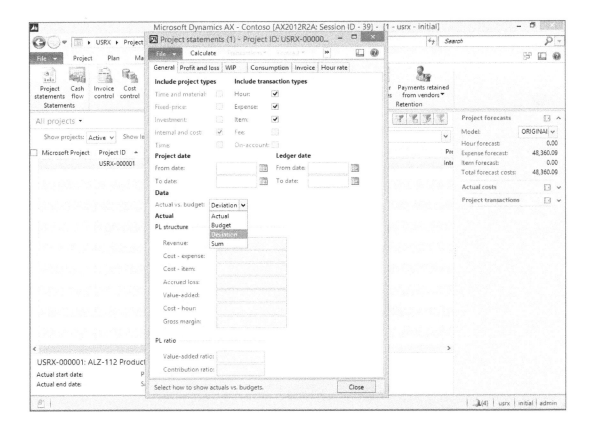

If you click on the dropdown list for the **Actual vs. Budget** field then you will be able to select a number of different comparison options. If you choose the **Deviation** option then you will be able to see the actual, budget, and deviation columns.

Creating Project Statements To Analyze Project Performance

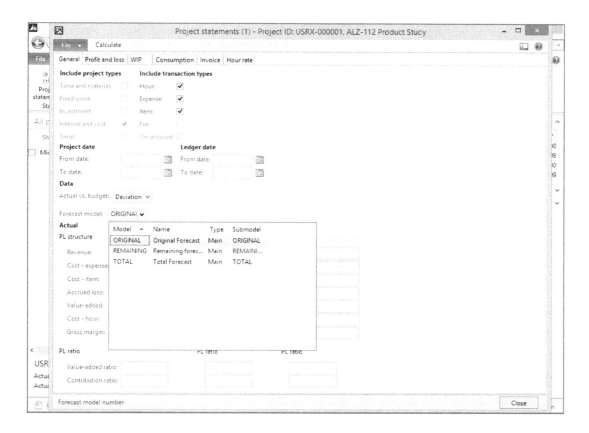

Also if you click on the **Forecast Model** dropdown list you can select from the different forecast models that you have created within Project Management.

Creating Project Statements To Analyze Project Performance

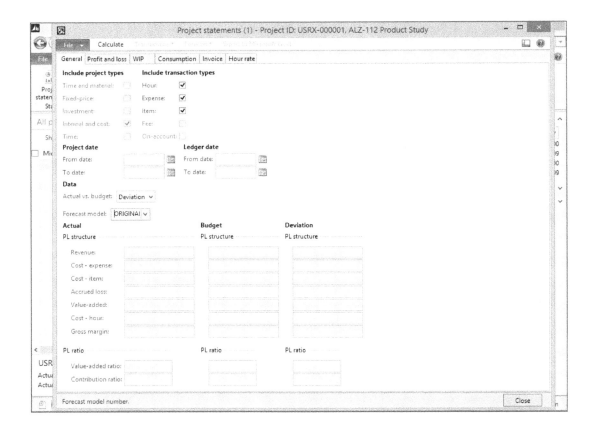

Once you have tweaked your Project Statement settings, click on the **Calculate** button within the menu bar.

Creating Project Statements To Analyze Project Performance

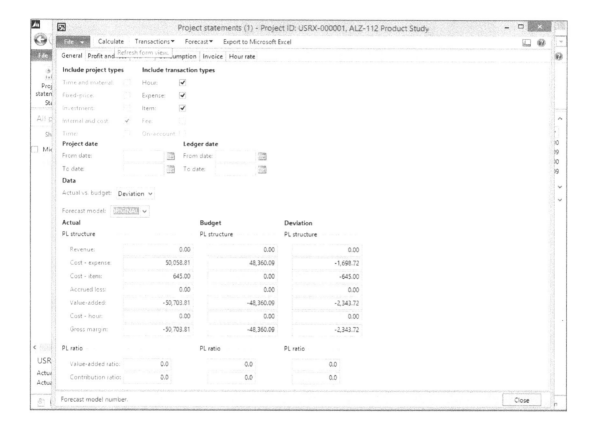

This will summarize all of your project actual and budgeted costs and revenue, giving you a quick view into the status of the project.

Creating Project Statements To Analyze Project Performance

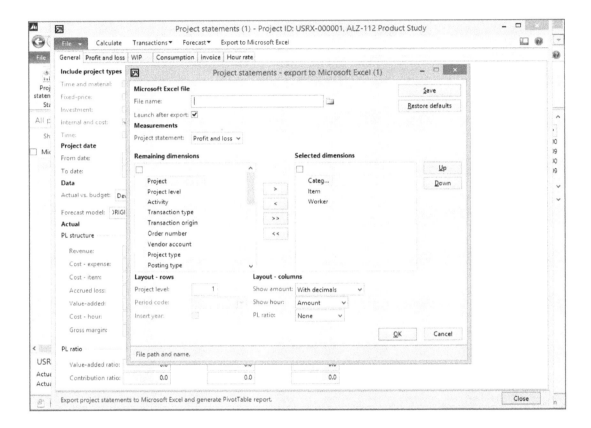

If you want to slice and dice the information even more, click on the **Export To Microsoft Excel** button in the menu bar. This will open up a **Project Statements Export** dialog box.

Click on the folder icon to the right of the **File Name** field.

Creating Project Statements To Analyze Project Performance

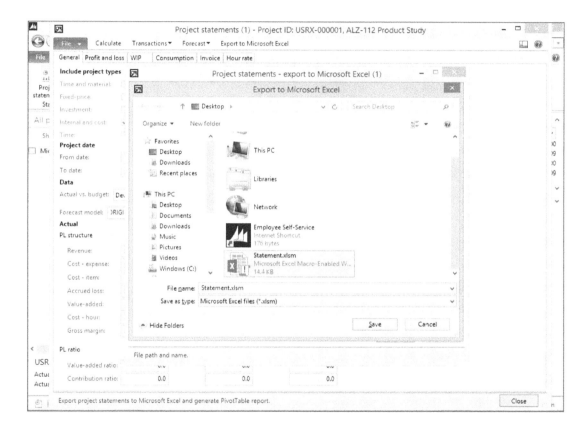

And then specify a location and filename for your Excel statement file and click the **Save** button.

Note: you don't have to have one located at the spot that you specify. If the file is not there then Dynamics AX will create it for you.

Creating Project Statements To Analyze Project Performance

Also, you can add or remove dimensions from the **Selected Dimensions** to simplify, or add more slicing and dicing options.

When you are ready, just click on the **OK** button.

Creating Project Statements To Analyze Project Performance

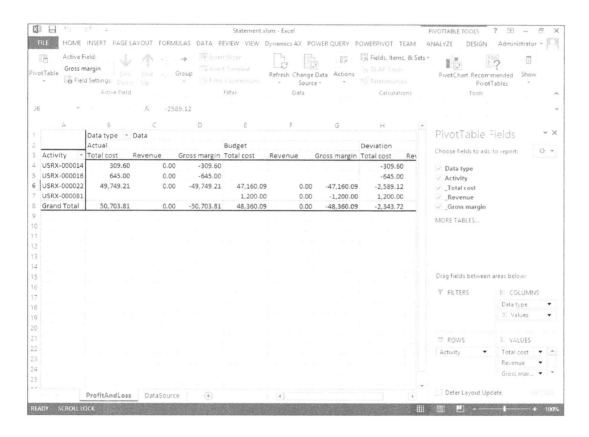

Dynamics AX will then export all of the statement information to Excel as a pivot table, and you will see a complete summary of your project.

How cool is that.

Creating Purchase Orders For Project Activities

You can add even more control to your projects by releasing out **Purchase Orders** from them based on your forecasts and estimates. This allows you to pick and choose what expenses you want to start approving for your projects rather than just having people post to them through journals.

Creating Purchase Orders For Project Activities

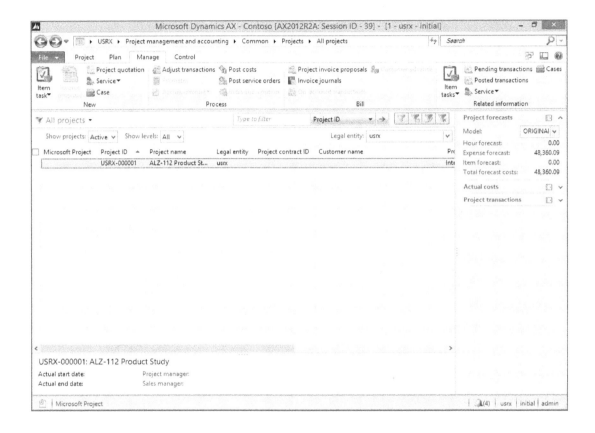

To do this, open up the **All Projects** list page and select the **Project** that you want to generate your Purchase Order for.

Creating Purchase Orders For Project Activities

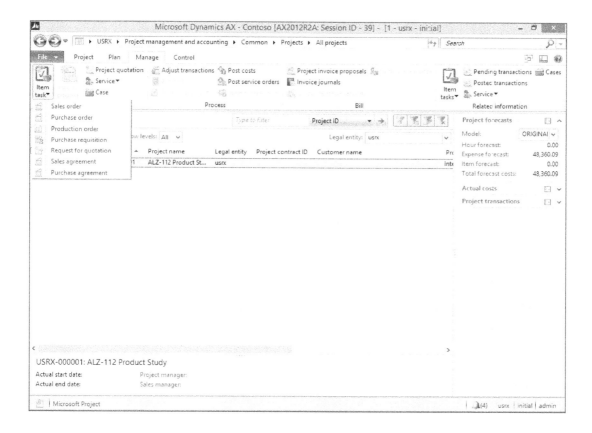

Click on the **Item Tasks** menu item within the **New** group of the **Manage** ribbon bar. This will show you a list of different items that you can create and associate with your project. Select the **Purchase Order** option.

Creating Purchase Orders For Project Activities

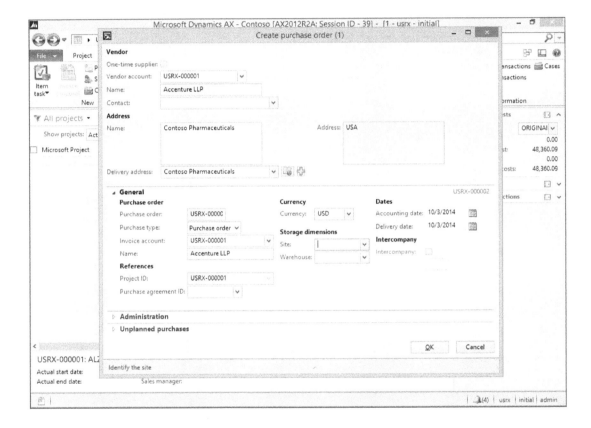

This will open up that **Create Purchase Order** dialog box for you with the Project ID already linked. Just click on the **OK** button to create the Purchase Order.

Creating Purchase Orders For Project Activities

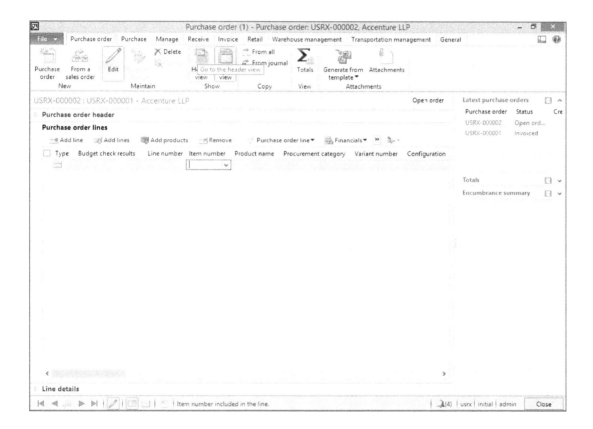

This will then take you directly to the **Purchase Order** detail form.

Creating Purchase Orders For Project Activities

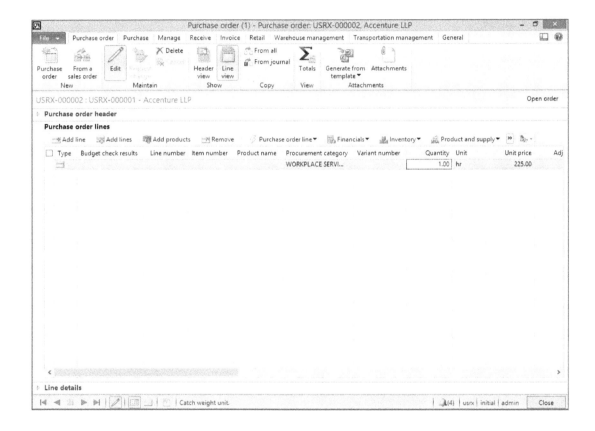

Just fill in the line details for the purchase order.

Creating Purchase Orders For Project Activities

Then expand out the **Line Details** tab at the bottom of the form, and switch to the **Projects** tab. This will allow you to select the **Activity Number** that you want to associate the Purchase Order Line to.

Creating Purchase Orders For Project Activities

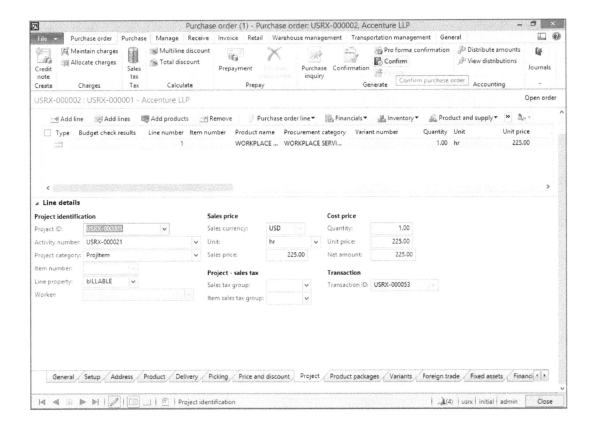

After you have done that you can just click on the **Confirm** button within the **Generate** group of the **Purchase** ribbon bar to confirm the purchase order.

Creating Purchase Orders For Project Activities

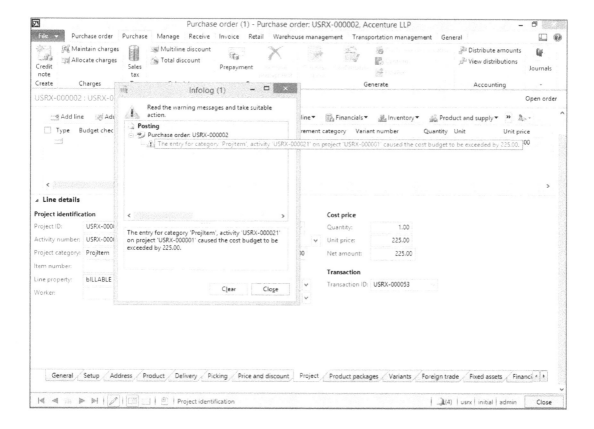

When the purchase order posts you may also notice that it is notifying you of any budget constraints that are being exceeded by the creation of this purchase order commitment.

Creating Purchase Orders For Project Activities

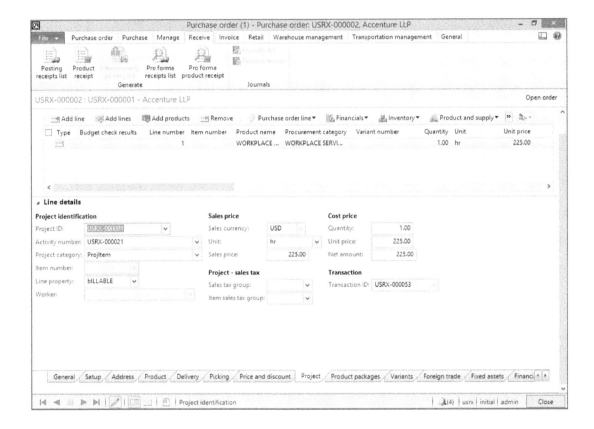

To see the impact of this Purchase Order on your project you can receive and invoice the lines. To do this, first click on the **Product Receipt** button within the **Generate** group of the **Receive** ribbon bar.

Creating Purchase Orders For Project Activities

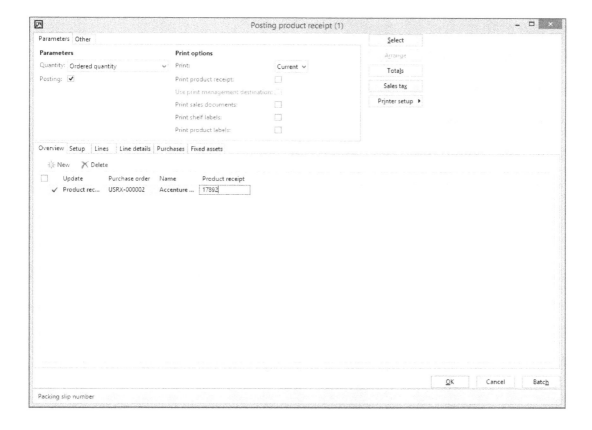

When the **Posting Product Receipt** dialog box is displayed, specify a **Product Receipt** tracking ID and then click on the **OK** button.

Creating Purchase Orders For Project Activities

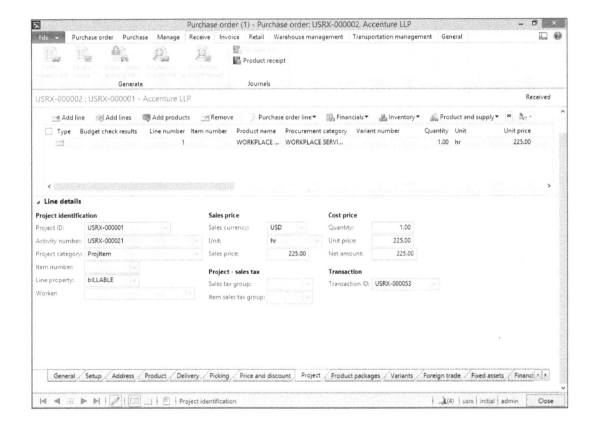

That should receive the product in full and close out all of the receiving options.

Creating Purchase Orders For Project Activities

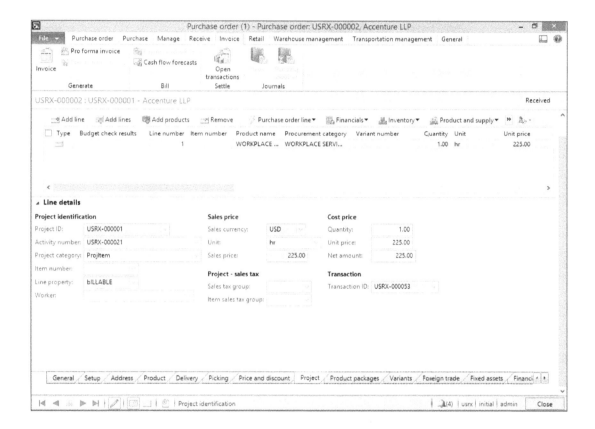

To finish the process, click on the **Invoice** button within the **Generate** group of the **Invoice** ribbon bar.

Creating Purchase Orders For Project Activities

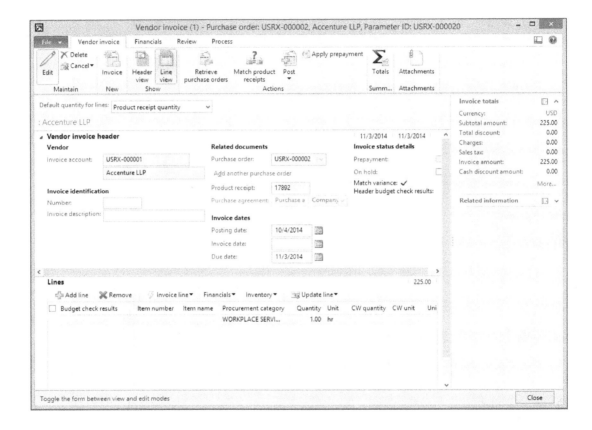

This will open up a **Vendor Invoice** details form.

Creating Purchase Orders For Project Activities

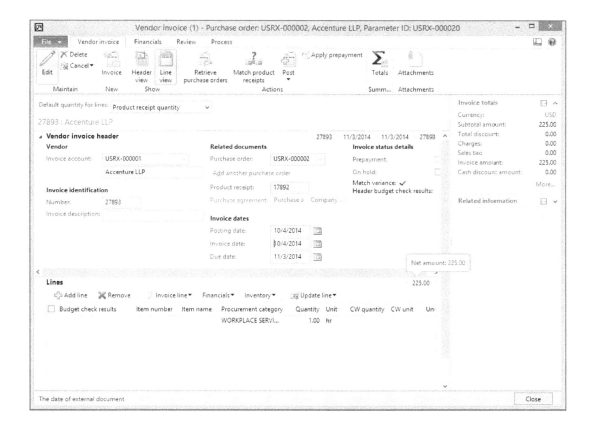

Enter a Invoice **Number**, and also specify and **Invoice Date**.

Creating Purchase Orders For Project Activities

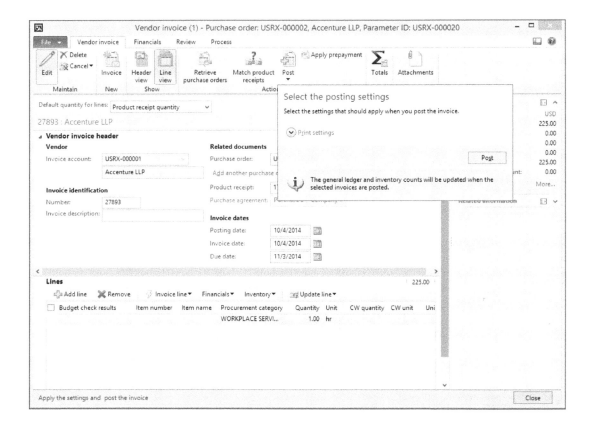

Then click on the **Post** button within the **Actions** group of the **Vendor Invoice** ribbon bar and click on the **Post** button within the confirmation dialog.

Creating Purchase Orders For Project Activities

This will post your invoice and also update the project details. Also notice that it is notifying you of any budget constraints that are being exceeded by the creation of this invoice.

Creating Purchase Orders For Project Activities

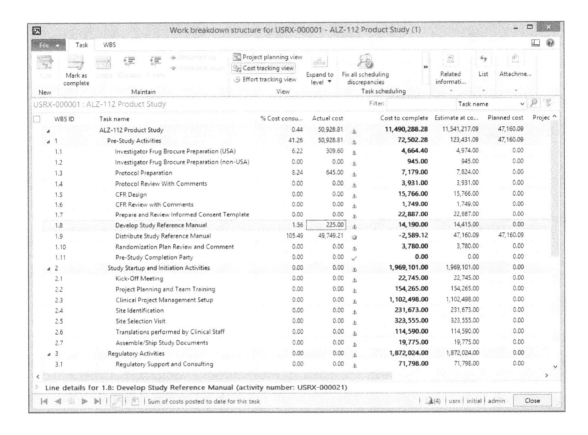

If you return to your **Cost Tracking View** for your project you will notice that the invoiced amount has been applied to your project costs.

Configuring Workers For Assignment To Projects

Tracking costs and expenses against projects is good, but you can take your project management to the next step by tracking resources and workers against the projects. This becomes even more useful since you can leverage all of the worker information that is already set up within Dynamics AX. All you need to do is configure the workers to allow them to work on projects.

Configuring Workers For Assignment To Projects

To do this, open up your **Worker** record and click on the **Project Setup** button within the **Setup** group of the **Project Management** tab.

Configuring Workers For Assignment To Projects

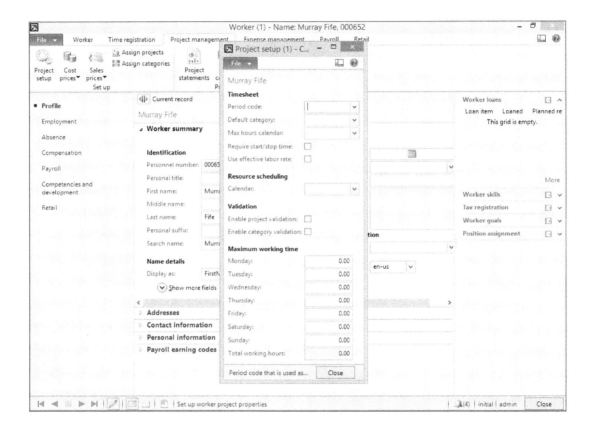

This will open up a **Project Setup** dialog box.

Configuring Workers For Assignment To Projects

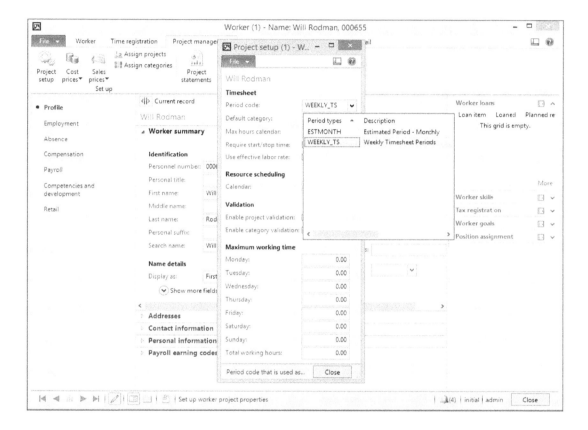

Click on the **Period Code** fields dropdown list and select the **WEEKLY_TS** period code that you created in the first chapter.

Configuring Workers For Assignment To Projects

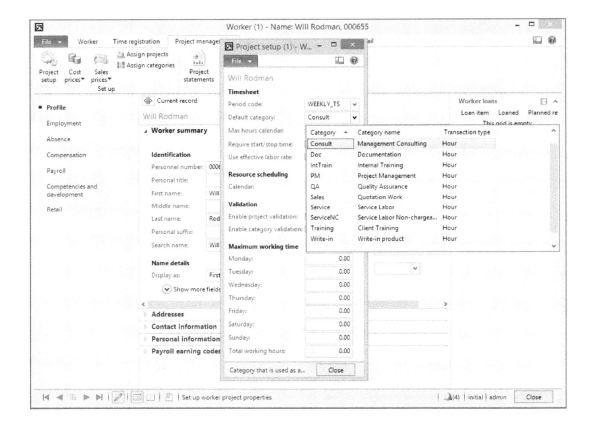

Then select a **Default Category** that will be used for the workers time.

Configuring Workers For Assignment To Projects

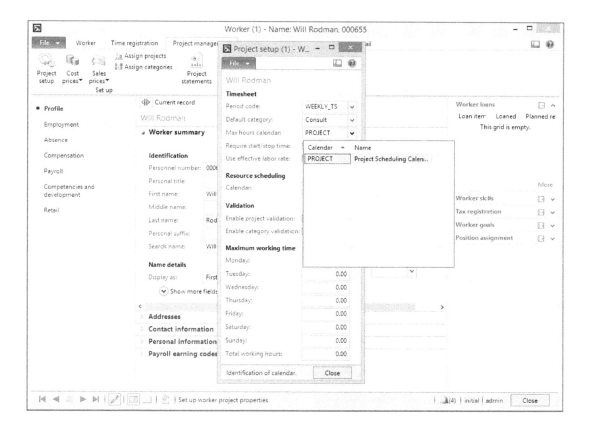

Then click on the **Max Hours Calendar** and select your Project Calendar that you want the worker to be able to post time against.

Configuring Workers For Assignment To Projects

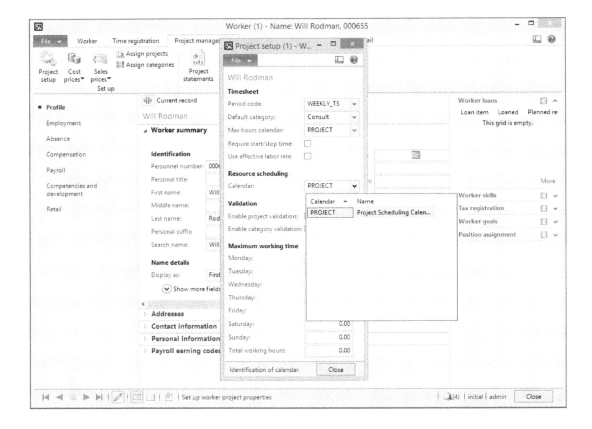

Now click on the **Calendar** field within the **Resource Scheduling** field group and select the **Calendar** that you want to use for scheduling.

Configuring Workers For Assignment To Projects

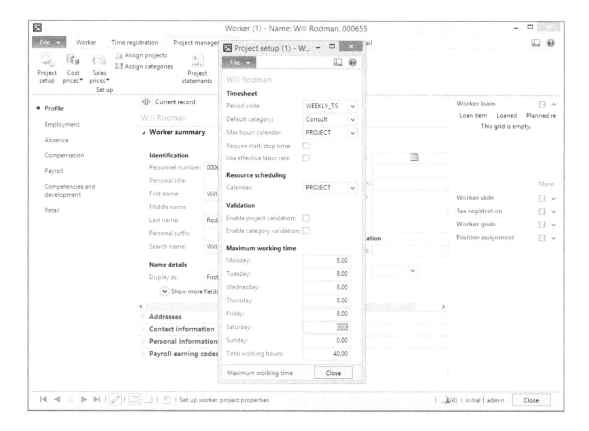

Finally update the **Maximum Working Time** for each day if you want to restrict the time that may be posted to an individual day.

After you have done that, just click on the **Close** button.

Configuring Project Role Templates

If you want to add a little more intelligence to your worker selection for certain tasks, then you can create **Project Rile Templates** which specify the skills that are required in order to considered for certain tasks. This is a great way to filter out workers that are not qualified for positions rather than having to keep all that knowledge in the head of the project manager.

Configuring Project Role Templates

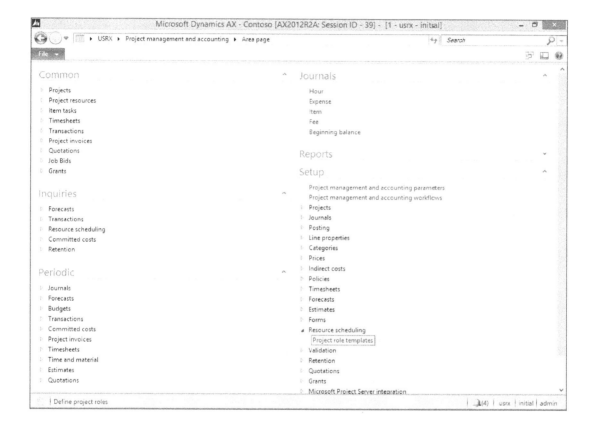

To do this, click on the **Project Role Templates** menu item within the **Resource Scheduling** folder of the **Setup** group within the **Project Management And Accounting** area page.

Configuring Project Role Templates

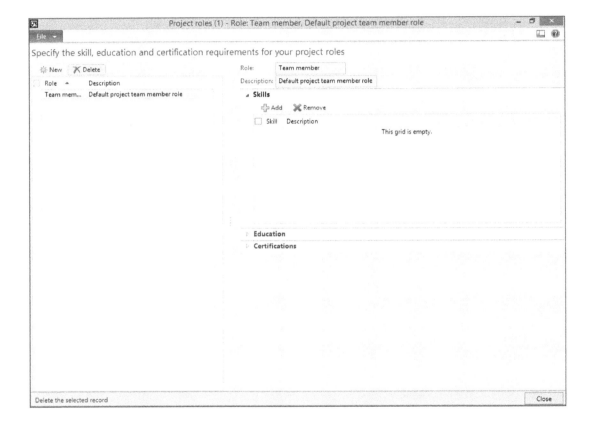

This will open up the **Project Roles** maintenance form, showing any existing roles.

Configuring Project Role Templates

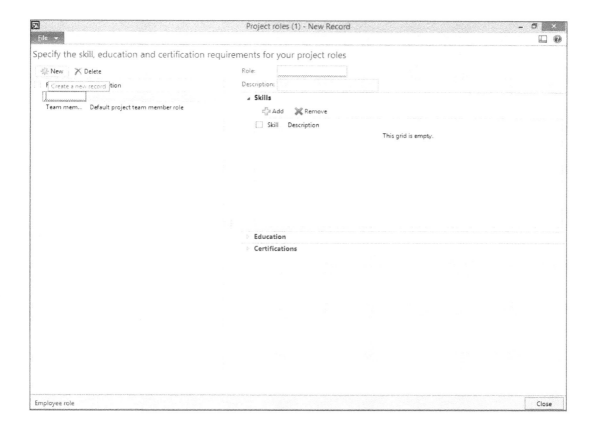

Click on the **New** button within the menu bar to create a new record.

Configuring Project Role Templates

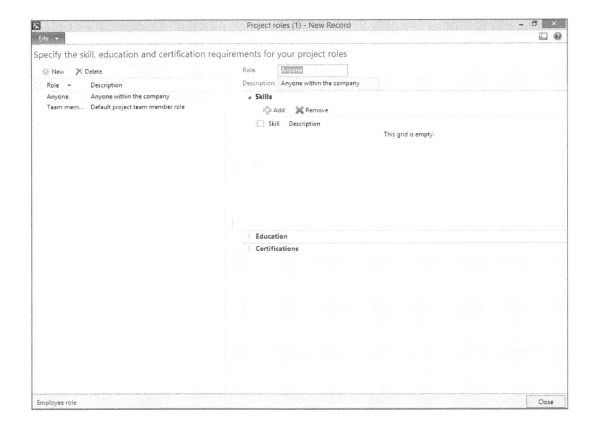

Then set the **Role** to be **Anyone** and the **Description** to **Anyone within the company**.

For this role we are not going to specify any required skills etc. so that we can use this to select anyone we like.

Configuring Project Role Templates

Click on the **New** button within the menu bar again to create another record.

For this record set the **Role** to be **PMP Certified** and the **Description** to **PMP Certified Team Members**.

Configuring Project Role Templates

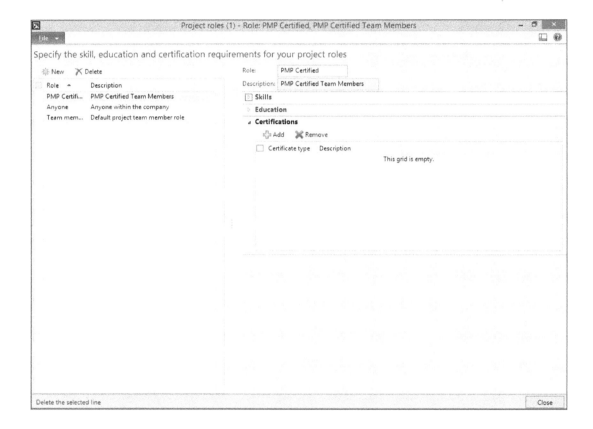

You can create filters for the roles based on **Skills, Education**, and **Certifications**. For this project role we want to select only workers that have a PMP certification so expand the **Certifications** tab group.

Configuring Project Role Templates

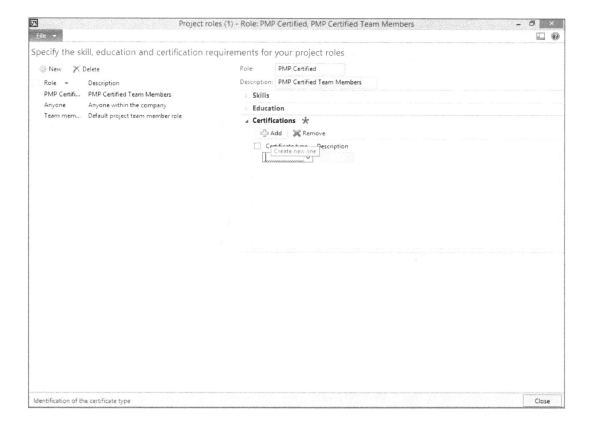

Now click on the **New** button within the **Certifications** tab group to create a new record.

Configuring Project Role Templates

Now click on the **Certification Type** dropdown list and select the **PMP** certification.

Configuring Project Role Templates

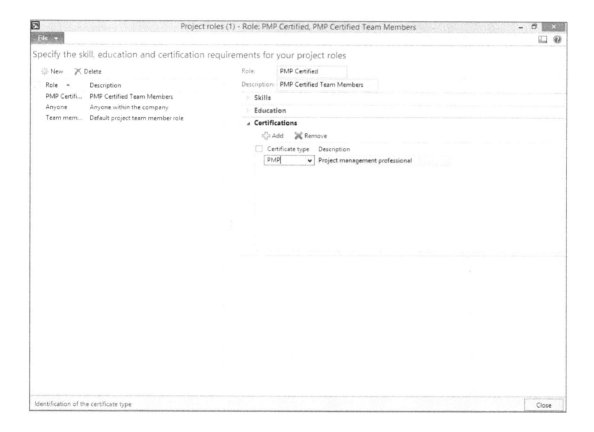

Now you have a certification mapping.

Configuring Project Role Templates

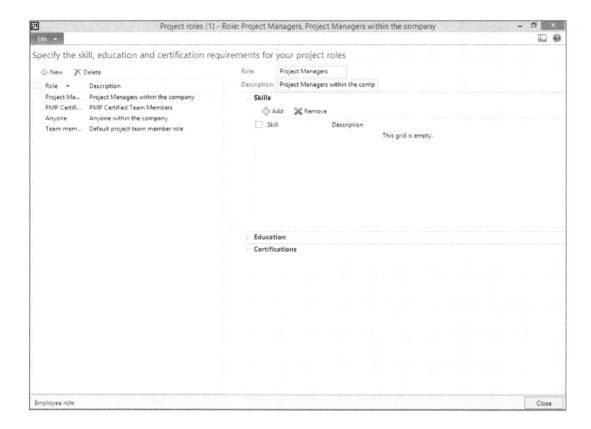

Click on the **New** button within the menu bar again to create another record.

For this record set the **Role** to be **Project Managers** and the **Description** to **Project Managers within the company**.

Configuring Project Role Templates

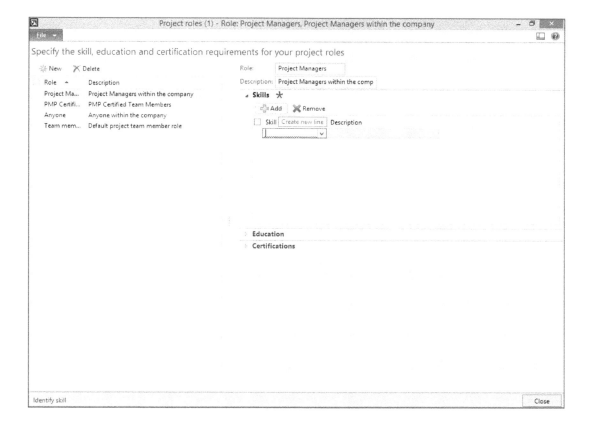

For this example, expand the **Skills** tab group and click on the **Add** button to add a new record.

Configuring Project Role Templates

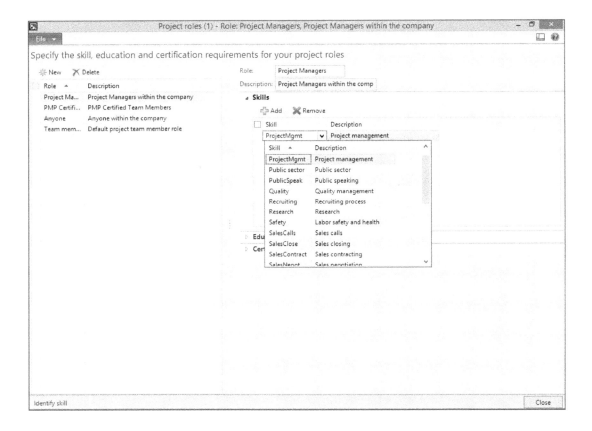

Then from the **Skill** dropdown box select the **ProjectMgmt** skill.

Configuring Project Role Templates

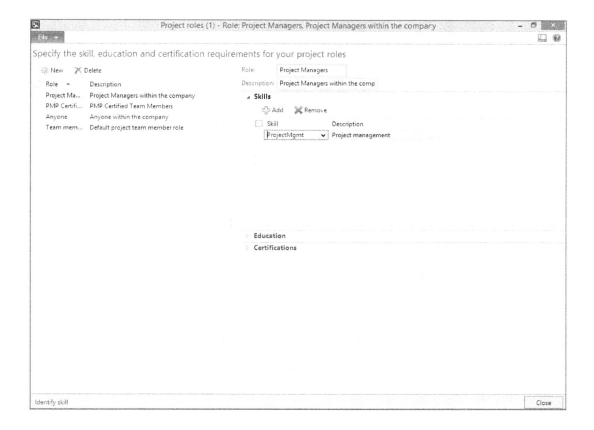

You can keep on adding roles to match your worker profiles, and when you are finished, just click on the **Close** button.

Adding Resources To The Project Using The Resource Scheduler

Once you have configured your workers and also you worker profiles, then you can start assigning them to your projects.

Adding Resources To The Project Using The Resource Scheduler

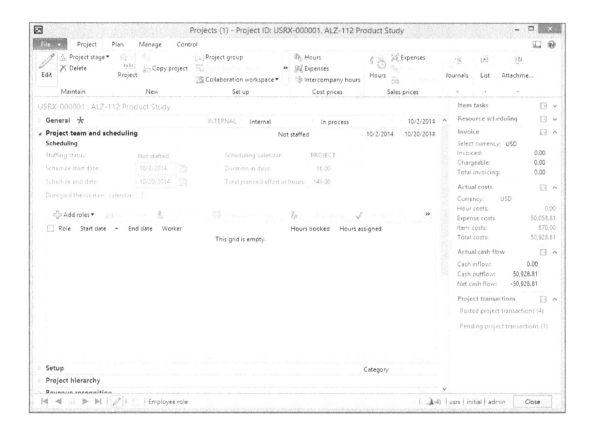

To do this, open up your **Project** in the detail view mode and expard out the **Project Team And Scheduling** tab.

Adding Resources To The Project Using The Resource Scheduler

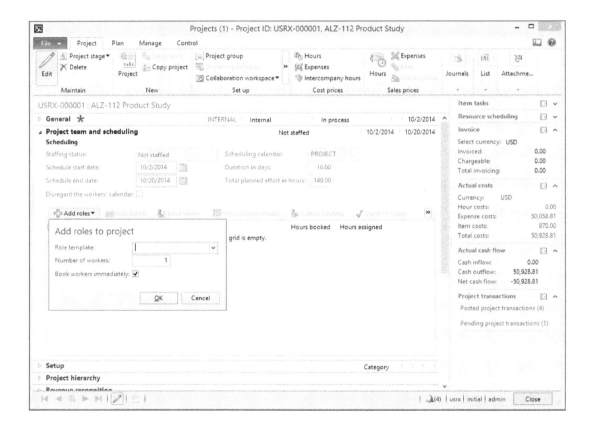

Click on the **Add Roles** button.

Adding Resources To The Project Using The Resource Scheduler

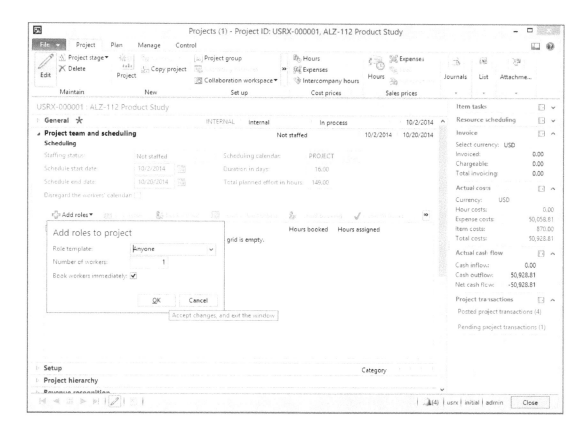

Then select the **Role Template** that you want to use to filter out the workers, and click the **OK** button.

Adding Resources To The Project Using The Resource Scheduler

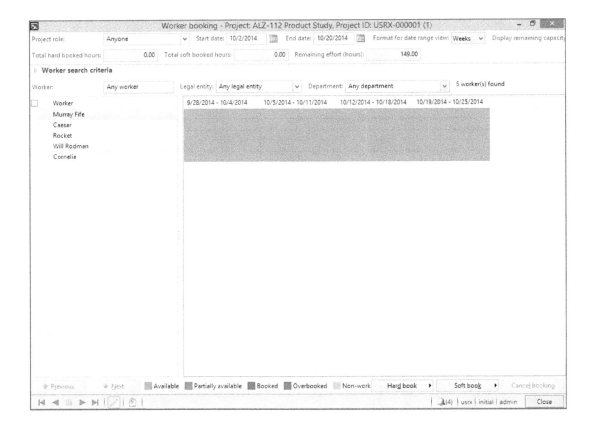

This will open up a scheduling view showing you all of the applicable resources and also their availability based on your selection.

Adding Resources To The Project Using The Resource Scheduler

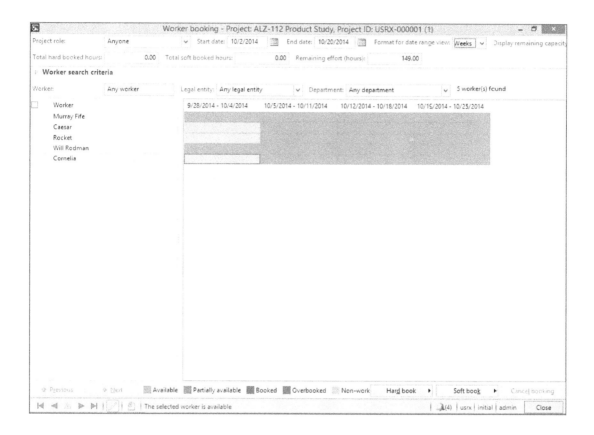

To assign the resources to the project, just click on the date range that you need them for.

Adding Resources To The Project Using The Resource Scheduler

To book then, click on either the **Hard Book**, or **Soft Book** buttons at the footer of the form and select the booking capacity that you want to use on them.

Adding Resources To The Project Using The Resource Scheduler

You will get a quick InfoLog that gives you an overview of the scheduling that has just been performed.

Adding Resources To The Project Using The Resource Scheduler

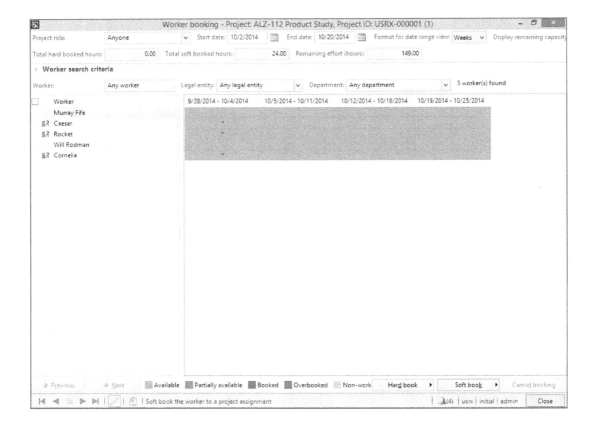

When you return to the **Worker Booking** form you will see that he workers have been marked for allocation to the project and you can click on the **Close** button to exit from the form.

Adding Resources To The Project Using The Resource Scheduler

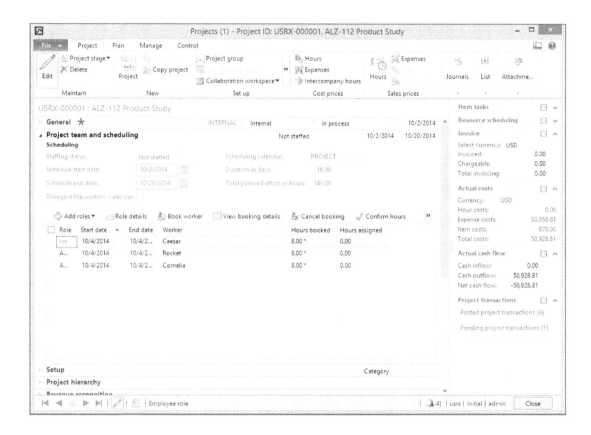

When you return to the project then you will see that the workers are also listed within the projects team.

Assigning Workers To Projects

Another way that you can control the workers that are to be used within your Project is to just assign them. This allows you to create a project team that will become the only resources that can post against the project.

Assigning Workers To Projects

To do this, open up your **Project** in the detail view and click on the **Assign Workers** button within the **Validations** group of the **Plan** ribbon bar.

Assigning Workers To Projects

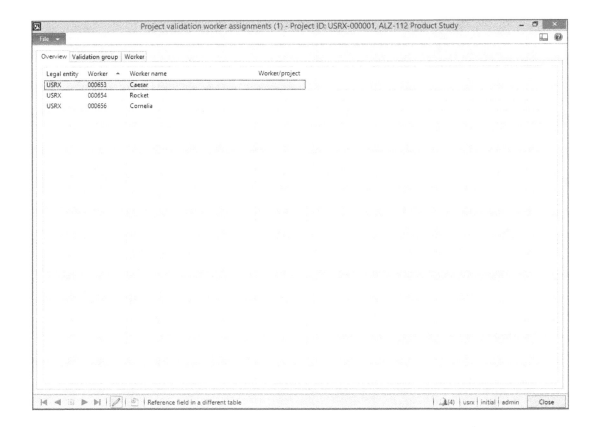

This will open up a **Worker Assignment** form showing you all of the workers that are associated with the project.

Assigning Workers To Projects

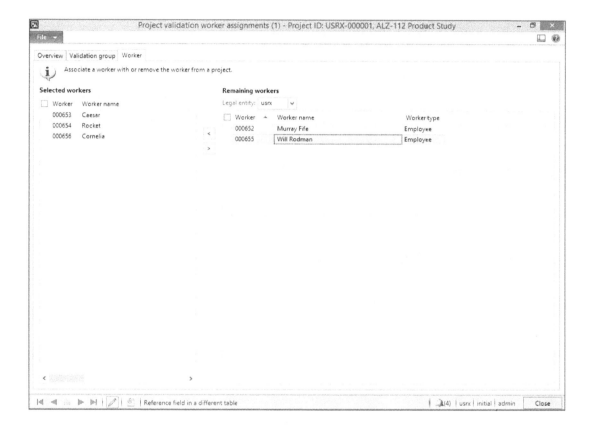

If you switch to the **Worker** tab you will be able to see all of the available workers that have not been assigned to the project.

Assigning Workers To Projects

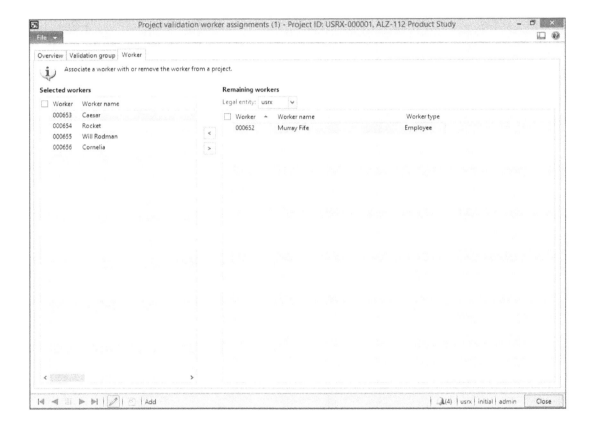

To add a worker, just select the record and click on the **<** button to move them into the **Selected Workers** group.

Assigning Workers To Projects

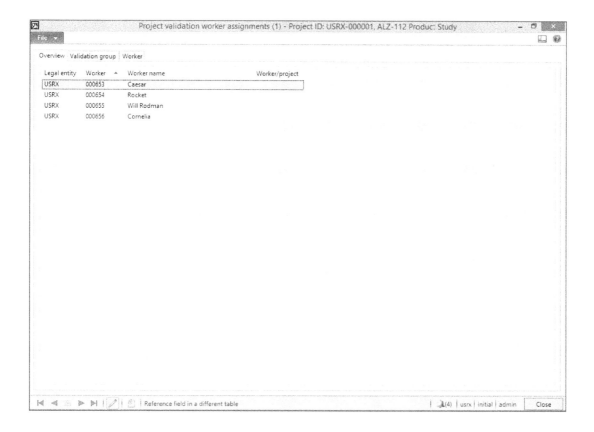

After you have assigned all of your workers to the project, just click on the **Close** button to exit from the form.

Saving Work Breakdown Structures As Templates

A lot of projects share similar work breakdown structures, and you can save a lot of time after creating your initial project by saving it off as a template. This will allow you to then re-use it for future project over and over again.

Saving Work Breakdown Structures As Templates

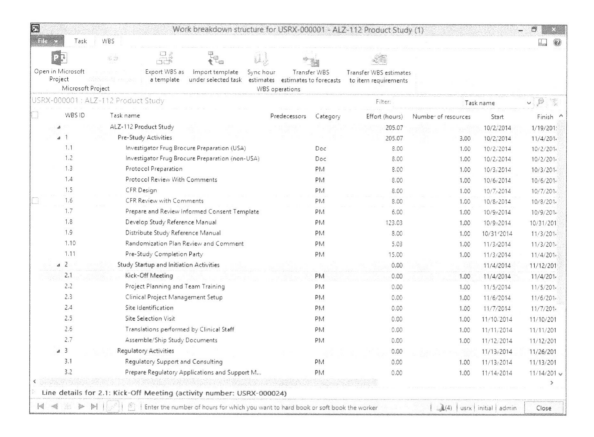

To do this, just open up your projects **Work Breakdown Structure** and click on the **Export WBS as a Template** button within the **WBS Operations** group of the **WBS** ribbon bar.

Saving Work Breakdown Structures As Templates

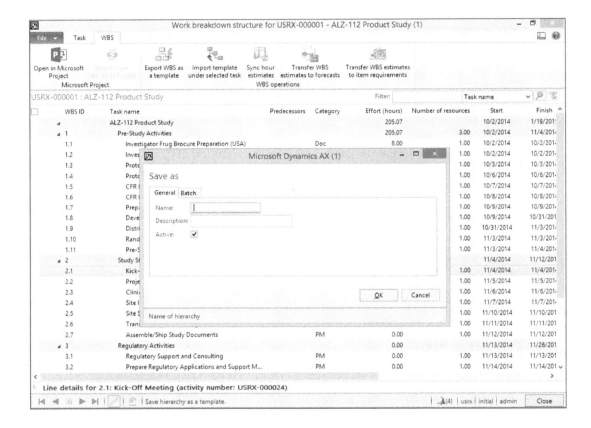

This will open up a **Save As** dialog box for your work breakdown structure.

Saving Work Breakdown Structures As Templates

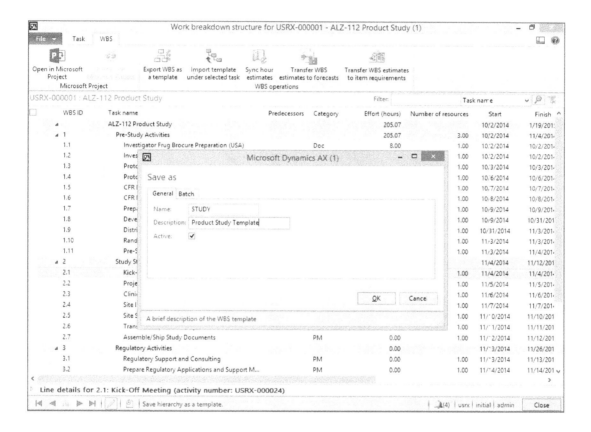

All you need to do is assign your template a **Name**, a **Description**, and also set the **Active** flag before clicking on the **OK** button.

Saving Work Breakdown Structures As Templates

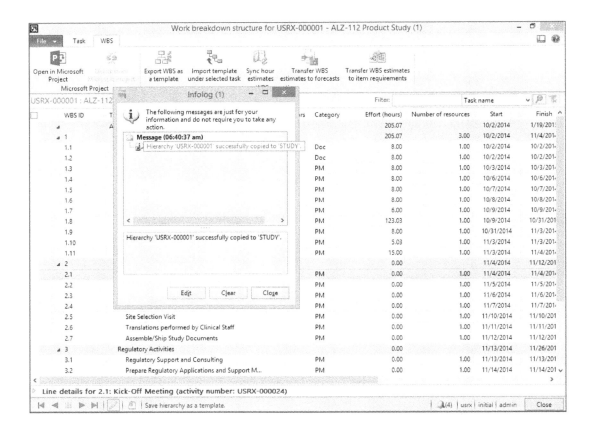

Now you will get an InfoLog saying that it has created your template for you and you are done.

Creating New Projects Using Templates

Once you have created your work breakdown structure template, creating new project using the template is a breeze.

Creating New Projects Using Templates

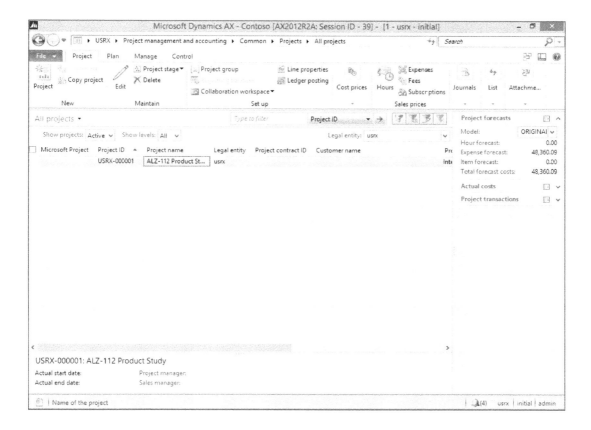

To do this, open up your **All Projects** list page and then click on the **Project** button within the **New** group of the **Project** ribbon bar.

Creating New Projects Using Templates

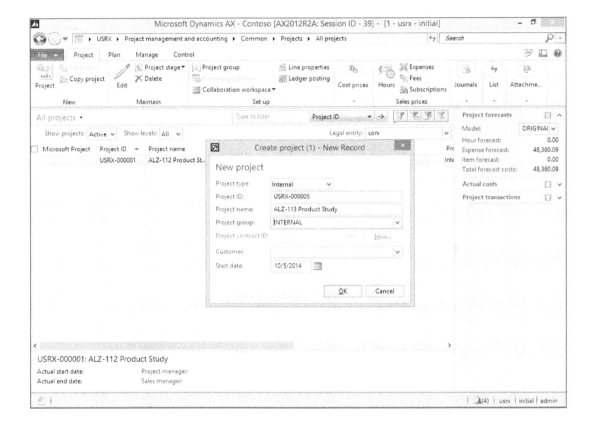

When the **Create Project** dialog box is displayed, assign your project a **Project Name** and also a **Project Group** and then click on the **OK** button.

Creating New Projects Using Templates

When the project detail form is displayed, click on the **Work Breakdown Structure** button within the **Activities** group of the **Plan** ribbon bar.

Creating New Projects Using Templates

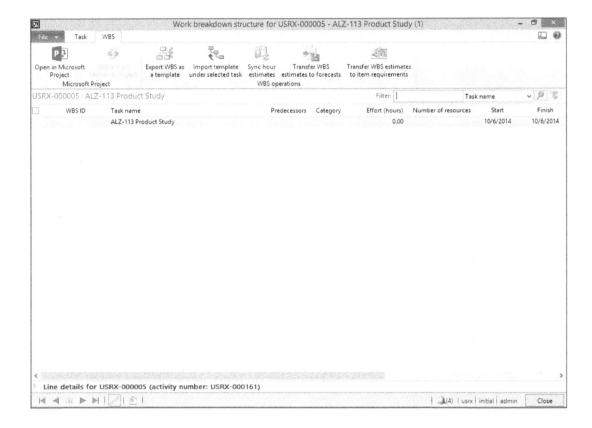

When the **Work Breakdown Structure** maintenance form is displayed, click on the **Import Template Under Selected Task** button within the **WBS Operations** group of the **WBS** ribbon bar.

Creating New Projects Using Templates

This will open up a **Copy From** dialog box and you can ten select the template that you just created from the **Name** dropdown list.

Creating New Projects Using Templates

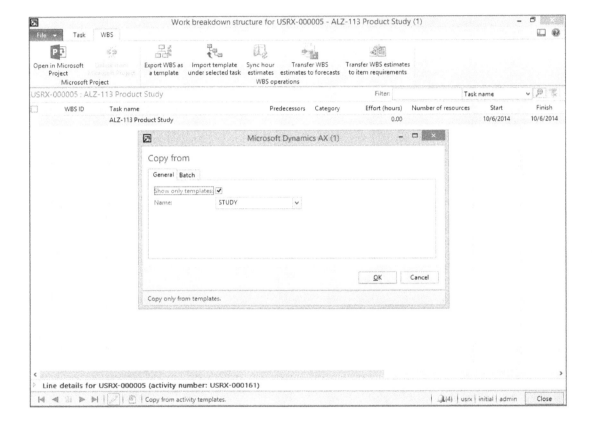

After selecting the **Name** click on the **OK** button.

Creating New Projects Using Templates

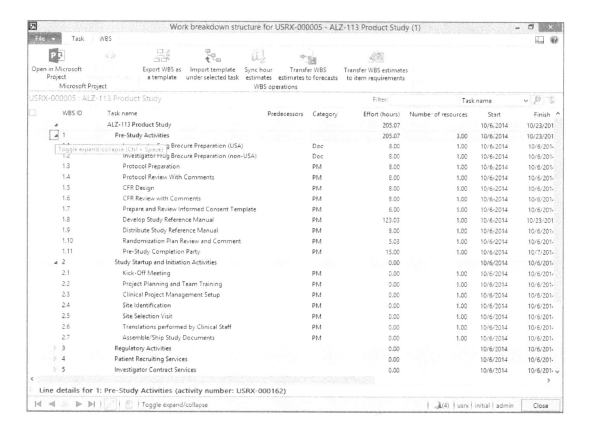

Now your work breakdown structure will be populated for you with all the details from the template.

How easy is that?

CONFIGURING PROJECT COLLABORATION WORKSPACES

When you create a project, there are usually a lot of people that want to track and contribute to the project that you may not necessarily have access to Dynamics AX. You may want to share documents, status reports, member notes and much more. A great way to do this is through SharePoint **Collaboration Workspaces** which you can create directly from your Dynamics AX projects.

In this chapter we will show how you can setup, create and use **Collaboration Workspaces** to share the unstructured data that you create for projects.

Configuring Collaboration Workspace Settings

Before you are able to create the Collaboration Workspaces though there is a little bit of setup required.

Configuring Collaboration Workspace Settings

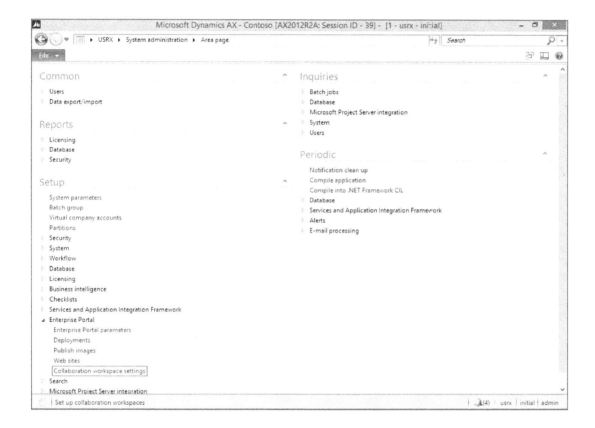

To do this, click on the **Collaboration Workspace Settings** menu item within the **Enterprise Portal** folder of the **Setup** group within the **System Administration** area page.

Configuring Collaboration Workspace Settings

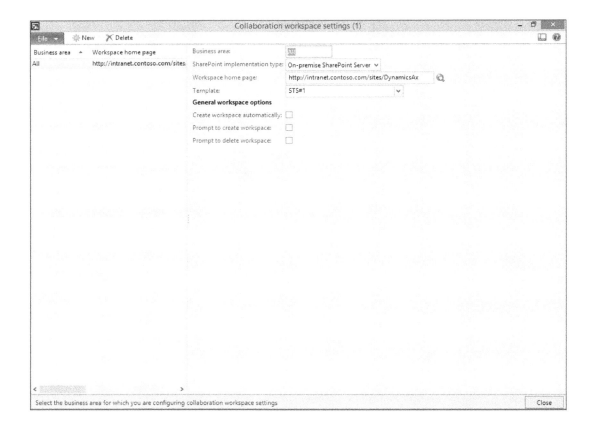

This will open up the **Collaboration Workspace Settings** maintenance form.

Configuring Collaboration Workspace Settings

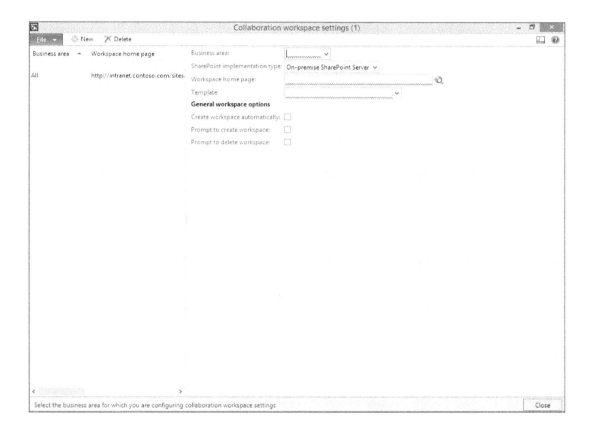

Click on the **New** button in the menu bar to create a new record.

Configuring Collaboration Workspace Settings

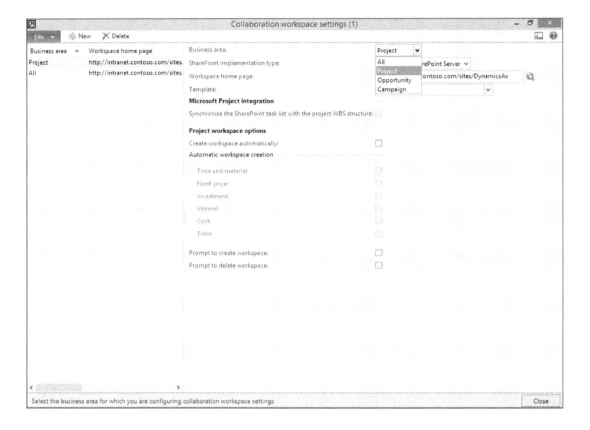

Click on the **Business Area** field dropdown list and select the **Project** option so that we will be configuring the Collaboration Workspace options just for the Projects.

Configuring Collaboration Workspace Settings

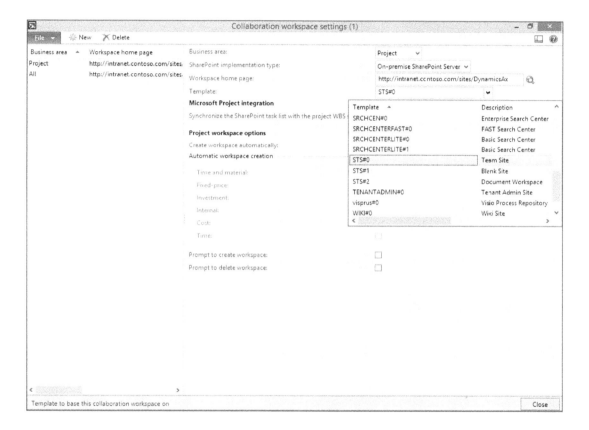

If you have not specified one already, set the **Workspace Home Page** to be your local Intranet SharePoint site.

Then from the **Template** dropdown list select the template that you want to use for your Project sites.

Configuring Collaboration Workspace Settings

If you want to automatically have the system ask you if you want to create a new Collaboration Workspace when you create a new project, then you can check the **Prompt To Create Workspace** flag.

If you want to automatically have the system ask you if you want to delete the Collaboration Workspace when you delete a project, then you can check the **Prompt To Delete Workspace** flag.

After you have done that, just click on the **Close** button to exit from the form.

Creating Collaboration Workspaces For Projects

Once you have configured your Collaboration Workspace settings, you can start creating them directly from your Projects.

Creating Collaboration Workspaces For Projects

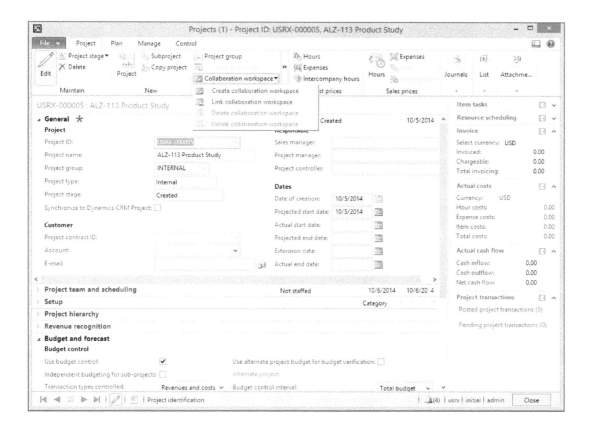

To do this, just open up your **Project**, and click on the **Collaboration Workspace** button within the **Setup** group of the **Project** ribbon bar and then click on the **Create Collaboration Workspace** menu item.

Creating Collaboration Workspaces For Projects

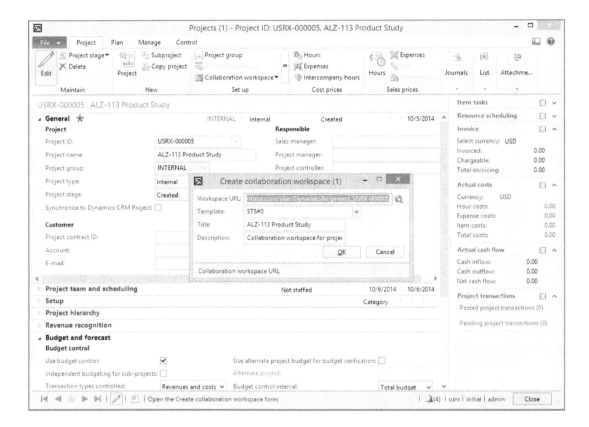

When the **Create Collaboration Workspace** dialog box is displayed, click on the **OK** button.

Creating Collaboration Workspaces For Projects

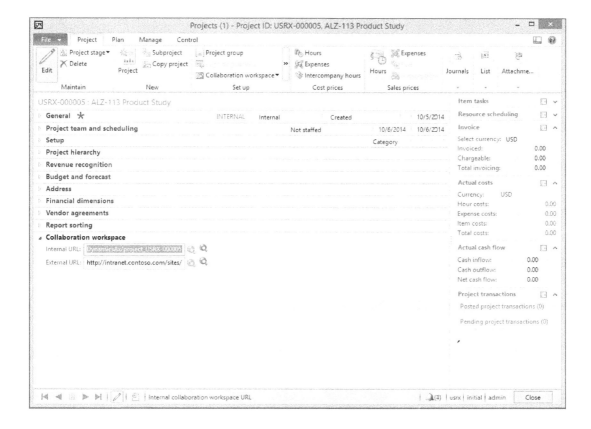

After a couple of seconds, Dynamics AX will finish provisioning the site for you and if you expand the **Collaboration Workspaces** tab you will see that the URL's for the site are populated within the **Internal URL** and **External URL** fields.

To view the site, just click on the web browser icon to the right of either of the fields.

Creating Collaboration Workspaces For Projects

This will take you directly to the **Collaboration Workspace** for that project.

Configuring Microsoft Project Integration To Use Collaboration Workspaces

When we initially configured the Microsoft Project Integration in this walkthrough, we just put all of the project plan files onto the network share. Although this is good in most cases, if you have configured your Collaboration Workspaces then you can do something even better than that, and save the project files directly to the Collaboration site.

Configuring Microsoft Project Integration To Use Collaboration Workspaces

To do this, click on the **Project Management And Accounting Parameters** menu item within the **Setup** group of the **Project Management And Accounting** area page.

Configuring Microsoft Project Integration To Use Collaboration Workspaces

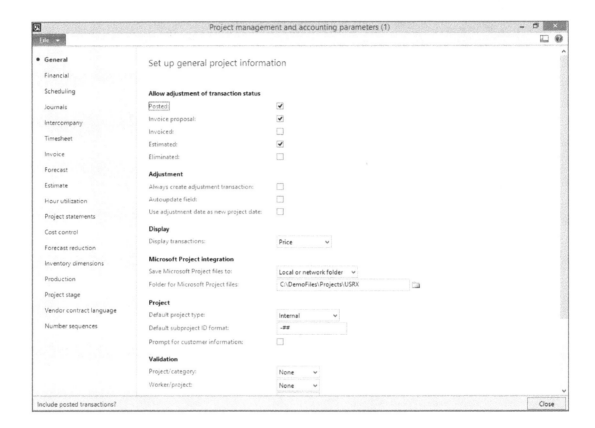

When the **Project Management And Accounting Parameters** form is displayed, select the **General** options page.

Configuring Microsoft Project Integration To Use Collaboration Workspaces

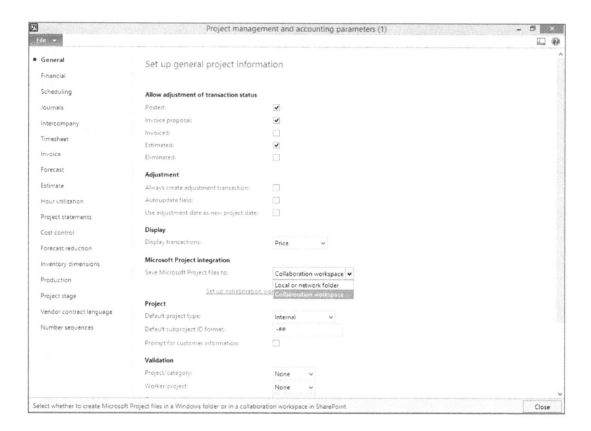

Within the **Microsoft Project Integration** field group, click on the **Save Microsoft Project Files to:** dropdown list and select the **Collaboration Workspace** opton.

Configuring Microsoft Project Integration To Use Collaboration Workspaces

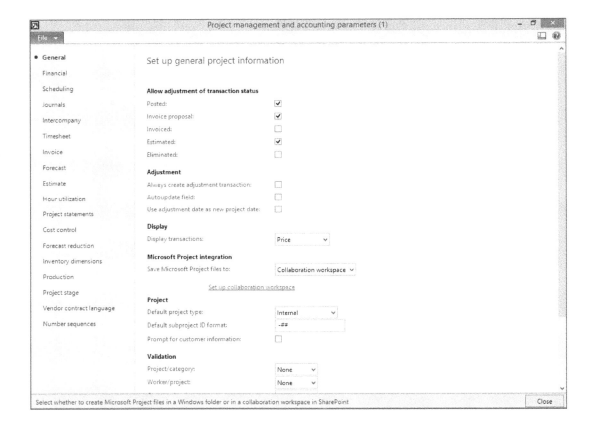

If you like you can double check your Collaboration Workspace settings by clicking on the **Set Up Collaboration Workspaces** link below the field.

Configuring Microsoft Project Integration To Use Collaboration Workspaces

This will take you back over to the **Collaboration Workspace Settings** maintenance form.

Click the **Close** button to exit from the form.

Configuring Microsoft Project Integration To Use Collaboration Workspaces

To test this out, click on the **Open In Microsoft Project** button within the **Activities** group of the **Plan** ribbon bar.

Configuring Microsoft Project Integration To Use Collaboration Workspaces

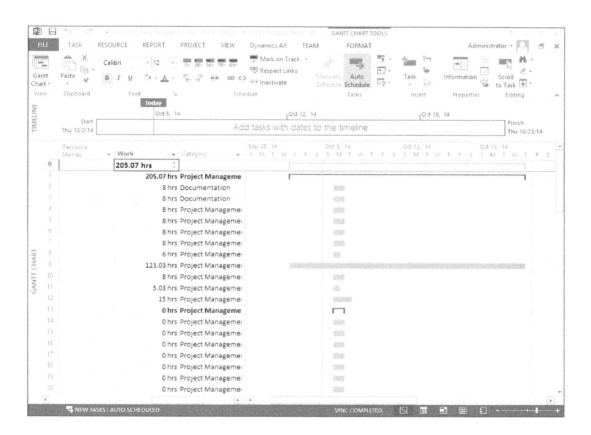

This will then create your Microsoft Project file and open it up for you.

Configuring Microsoft Project Integration To Use Collaboration Workspaces

If you click on the **Files** option though you will see that it is actually being stored on SharePoint now.

Configuring Collaboration Workspaces To Use SharePoint Online

You don't have to host your **Collaboration Workspaces** locally on your intranet either. If you are subscribed to **Office 365** and have a **SharePoint Online** account then you can make the collaboration site even more accessible by creating the site there.

Configuring Collaboration Workspaces To Use SharePoint Online

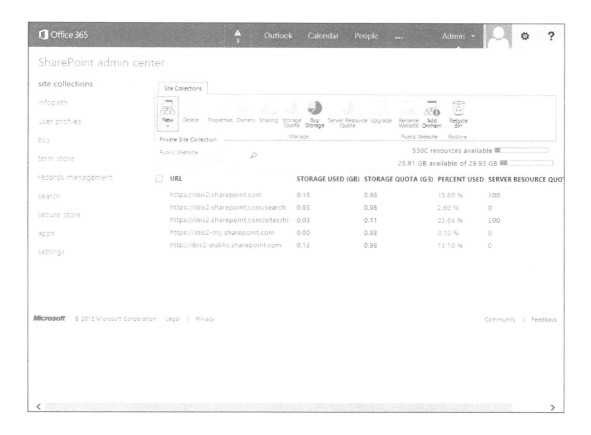

Before we do this though you may want to create a new Site on Office 365 that you will use just for your Projects, To do that, open up Office 365 and then go to the **SharePoint Admin Center**.

From there, click on the **New** button within the **Manage** group of the **Site Collections** ribbon bar and select the **Private Site Collection** option.

Configuring Collaboration Workspaces To Use SharePoint Online

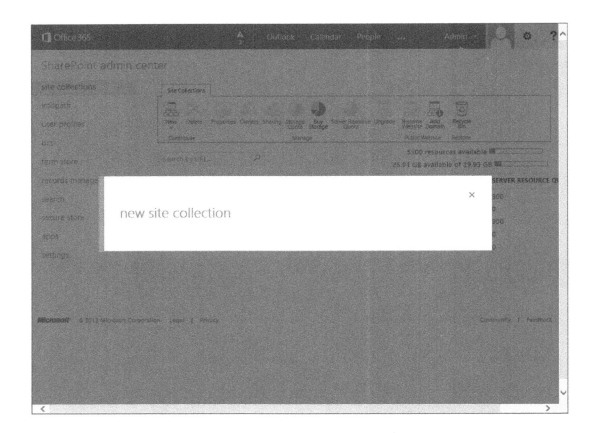

When the **New Site Collection** confirmation box is displayed, click on the **New Site Collection** link.

Configuring Collaboration Workspaces To Use SharePoint Online

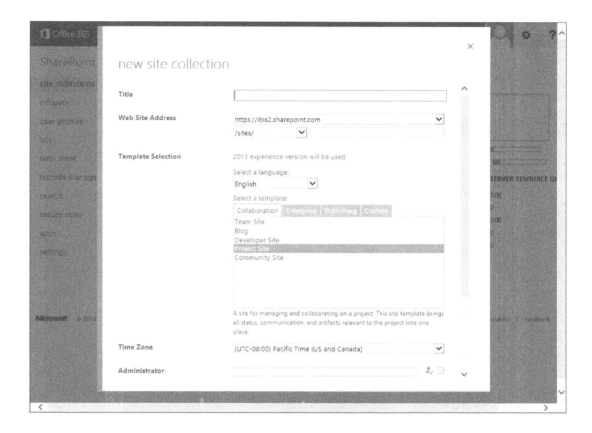

This will open up the **New Site Collection** dialog box.

Configuring Collaboration Workspaces To Use SharePoint Online

Give your new site a **Title** and also a subdomain.

Configuring Collaboration Workspaces To Use SharePoint Online

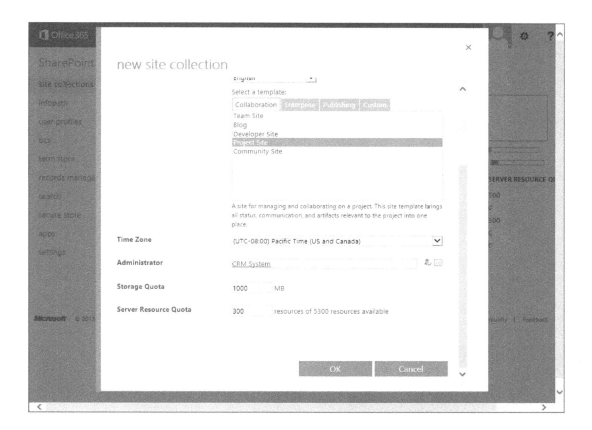

Also, make sure that the **Template** is set to **Project Site**.

Then assign an **Administrator** to the site and also set a **Storage Quota** for the site before clicking on the **OK** button.

Configuring Collaboration Workspaces To Use SharePoint Online

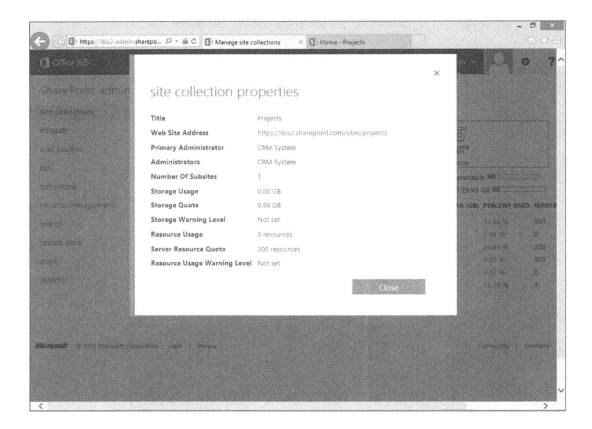

Configuring Collaboration Workspaces To Use SharePoint Online

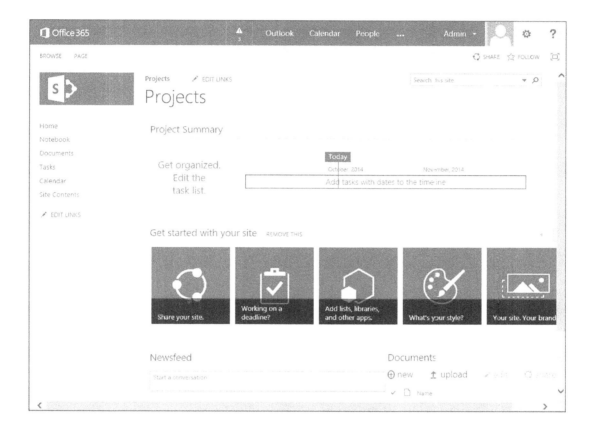

After a few minutes you will have a new site on Office 365.

Configuring Collaboration Workspaces To Use SharePoint Online

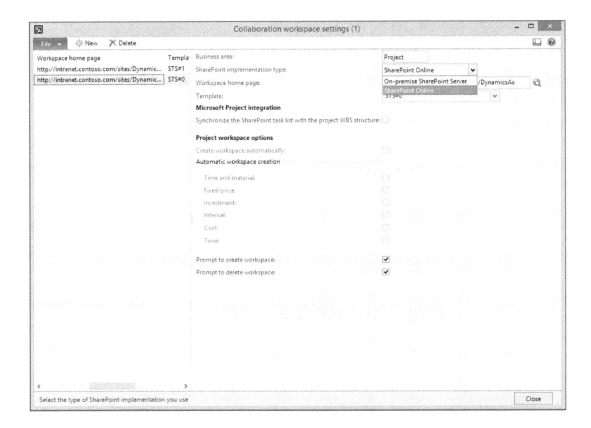

Now return back to the **Collaboration Workspace Settings** and change the **SharePoint Implementation Type** to **SharePoint Online.**

Configuring Collaboration Workspaces To Use SharePoint Online

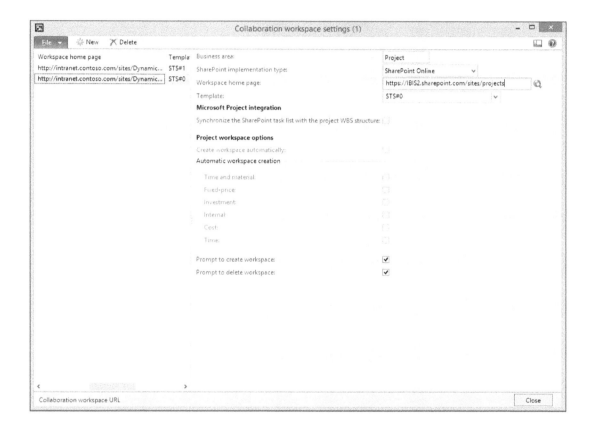

Then set the **Workplace Home Page** to be the URL for your new Project Site.

Configuring Collaboration Workspaces To Use SharePoint Online

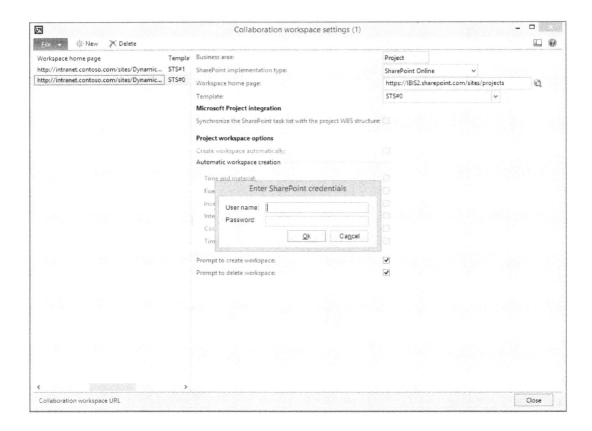

As soon as you do that you will be asked to type in your credentials to authenticate against the site.

Configuring Collaboration Workspaces To Use SharePoint Online

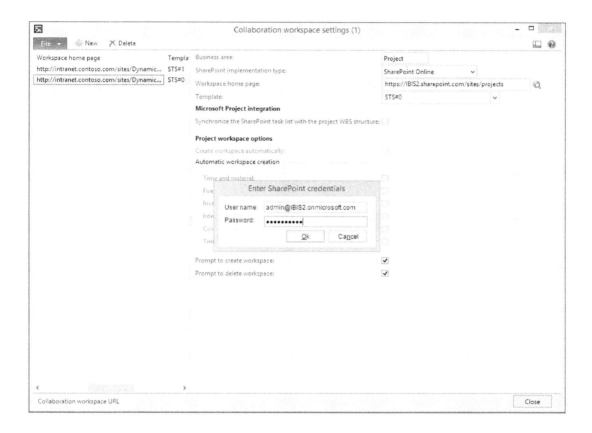

Type them in and then click on the **OK** button.

Configuring Collaboration Workspaces To Use SharePoint Online

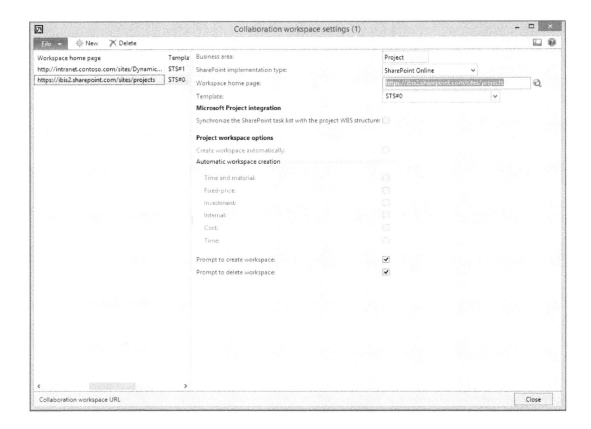

If everything worked for you then the system will return back to the **Collaboration Workspaces** page.

Configuring Collaboration Workspaces To Use SharePoint Online

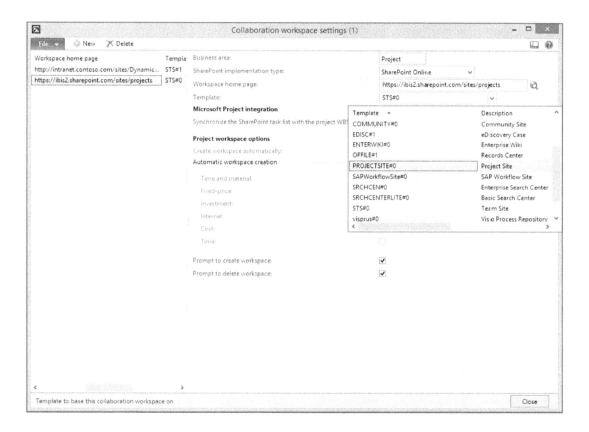

Now click on the **Template** dropdown list and select the **PROJECTSITE#0** template.

Configuring Collaboration Workspaces To Use SharePoint Online

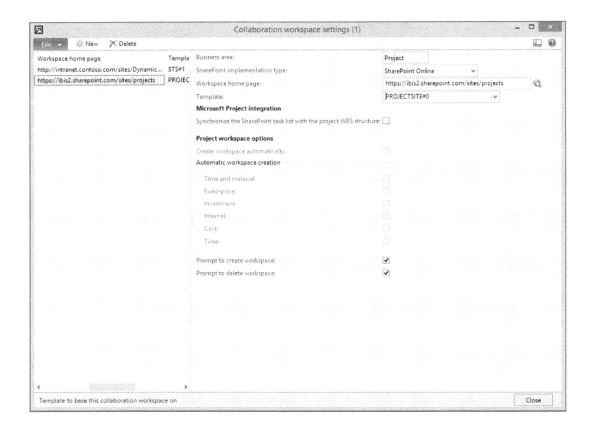

After you have done that, just click on the **Close** button to exit from the form.

Configuring Collaboration Workspaces To Use SharePoint Online

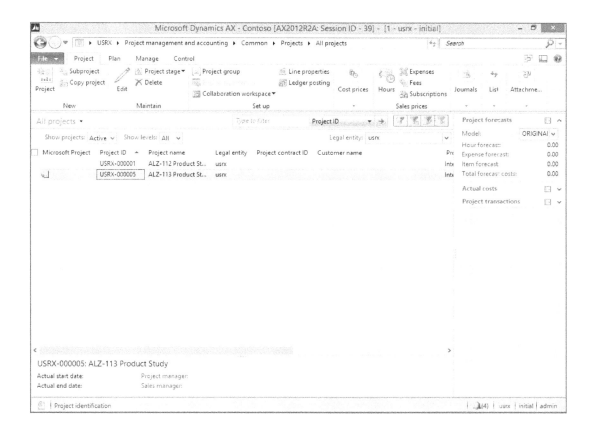

Now open up your **Project**, and click on the **Collaboration Workspace** button within the **Setup** group of the **Project** ribbon bar and then click on the **Create Collaboration Workspace** menu item.

Configuring Collaboration Workspaces To Use SharePoint Online

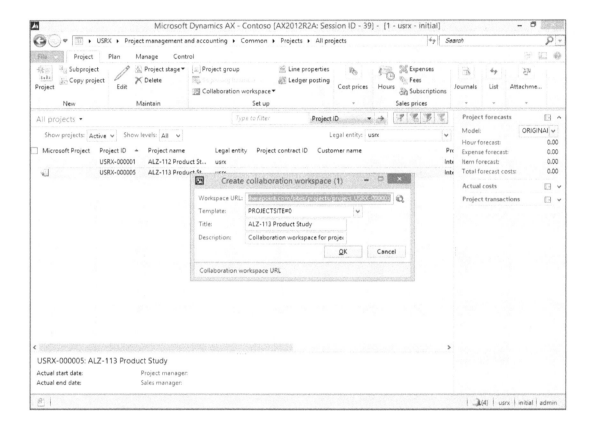

When the **Create Collaboration Workspace** dialog box is displayed, click on the **OK** button.

Configuring Collaboration Workspaces To Use SharePoint Online

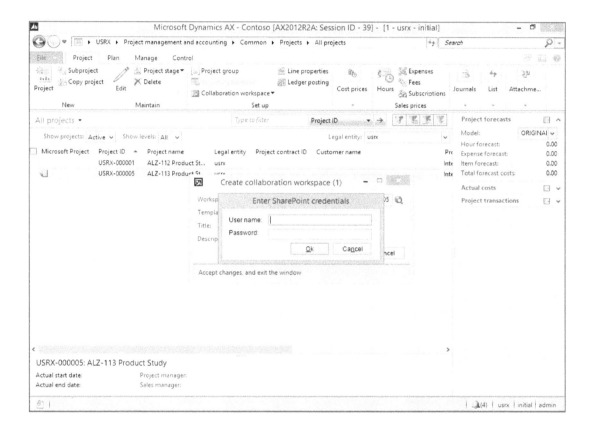

As soon as you do that you will be asked to type in your credentials to authenticate against the site.

Configuring Collaboration Workspaces To Use SharePoint Online

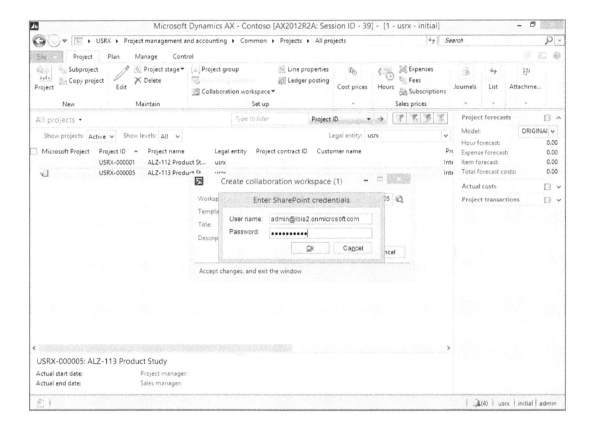

Type them in and then click on the **OK** button.

Configuring Collaboration Workspaces To Use SharePoint Online

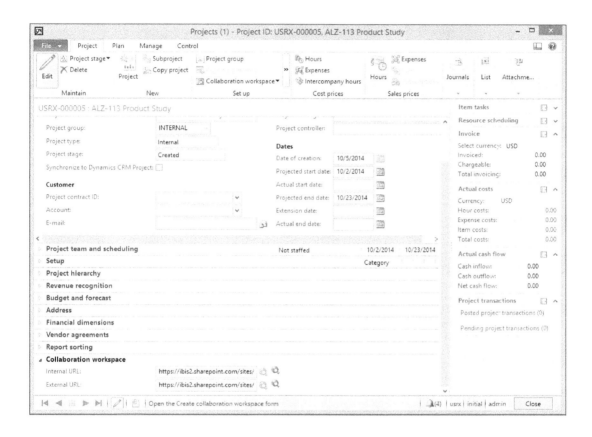

Now you will notice that the **Collaboration Workspaces** are linked to your SharePoint Online account.

Configuring Collaboration Workspaces To Use SharePoint Online

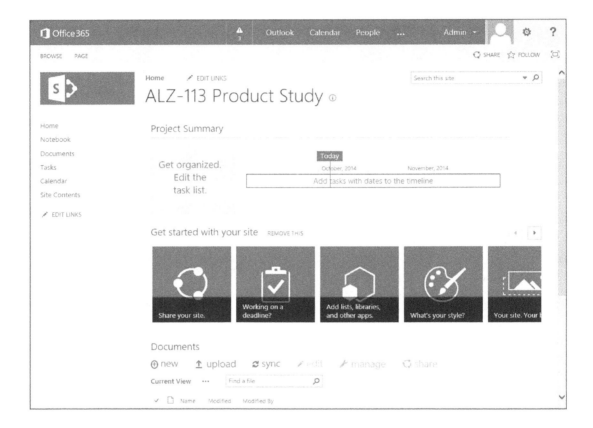

If you click on the URL's then you will be taken to the projects collaboration workspace on SharePoint Online.

Publishing Microsoft Project Tasks To SharePoint Online Collaboration Workspaces

One of the benefits of using SharePoint Online is that you can then share your project details easily with other people and you don't have to worry about setting up security within the organization to give them access. One of the items that you may want to share is the Project Plan, and one of the ways that you can do that is directly from Microsoft Project.

Publishing Microsoft Project Tasks To SharePoint Online Collaboration Workspaces

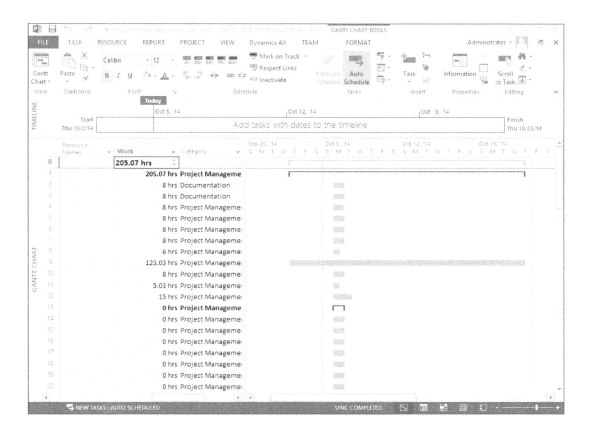

To do this, just start off by opening up your work breakdown structure within Microsoft Project.

Publishing Microsoft Project Tasks To SharePoint Online Collaboration Workspaces

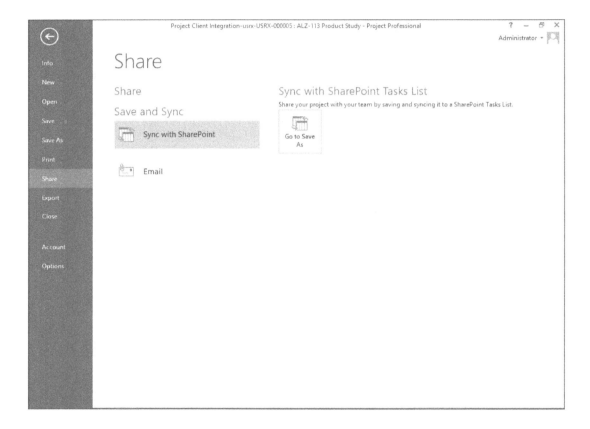

Then click on the **File** menu and select the **Share** option. Then click on the **Sync with SharePoint** option and click on the **Go To Save As** button.

Publishing Microsoft Project Tasks To SharePoint Online Collaboration Workspaces

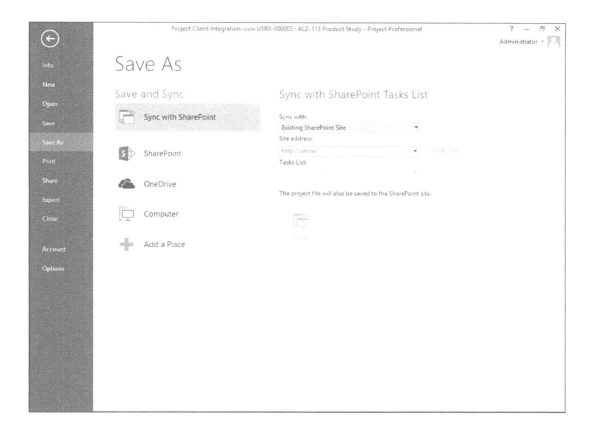

When the **Save As** options are shown you will notice that you can specify your SharePoint URL.

Publishing Microsoft Project Tasks To SharePoint Online Collaboration Workspaces

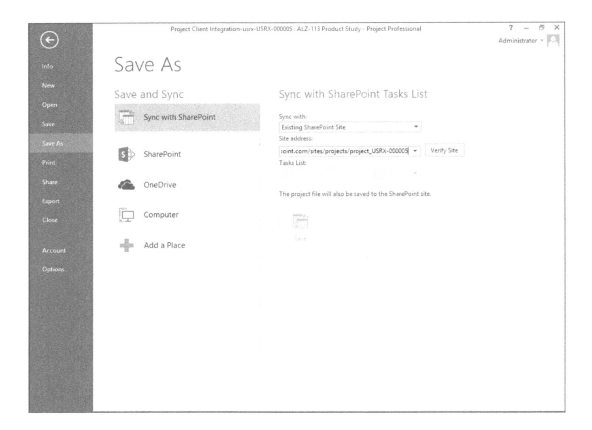

Paste in the URL for your Project Collaboration Workspace into the **Site Address** field and click on the **Verify Site** button.

Publishing Microsoft Project Tasks To SharePoint Online Collaboration Workspaces

This will open up a **Sign In** dialog for your online site.

Publishing Microsoft Project Tasks To SharePoint Online Collaboration Workspaces

Publishing Microsoft Project Tasks To SharePoint Online Collaboration Workspaces

Just type in your **User ID** and **Password** and then click on the **Sign In** button.

Publishing Microsoft Project Tasks To SharePoint Online Collaboration Workspaces

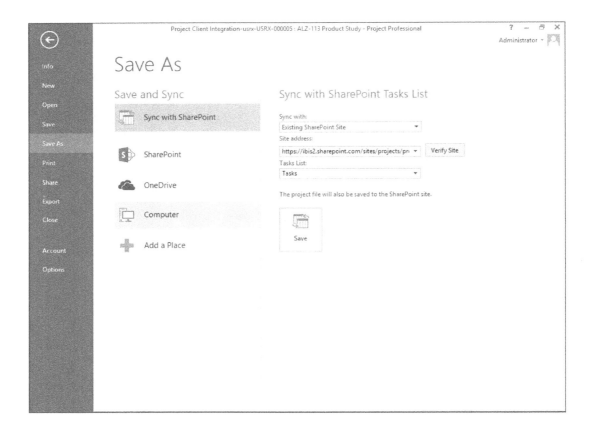

If all of your credentials are OK then you will be able to click on the **Save** button.

Publishing Microsoft Project Tasks To SharePoint Online Collaboration Workspaces

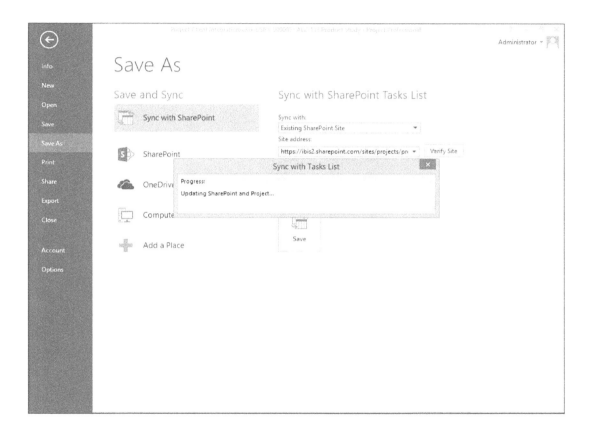

Then Microsoft Project will publish the entire plan up to SharePoint Online.

Publishing Microsoft Project Tasks To SharePoint Online Collaboration Workspaces

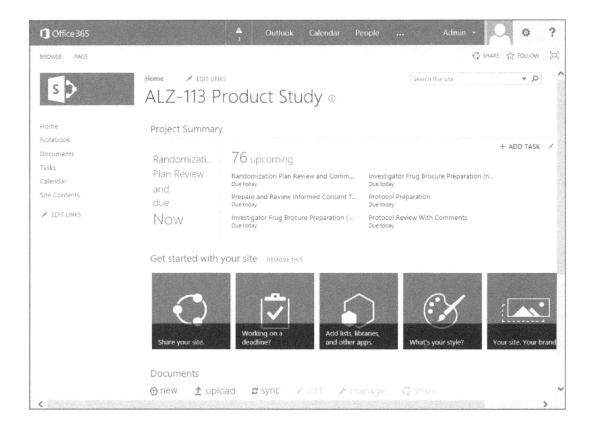

The next time you open up your Collaboration Workspace you will see the project summary is listed there with all of the items from your Work Breakdown Structure.

Publishing Microsoft Project Tasks To SharePoint Online Collaboration Workspaces

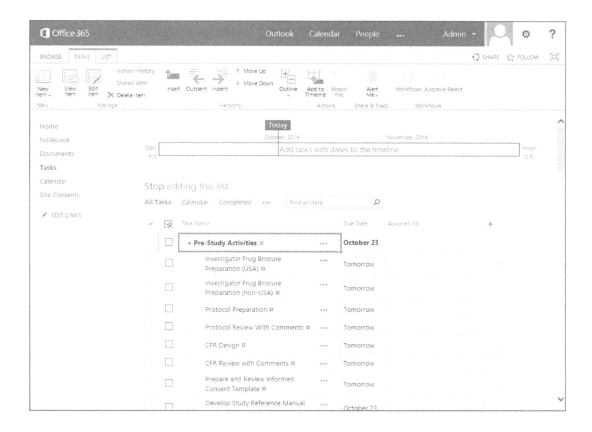

If you drill into the items you will also be able to see all of the tasks and the due dates.

What a great way to publish project details.

USING MS PROJECT TO MANAGE PROJECT DETAILS

In the previous sections we showed you how you could use **Microsoft Project** to manage some of the project details, but if you want you can actually use it a lot more. Since the it is integrated with Dynamics AX through the Office Add-Ins, you can use some of the other features in Microsoft Project such as resource management and scheduling to make your projects even more streamlined.

In this chapter we will look at a couple more options on how you can use Microsoft Project in conjunction with your Dynamics AX projects.

Adding Resources To Microsoft Project Plans

When you transfer the Project data over to Microsoft Project, you are not just linking all of the work breakdown structure activities over to it, but also a lot of the metadata that is embedded in the project itself like the resources and workers. That means that you can take advantage of this and add resources directly within Microsoft Project.

Adding Resources To Microsoft Project Plans

To start off, open up your project and click on the **Open In Microsoft Project** button within the **Activities** group of the **Plan** ribbon bar.

Adding Resources To Microsoft Project Plans

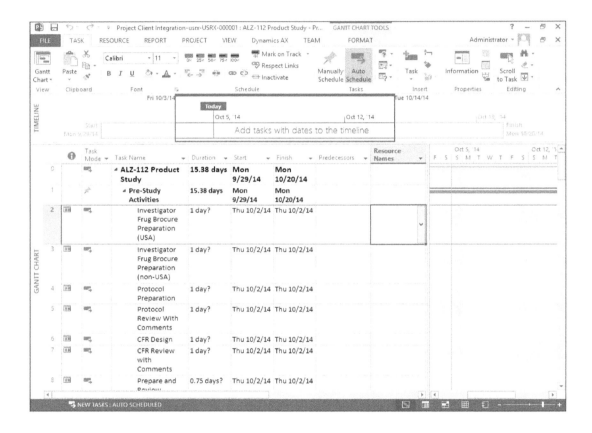

This will create your project file within Microsoft Project, and build all of your activities for you.

Adding Resources To Microsoft Project Plans

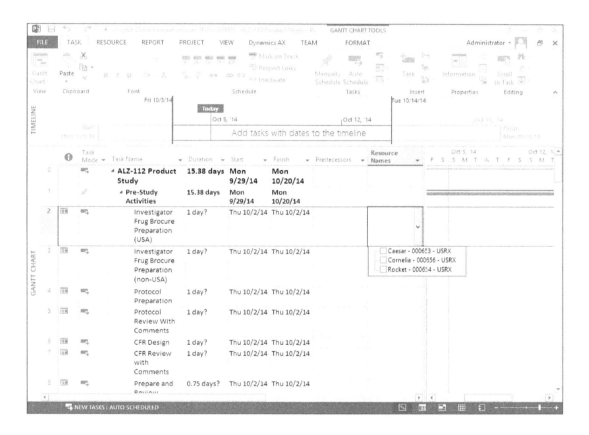

If you click on the dropdown box within the **Resource Names** field on your project plan then you will notice that all of the workers that have been assigned to the project will show up as resources that you can assign to the tasks.

Adding Resources To Microsoft Project Plans

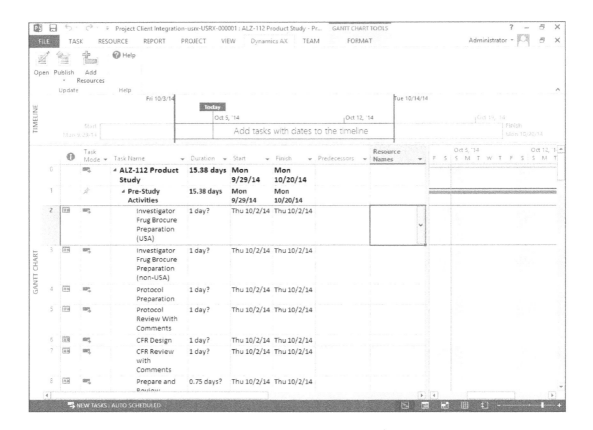

Notice also that there is a Dynamics AX ribbon bar as well.

Note: If you don't have this ribbon bar then you just need to install the Office Add-Ins for Dynamics AX.

If you want to allow more resources to be assigned to the project then just click on the **Add Resources** button within the **Update** group of the **Dynamics AX** ribbon bar.

Adding Resources To Microsoft Project Plans

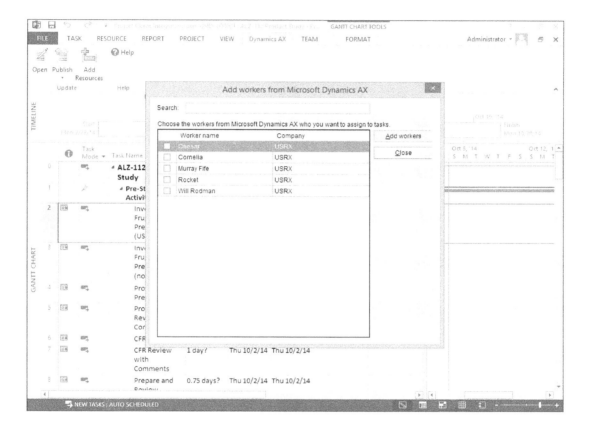

This will open up a list of resources that you can assign to the project – coming directly from Dynamics AX.

Adding Resources To Microsoft Project Plans

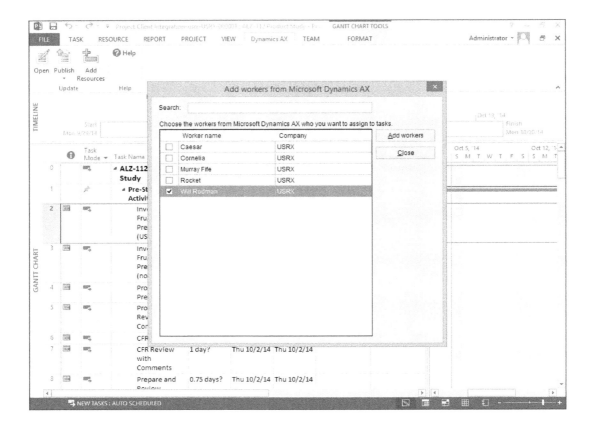

To add a worker, just check the checkbox beside their name and click on the **Add Workers** button.

Adding Resources To Microsoft Project Plans

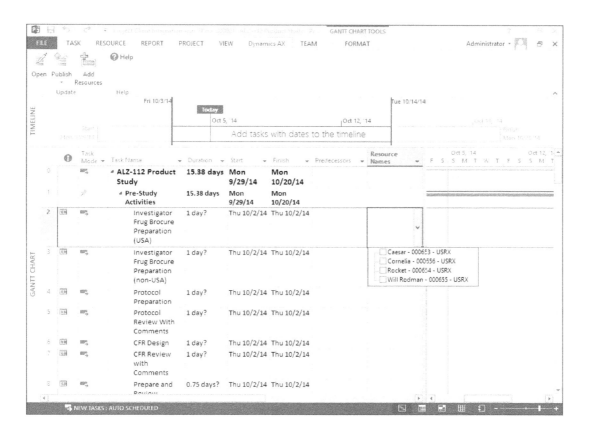

When you return back to the **Resource Names** you will see the new worker is able to be assigned to your projects.

Assigning Workers To Activities Through Microsoft Project

Once you have all of the workers that you want assigned to your project you can then just add them as resources to your work breakdown structure tasks.

Assigning Workers To Activities Through Microsoft Project

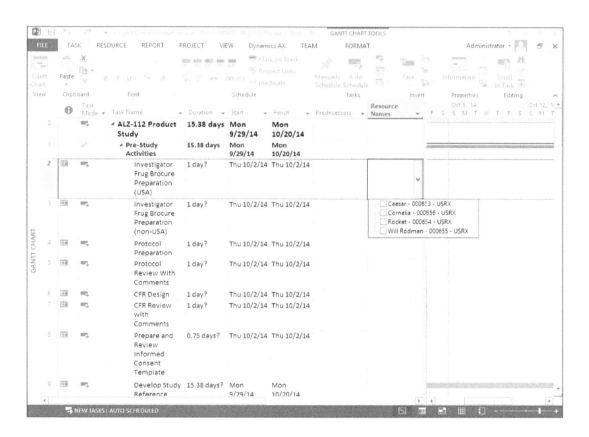

To do this, open up your Microsoft Project plan and click on the dropdown list for the **Resource Names** on the task that you want to assign the resources to.

Assigning Workers To Activities Through Microsoft Project

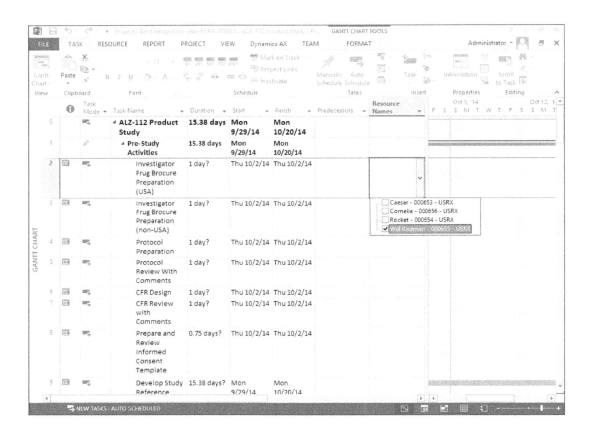

To add a resource, just select them by checking the box beside their name.

Assigning Workers To Activities Through Microsoft Project

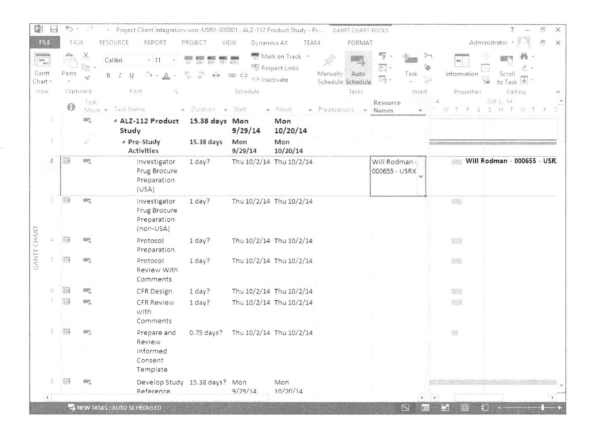

When you exit from the field they will be associated with the task.

Managing Resource Scheduling Through Microsoft Project

Microsoft Project has a lot of inbuilt scheduling features that are great when it comes to leveling out your project resources and making sure that you don't have resources tasks that overlap.

Managing Resource Scheduling Through Microsoft Project

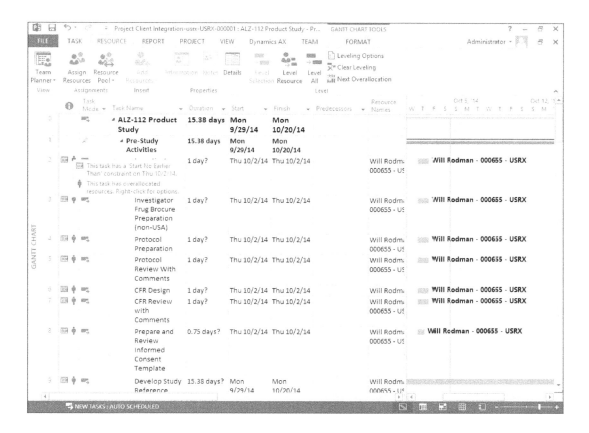

To see this in action, start with a project where you have assigned resources to all of your tasks, but have not added any dependencies on the tasks. All you need to do is click on the **Level Resource** button within the **Level** group of the **Resource** ribbon bar.

Managing Resource Scheduling Through Microsoft Project

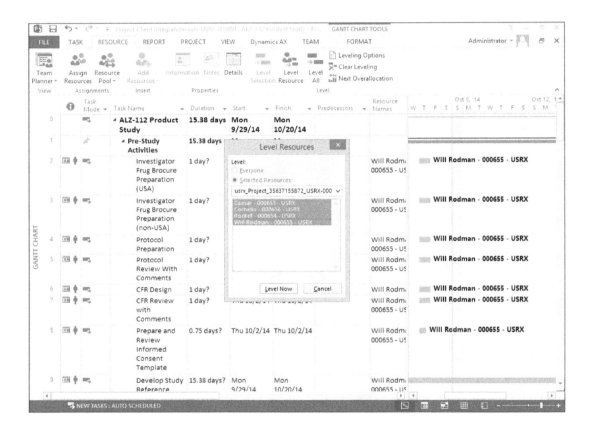

When the **Level Resources** dialog box is displayed you can select the resources that you want to manage the capacity for – in this case we will just choose everyone – and then click the **Level Now** button.

Managing Resource Scheduling Through Microsoft Project

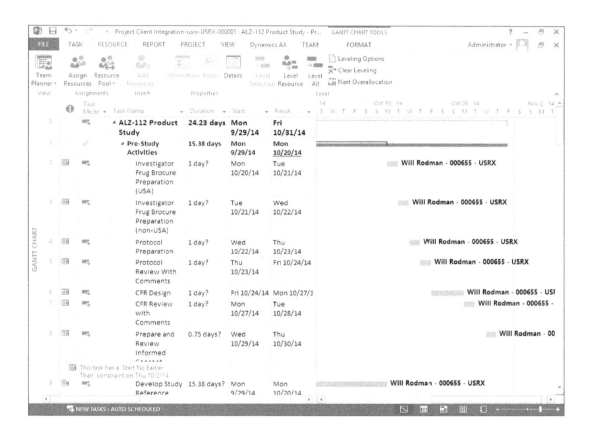

Like project management magic, now all of the resource tasks are leveled out with no overlap.

Organizing Workbreakdown Activities Through Microsoft Project

Microsoft Project is really an easier way to manage your project structures because of the drag and drop capabilities, and also the editing features for the project definition. It has been designed from the ground up for editing projects, so why not take full advantage of it.

Organizing Workbreakdown Activities Through Microsoft Project

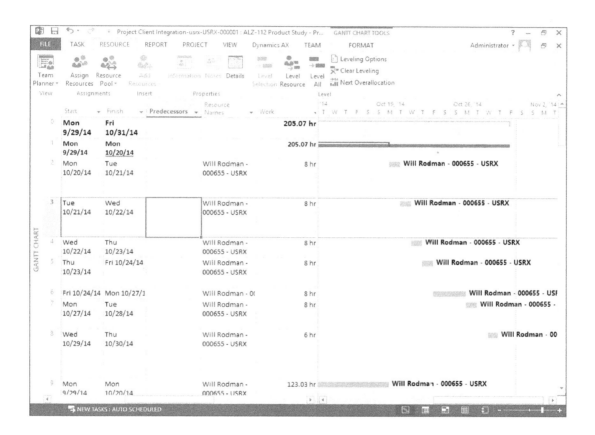

One example is the ability to link the work breakdown structure activities together. To do this start off by opening up your project in Microsoft Project and selecting the activity that you want to link.

Organizing Workbreakdown Activities Through Microsoft Project

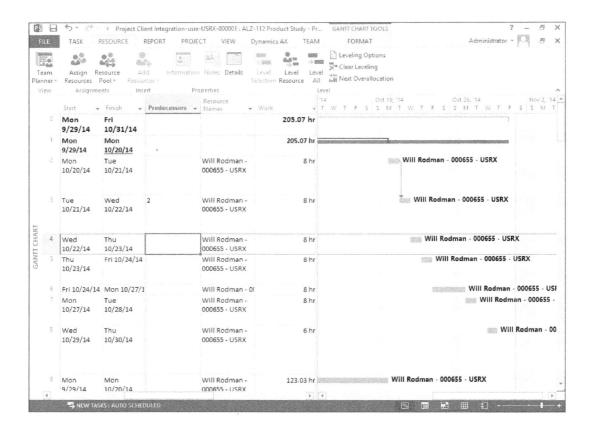

Then within the **Predecessor** field enter in the previous task that you want to link the current task to.

Organizing Workbreakdown Activities Through Microsoft Project

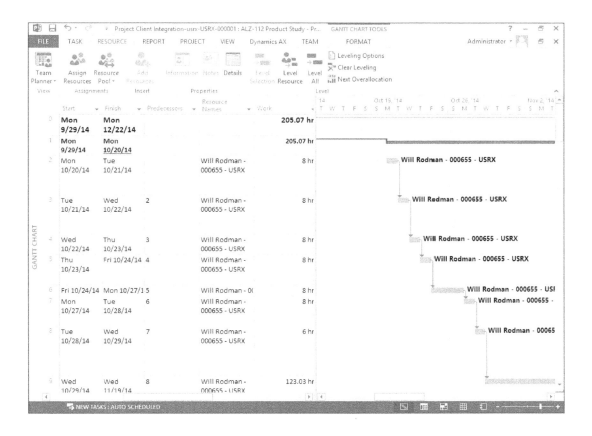

If you keep on working through the tasks that way then you can quickly see all of the tasks being visually linked within the Gantt chart on the right.

Organizing Workbreakdown Activities Through Microsoft Project

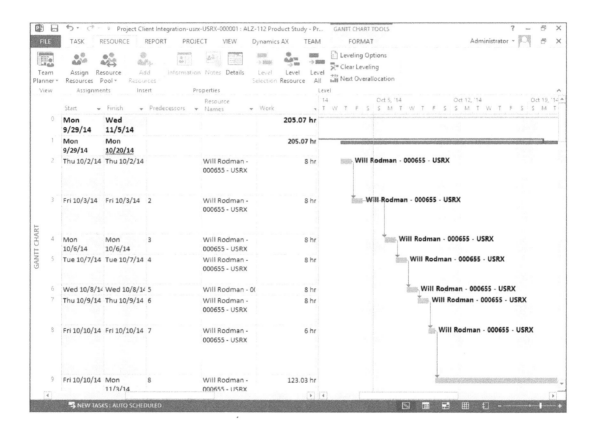

Organizing Workbreakdown Activities Through Microsoft Project

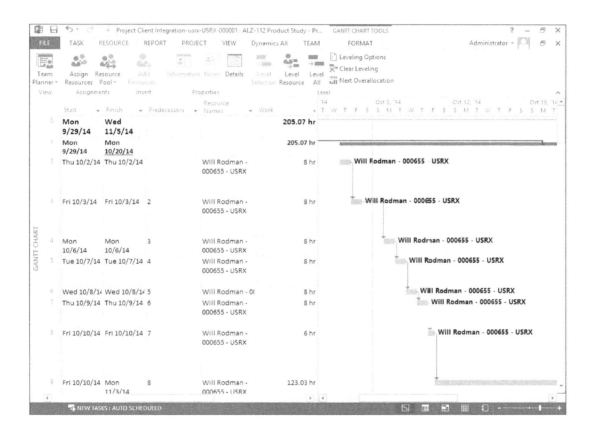

If you notice that the project plan is a little skewed after you have changed the task links, then just click on the **Level All** button within the **Level** group of the **Resource** ribbon bar.

Organizing Workbreakdown Activities Through Microsoft Project

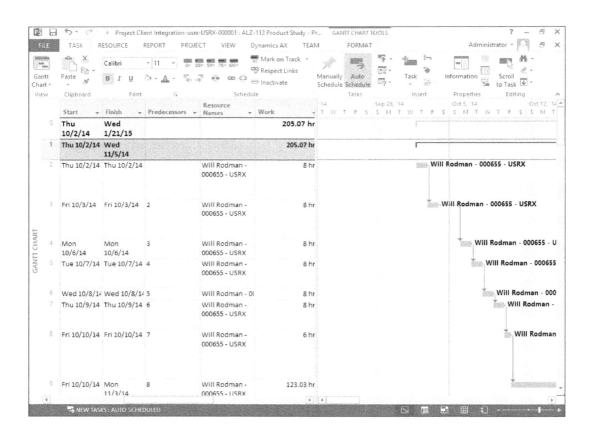

That will adjust all of the tasks and bring them back in line with the project.

Organizing Workbreakdown Activities Through Microsoft Project

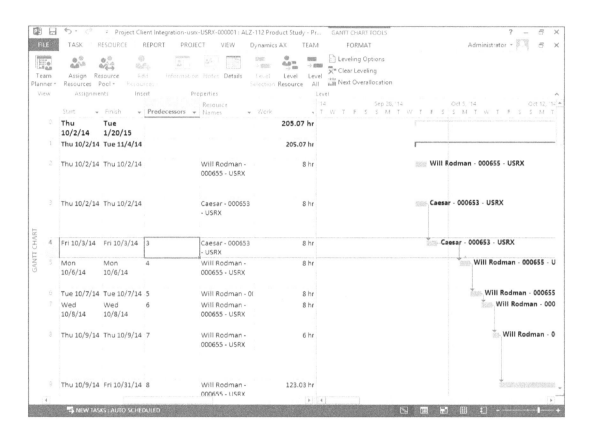

If you have a project where multiple resources are involved within the project then the leveling will work even better because the tasks can now overlap if different people can perform the tasks.

Organizing Workbreakdown Activities Through Microsoft Project

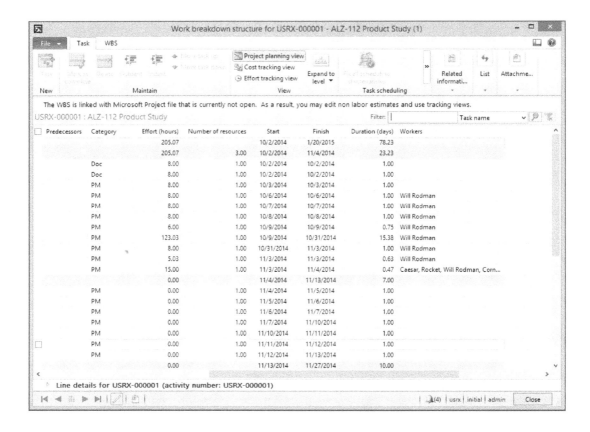

When you save your project then all of your scheduling and resource assignments will be updated within Dynamics AX.

How cool is that?

Unlinking Projects From Microsoft Project

You may have noticed that when you link the Dynamics AX project over to Microsoft Project, then you loose the ability to edit the project work breakdown structure within Dynamics AX. This is just a precaution that Dynamics puts in place to make sure that there aren't too many cooks in the kitchen. But if you decide that you want to return back to the traditional way of editing your work breakdown structures then don't worry – unlinking projects from Microsoft Project is just a click of a button away.

Unlinking Projects From Microsoft Project

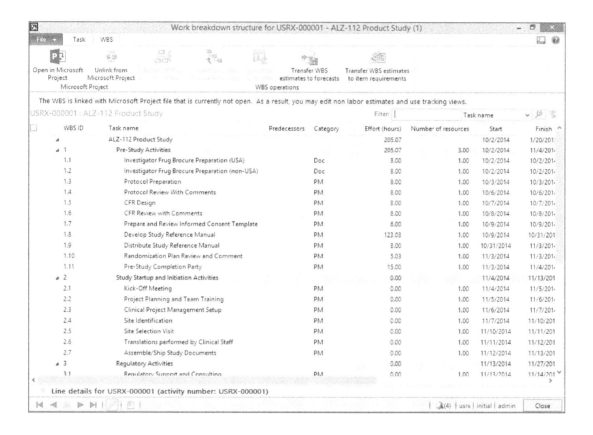

All you need to do is open up your project that is linked with Microsoft Project and then click on the **Unlink From Microsoft Project** button within the **Microsoft Project** group of the **WBS** ribbon bar.

Unlinking Projects From Microsoft Project

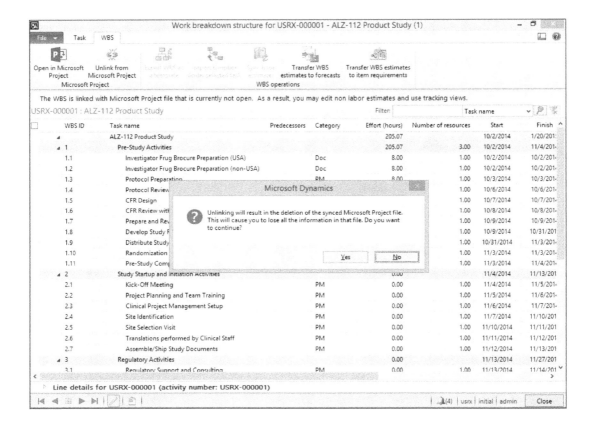

When the warning dialog is displayed, just click on the **Yes** button.

Unlinking Projects From Microsoft Project

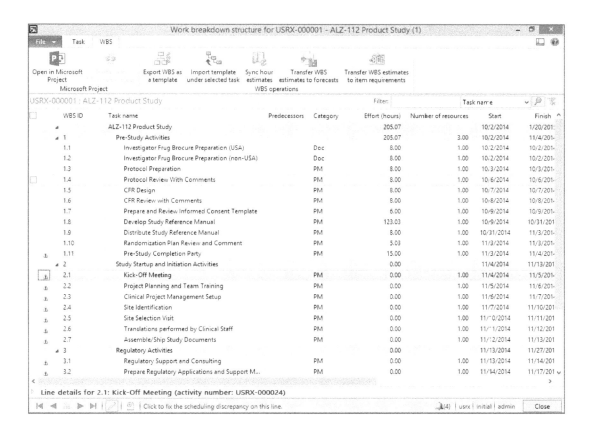

When you return back to your project it will be editable within Dynamics AX.

CONFIGURING PROJECT BUDGETS

If you want tighter control over your projects and also the expenses that are posted to the projects then you may want to use the budgeting feature within Dynamics AX. This allows you to import all of your forecasted expenses into a project budget, adjust them and then control how the budget is used to control other peoples charges.

In this chapter we will show you how you can set up budgets to work alongside your projects.

Configuring Budget Forecast Models

The first thing that we need to do is add a few more **Budget Forecast Models** that we will use for our budgeting.

Configuring Budget Forecast Models

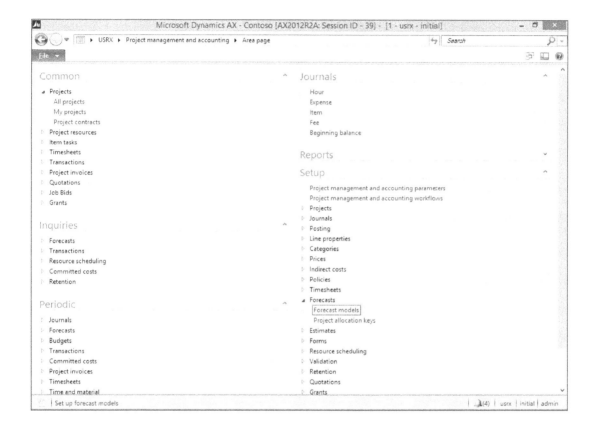

To do this, click on the **Forecast Models** menu item within the **Forecasts** folder of the **Setup** group within the **Project Management And Accounting** area page.

Configuring Budget Forecast Models

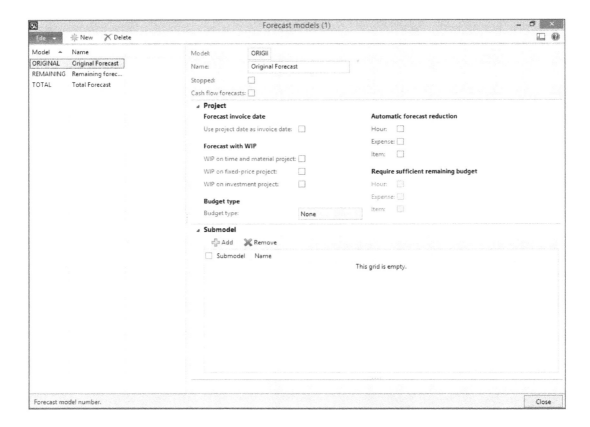

When the **Forecast Models** maintenance form is displayed, click on the **New** button in the menu bar to create a new record.

Configuring Budget Forecast Models

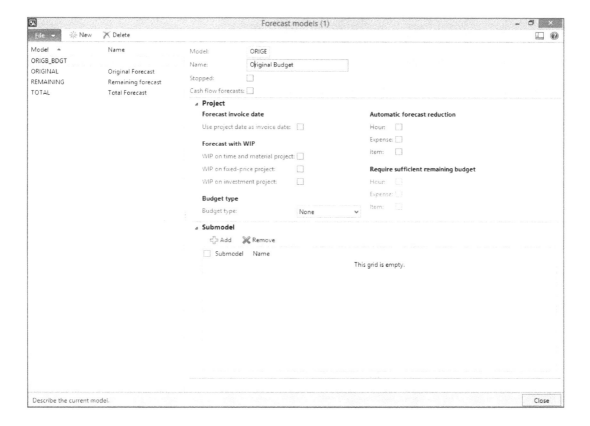

Set the **Model** code to be **ORIGBDGT** and the **Name** to be **Original Budget**.

Configuring Budget Forecast Models

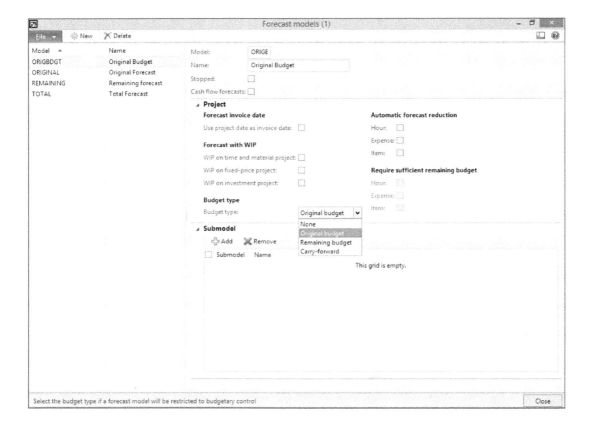

Then change the **Budget Type** to be **Original Budget**.

Configuring Budget Forecast Models

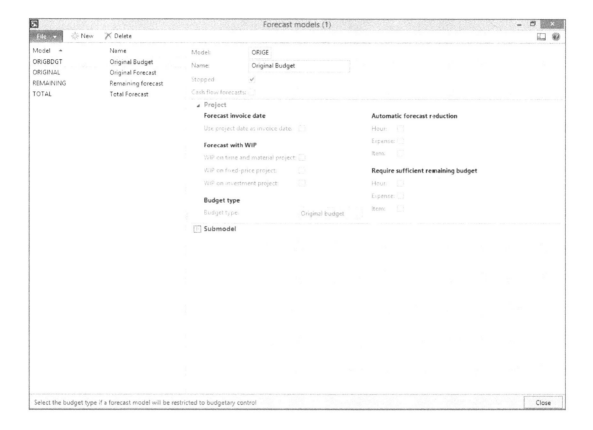

This will automatically set the budget up for you and you don't need to check anything else.

Configuring Budget Forecast Models

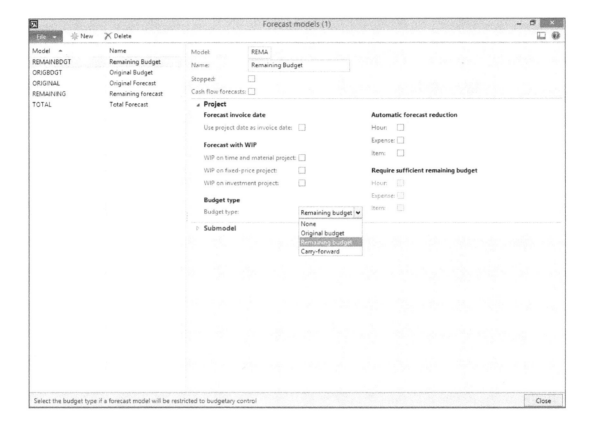

Click on the **New** button again to create a new record and for this one set the **Model** code to **REMAINBDGT**, the **Name** to **Remaining Budget** and the **Budget Type** to **Remaining Budget**.

Configuring Budget Forecast Models

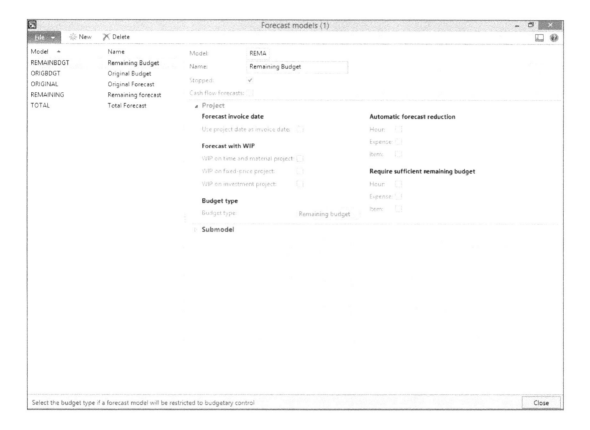

Again, this will automatically set the budget up for you and you don't need to check anything else.

Configuring Budget Forecast Models

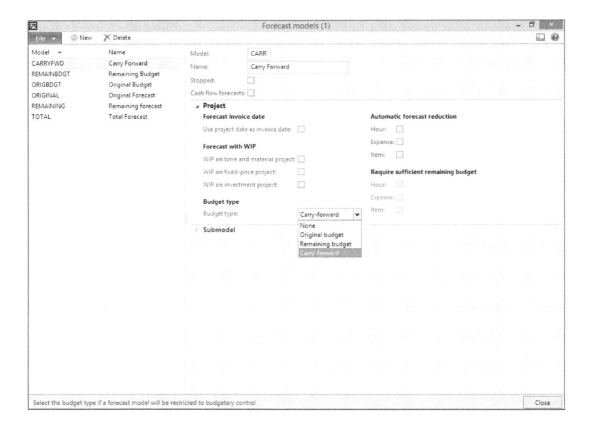

Finally, click on the **New** button again to create one last record and for this one set the **Model** code to **CARRYFWD**, the **Name** to **Carry Forward** and the **Budget Type** to **Carry Forward**.

Configuring Budget Forecast Models

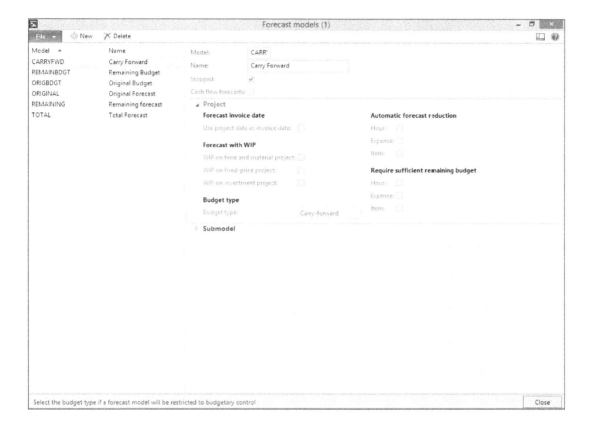

This will also automatically set the budget up for you and you don't need to check anything else.

Now click on the **Close** button to exit from the form.

Creating A Project Budget

Now that we have our budget models we can create a **Project Budget**.

Creating A Project Budget

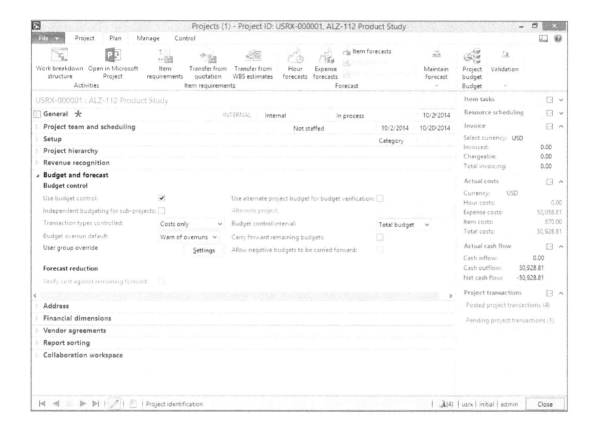

To do this, open up your **Project** and click on the **Project Budget** button within the **Budgets** group of the **Plan** ribbon bar.

Creating A Project Budget

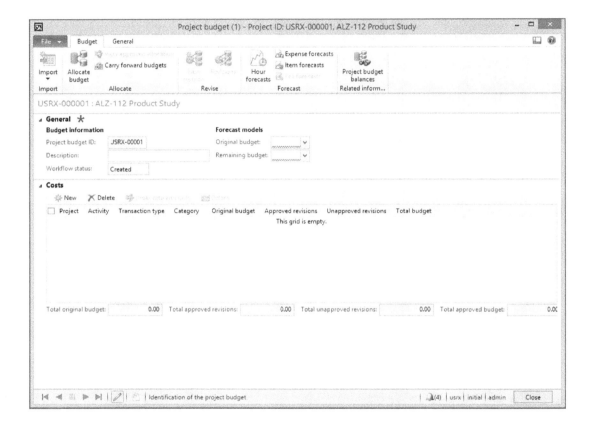

This will open up the **Project Budgets** maintenance form.

Creating A Project Budget

Give your **Project Budget** and **Description.**

Creating A Project Budget

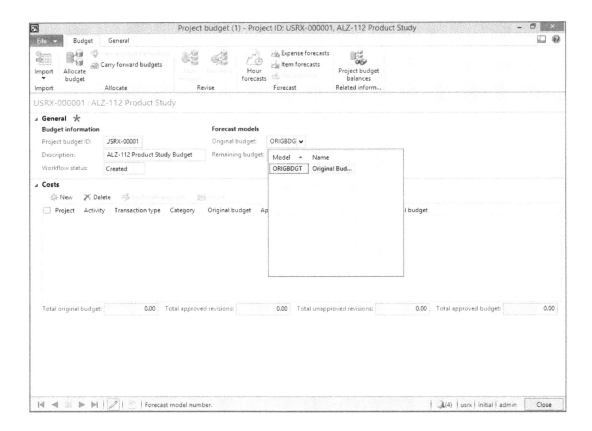

Then set the **Original Budget** code to be **ORIGBDGT.**

Creating A Project Budget

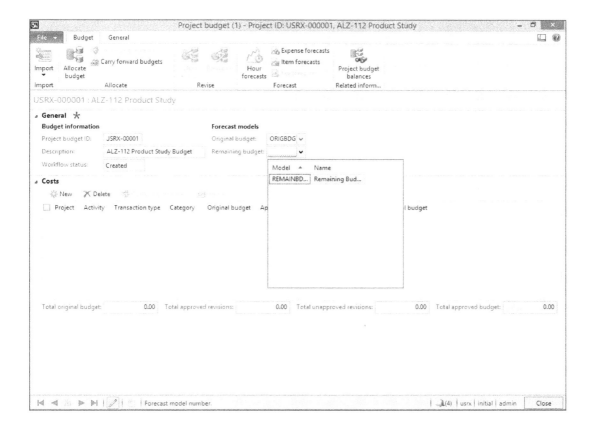

And set the **Remaining Budget** code to be **REMAINBDGT**.

Creating A Project Budget

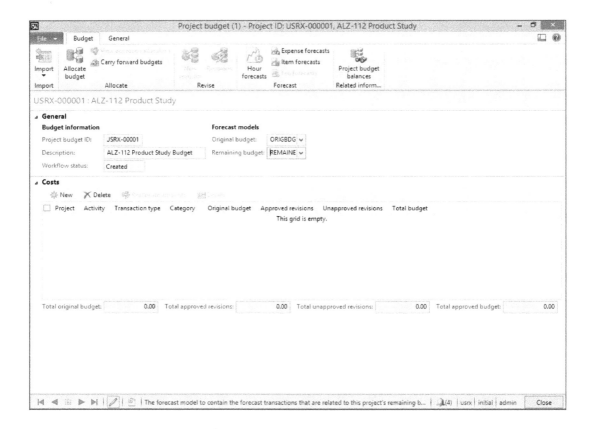

After you have done that you can save the budget.

Importing Forecasts Into Project Budgets

Once you have a **Project Budget** configured you can then import in all of your forecasts to create the initial budget details.

Importing Forecasts Into Project Budgets

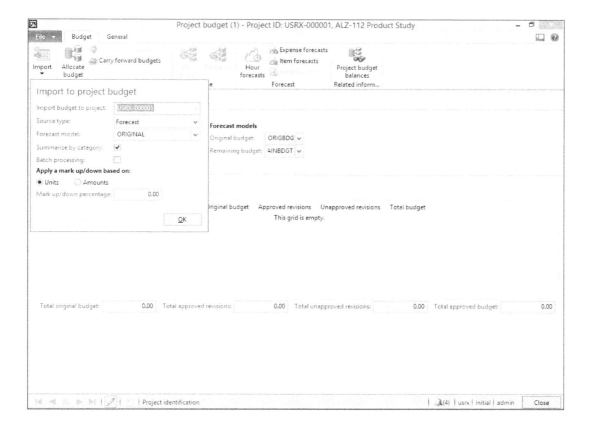

To do this, click on the **Import** button within the **Import** group of the **Budget** ribbon bar. This will open up a **Import To Project Budget** dialog box.

Importing Forecasts Into Project Budgets

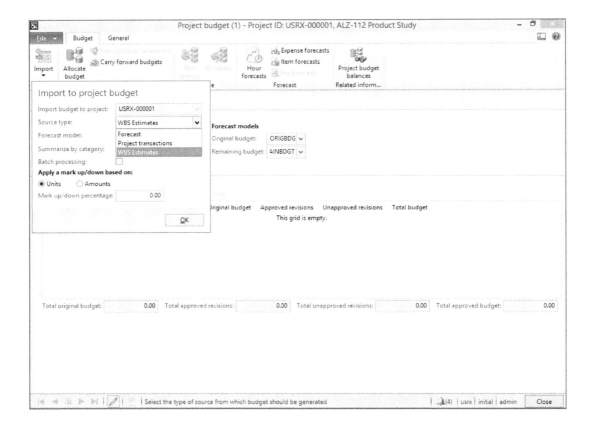

If you click on the **Source** type you will see all of the different sources that you can import your budget from. In this case we will select the **WBS Estimates** as our source type.

Importing Forecasts Into Project Budgets

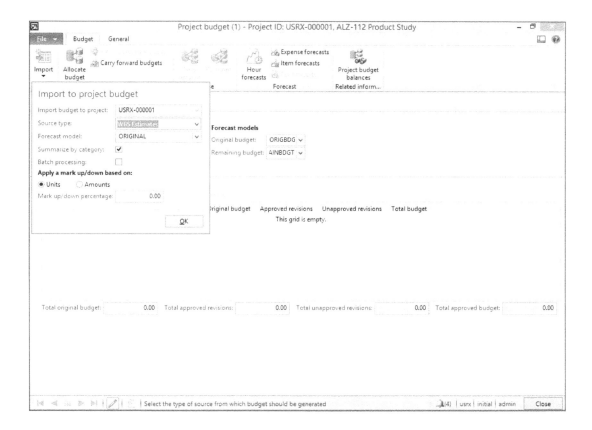

After you have done that, just click on the **OK** button to start the import.

Importing Forecasts Into Project Budgets

You will see that all of your costs have now been copied down to the budget. By default though these are broken out by category.

Importing Forecasts Into Project Budgets

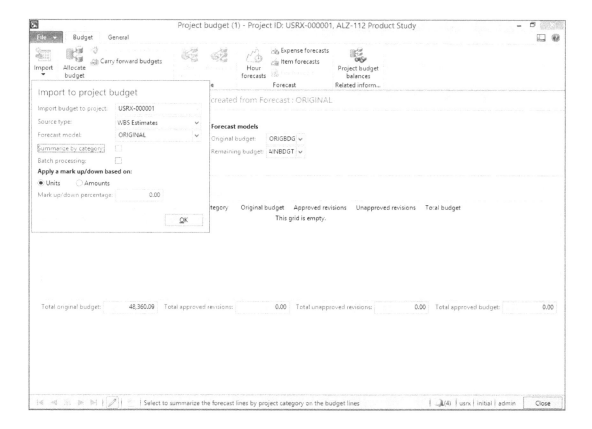

If you want to budget at a lower level and do so by Activity, then just rerun the import process, but this time, uncheck the **Summarize By Category** flag.

Importing Forecasts Into Project Budgets

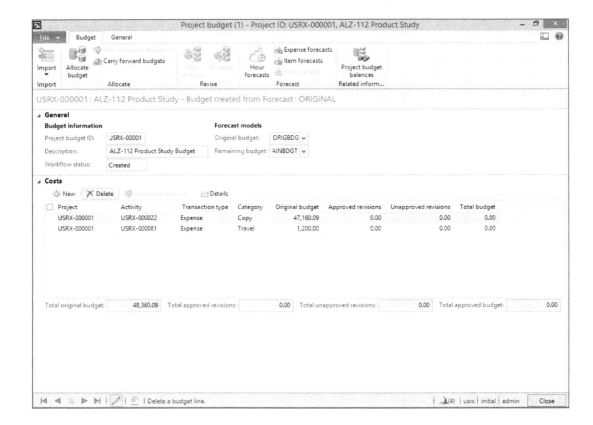

Now we will have all of your budgets configured down to the actual activity.

CONFIGURING TIMESHEET REPORTING FOR PROJECTS

Dynamics AX has inbuilt timesheet reporting which is great, but this is even more useful because it automatically links up to **Project Management And Accounting** allowing all of the time posted on time sheets to be posted to your projects as well so that you can track resources and the work that they have performed. Having the workers enter in their own time may be a chore for them, but it means that you don't have to do it which is better in the long run.

Giving Employees Full Access To The Employee Self Service Portal

There are a couple of ways that you can post time through timesheets. The most accessible way is through the **Employee Self Service Portal** which allows the workers (and contractors) just to sign in through a web portal and start entering in their timesheets. First though you need to make sure that they have access to it through their security profile.

Giving Employees Full Access To The Employee Self Service Portal

Start off by navigating to the Employee Self Service Portal. If you have limited rights, then you may only be able to see the **Timesheets** group on the page. If this is all that you want to give the user access to then that's fine.

Giving Employees Full Access To The Employee Self Service Portal

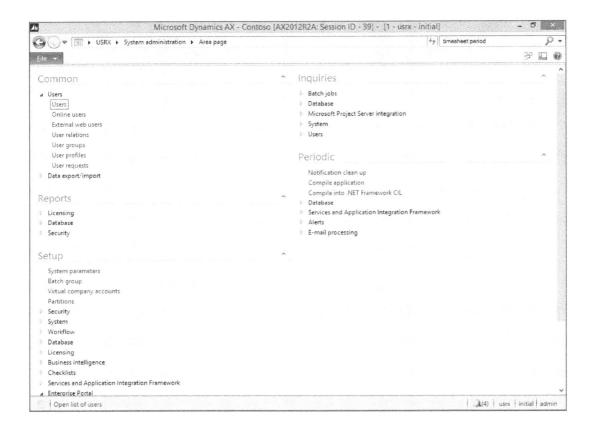

If you want to give the worker more access though you will need to set them up with an **Employee** role. To do that, click on the **Users** menu item within the **Users** folder of the **Common** area within the **System Administration** area page.

Giving Employees Full Access To The Employee Self Service Portal

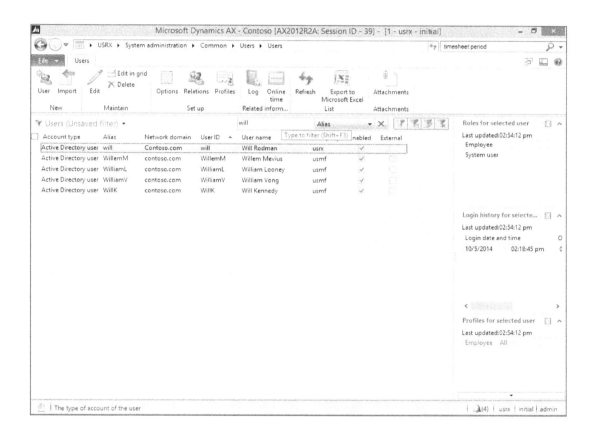

When the **Users** list page is displayed, double click on the user that you want to add more profiles to.

Giving Employees Full Access To The Employee Self Service Portal

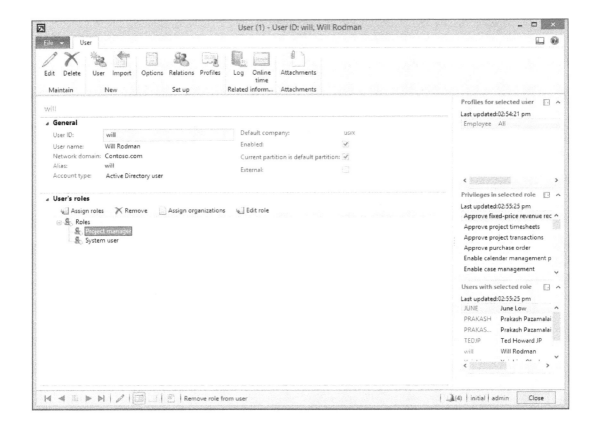

This will open up the User detail page. Now click on the **Assign Roles** button within the **User Roles** tab menu bar.

Giving Employees Full Access To The Employee Self Service Portal

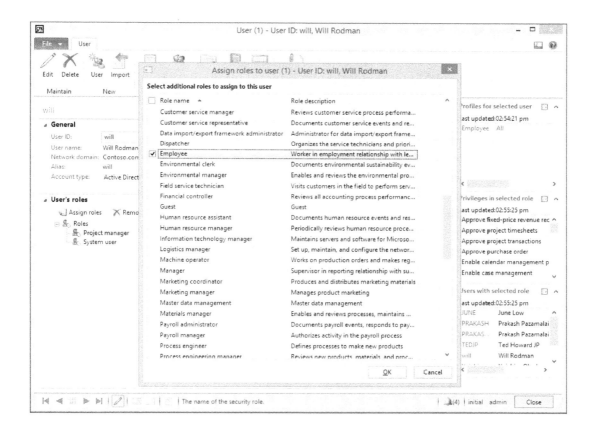

When the **Assign Roles To User** dialog box is displayed, check the **Employee** role and then click on the **OK** button.

Giving Employees Full Access To The Employee Self Service Portal

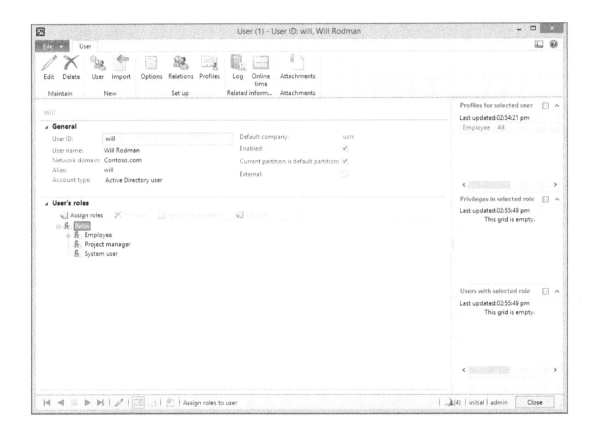

When you return to the User form they should now have an additional role for the **Employee.**

Giving Employees Full Access To The Employee Self Service Portal

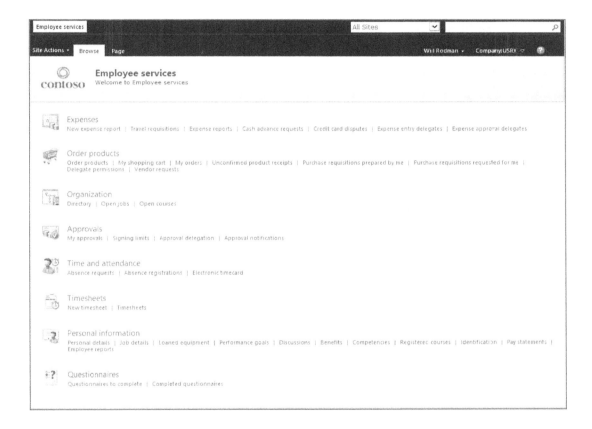

Now when they log into the **Employee Self Service Portal** they will see a not more options for them to access.

Posting Time To Projects Using The Employee Self Service Portal

Once the user is configured to have access to the **Employee Self Service Portal** they can start using it to post time.

Posting Time To Projects Using The Employee Self Service Portal

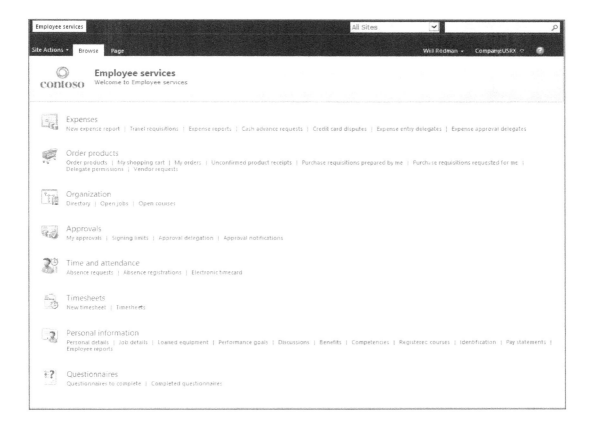

To do that they just need to access the **Employee Self Service Portal** and then click on the **New Timesheet** link within the **Timesheets** menu group.

Posting Time To Projects Using The Employee Self Service Portal

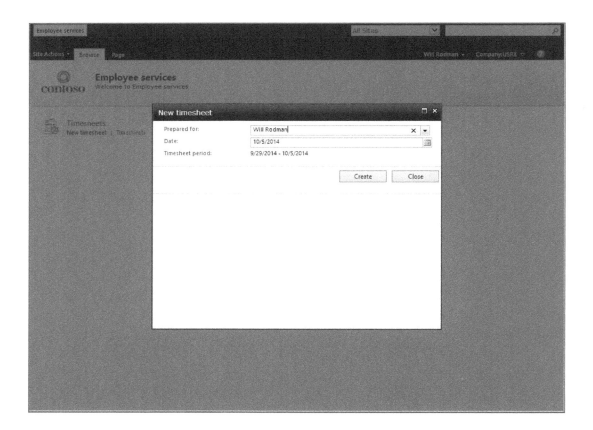

When the **New Timesheet** dialog box is displayed, the date and timesheet period will already be populated based off the timesheet period that you defined for the worker. Just click the **Create** button.

Posting Time To Projects Using The Employee Self Service Portal

This will open up the **Timesheet Entry** form for you.

Posting Time To Projects Using The Employee Self Service Portal

To add a new record, just click on the **New Line** button within the **Timesheet Lines** tab group.

Posting Time To Projects Using The Employee Self Service Portal

To associate the time against a project, just click on the **Project** dropdown list and you will see a list of all the active projects.

Posting Time To Projects Using The Employee Self Service Portal

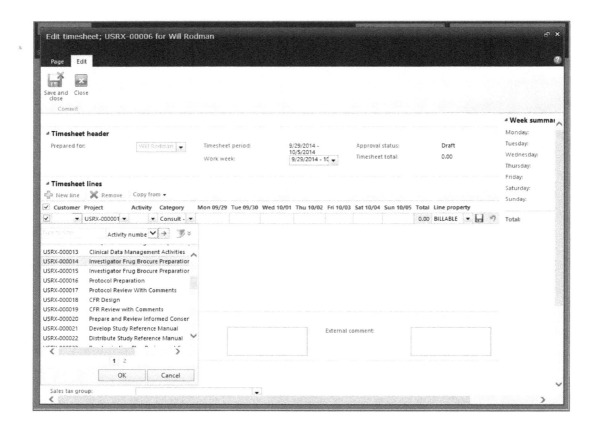

After you select a Project, you can then select an **Activity** that you worked on.

Posting Time To Projects Using The Employee Self Service Portal

All that is left is for you to fill in the hours that were worked on the activity.

When you are done, just click the **Save** icon.

Posting Time To Projects Using The Employee Self Service Portal

After you have posted your time, just click on the **Save And Close** button within the **Commit** group of the **Edit** ribbon bar.

Viewing Time Sheets Through The Employee Self Service Portal

After you have posted your time through the **Employee Self Service Portal** you can always return and revise the time sheets.

Viewing Time Sheets Through The Employee Self Service Portal

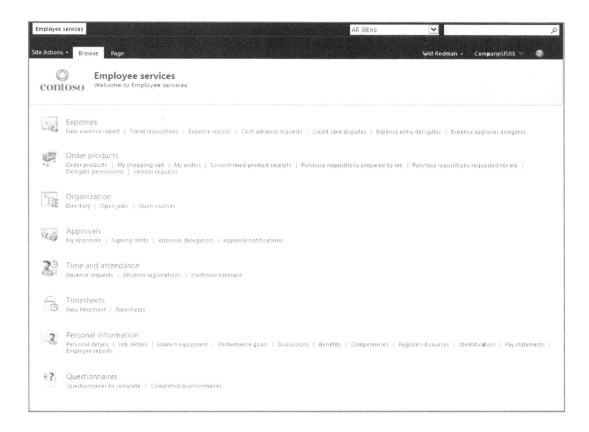

To do that they just need to access the **Employee Self Service Portal** and then click on the **Timesheets** link within the **Timesheets** menu group.

Viewing Time Sheets Through The Employee Self Service Portal

This will show you a list of all the timesheets that you have entered and you can edit them if you like.

Posting Time Through The Rich Client

If you have access to the **Rich Client** then you can also post your timesheets through there as well, giving you another option for submitting time.

Posting Time Through The Rich Client

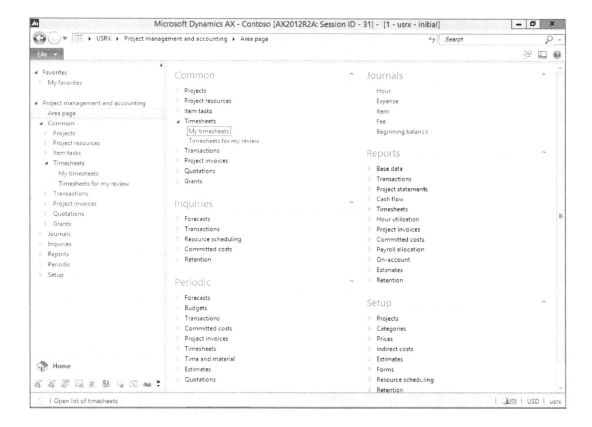

To do this, click on the **My Timesheets** menu item within the **Timesheets** folder of the **Common** group within the **Project Management And Accounting** area page.

Posting Time Through The Rich Client

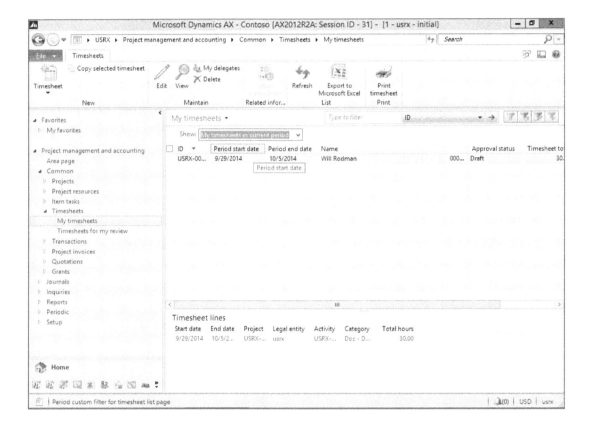

When the **My Timesheets** list page is displayed you will be able to see all of your timesheets, including the ones that were posted through the **Employee Self Service Portal.**

You can create new time sheets just by clicking on the **Timesheet** button within the **New** group of the **Timesheets** ribbon bar, or edit existing ones just by double clicking on them.

Posting Time Through The Rich Client

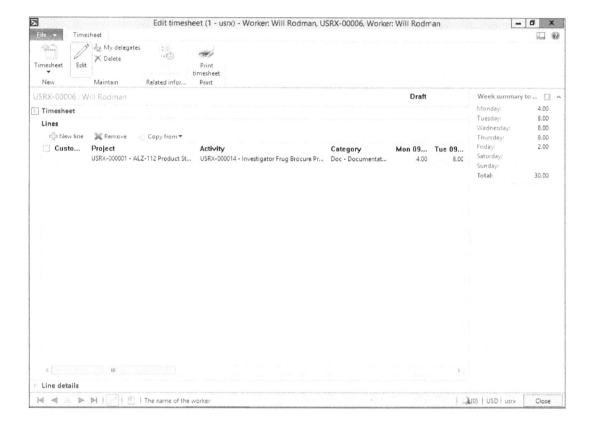

When you open up an existing timesheet you will see all of the time is laid out the same way as it was within the **Employee Self Service Portal**.

Posting Time Through The Rich Client

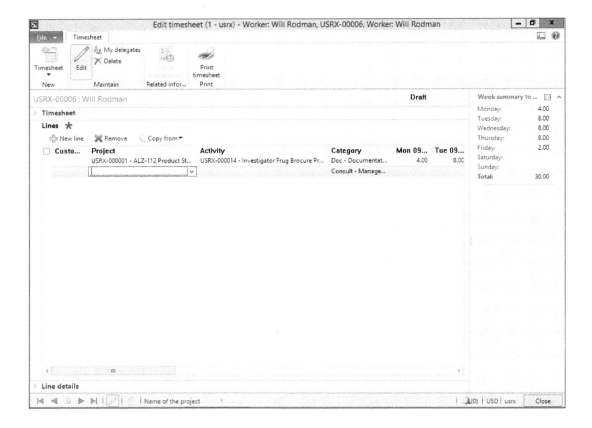

If you want to add a new line, then just click on the **New Line** button within the **Lines** tab group menu bar,

Posting Time Through The Rich Client

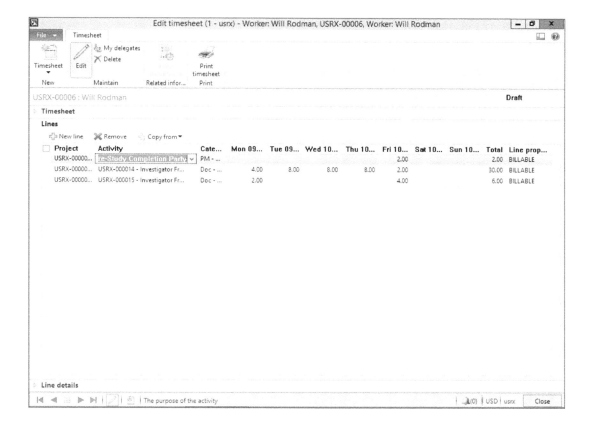

You can select the **Project** and **Activity** just the same way and then specify the time by work day.

If you want to print a copy of your timesheet then just click on the **Print Timesheet** button within the **Print** group of the **Timesheet** ribbon bar.

Posting Time Through The Rich Client

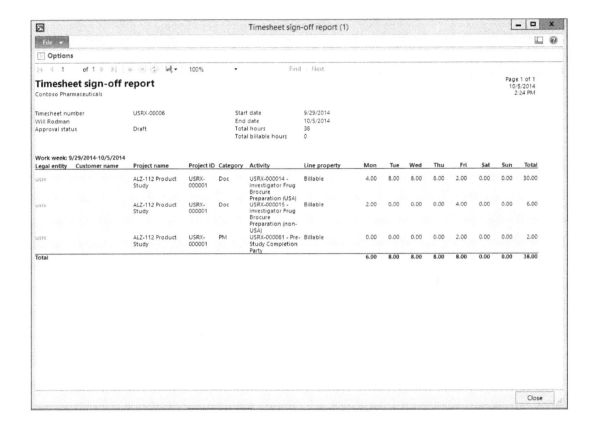

This will create a hardcopy report of your timesheet for you.

Creating A Timesheet Approval Workflow

A benefit of posting time through the Timesheet function within Dynamics AX is that you can then associate a workflow to it for approval. This allows you to streamline the timesheet entry and approval process by making it completely electronic.

Creating A Timesheet Approval Workflow

To do this, click on the **Project Management And Accounting Workflows** menu item within the **Setup** group of the **Project Management And Accounting** area page.

Creating A Timesheet Approval Workflow

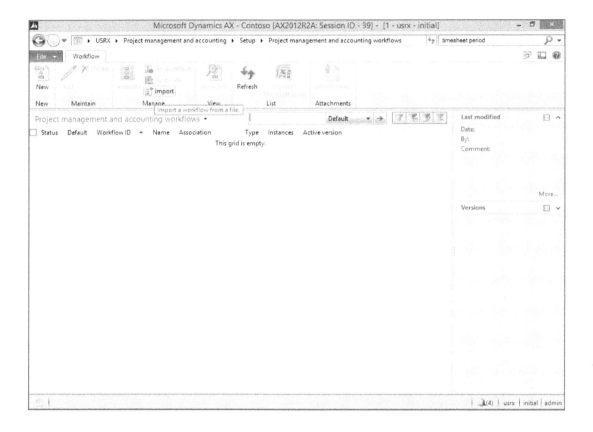

When the **Project Management And Accounting Workflows** maintenance form is displayed, click on the **New** button within the **New** group of the **Workflow** ribbon bar.

Creating A Timesheet Approval Workflow

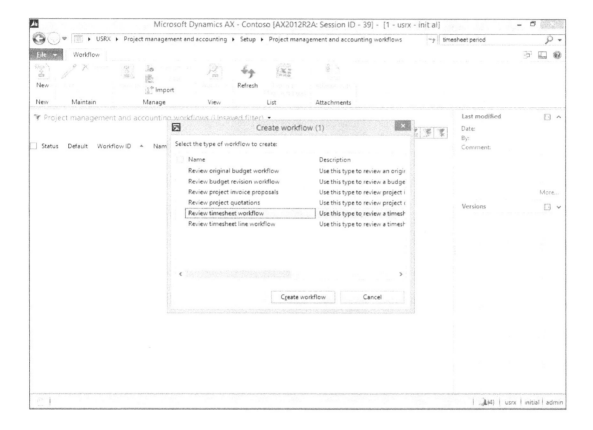

When the **Create Workflow** dialog box is displayed, you will see that there are a number of different workflows that you can choose from. Select the **Review Timesheet Workflow** from the list and then click on the **Create Workflow** button.

Creating A Timesheet Approval Workflow

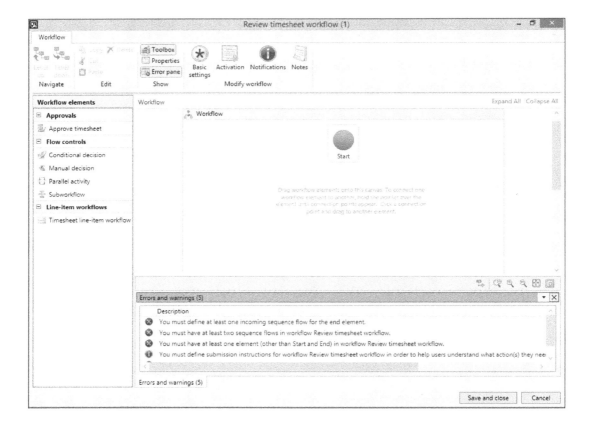

This will take you straight to the workflow designer canvas.

Creating A Timesheet Approval Workflow

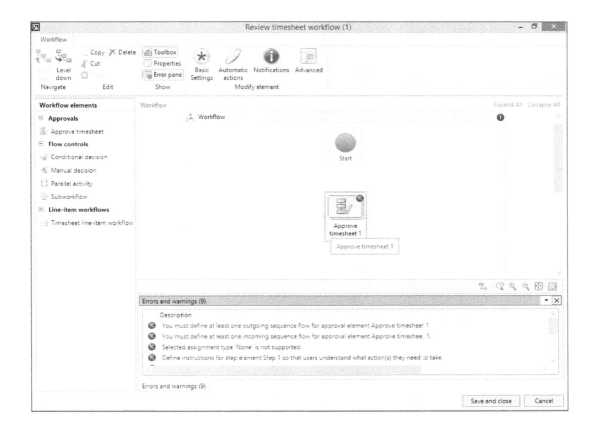

From the palette on the left, drag the **Approve Timesheet** element onto the canvas.

Creating A Timesheet Approval Workflow

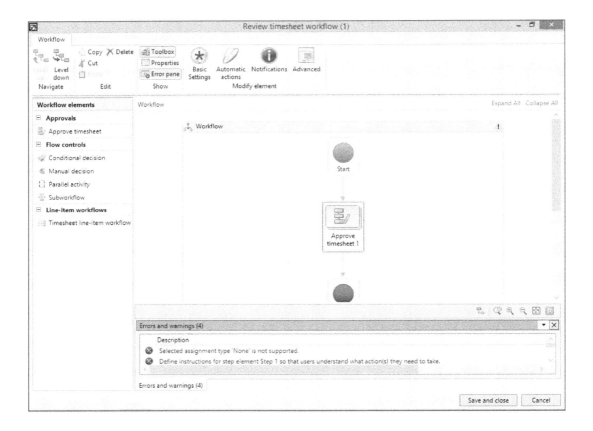

Then link the **Start** and **End** elements to the workflow to create a connected workflow.

Notice that within the bottom section of the Workflow designer is a list of loose ends that you need to tidy up. Double click on the first one.

Creating A Timesheet Approval Workflow

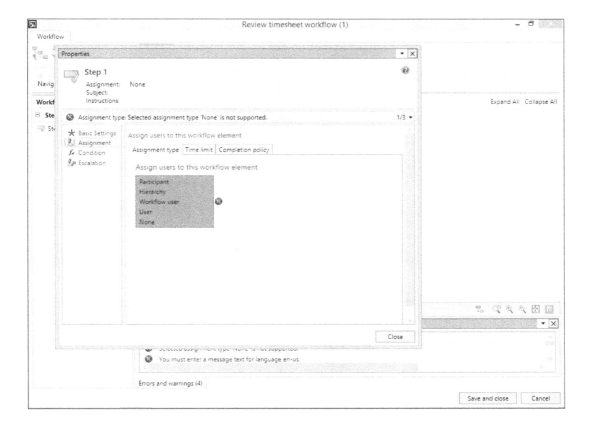

That will take you into a **Properties** page where you need to assign the person that will approve the timesheet.

Creating A Timesheet Approval Workflow

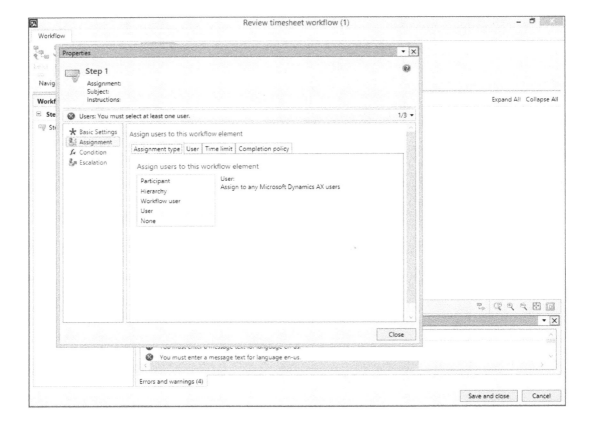

Within the **Assignment Type** list, click on the **User** option to assign the timesheet approval just to one person.

Creating A Timesheet Approval Workflow

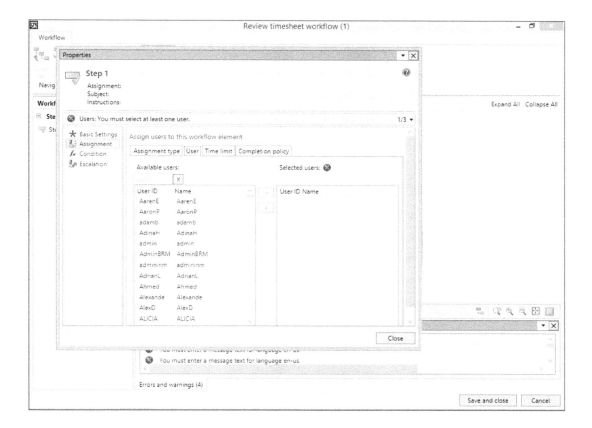

Now switch to the **User** tab.

Creating A Timesheet Approval Workflow

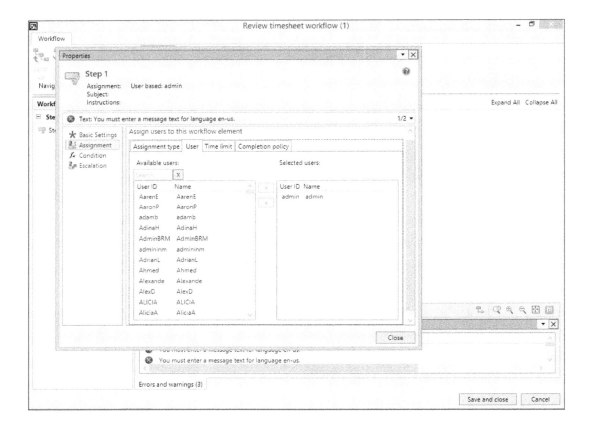

Select the user that you want to approve the timesheet from the list of **Available Users** and then click on the **>** button to assign them to the **Selected Users.**

Creating A Timesheet Approval Workflow

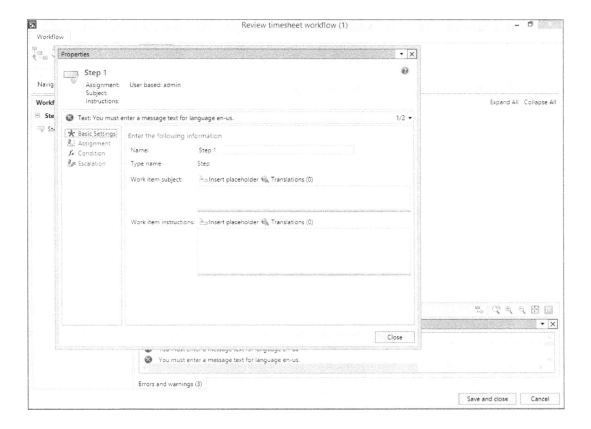

Now click on the **Basic Settings** on the left hand side of the dialog box, and you will see that there are a few more fields that need to be updated.

Creating A Timesheet Approval Workflow

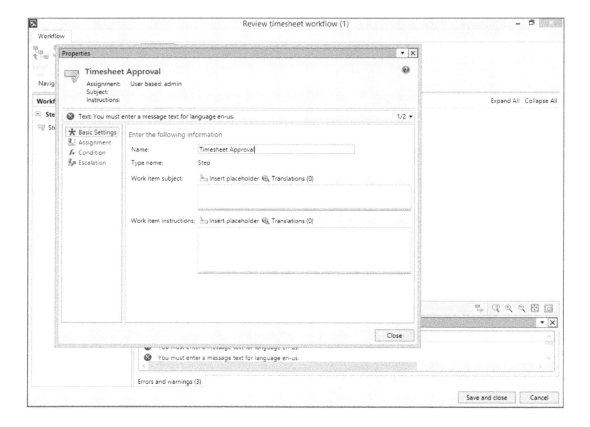

Give your step a more descriptive **Name**.

Creating A Timesheet Approval Workflow

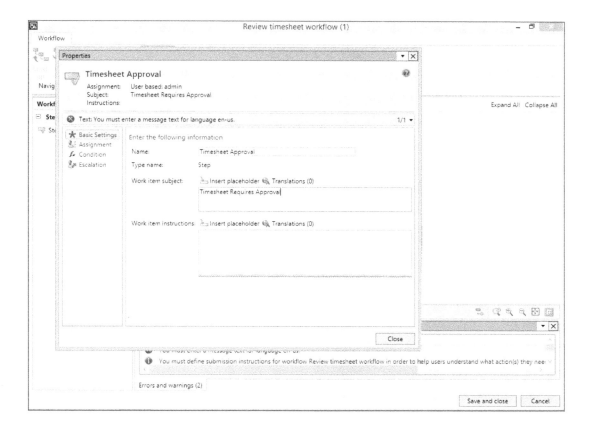

Then within the **Work Item Subject** enter in a quick description of the task which will show in the alerts and subjects of emails.

Creating A Timesheet Approval Workflow

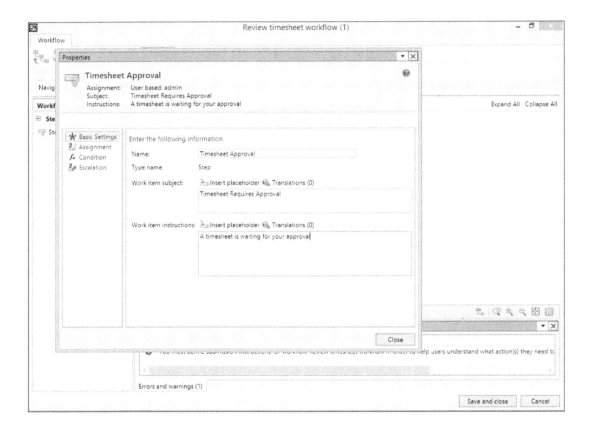

Finally, add some **Work Item Instructions** for a more detailed explanation of what the user needs to do in order to complete the workflow.

After you have done that, click on the **Close** button to exit from the form.

Creating A Timesheet Approval Workflow

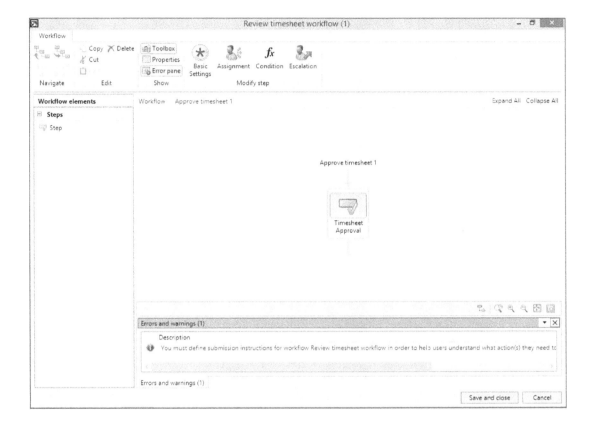

When you return to the canvas you will see that there is still one more warning in the **Errors And Warnings** panel. Just double click on it.

Creating A Timesheet Approval Workflow

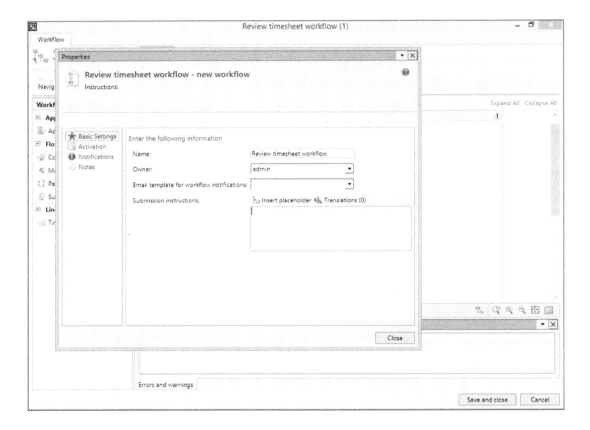

This will take you to a properties page for the workflow where the **Submission Instructions** are required.

Creating A Timesheet Approval Workflow

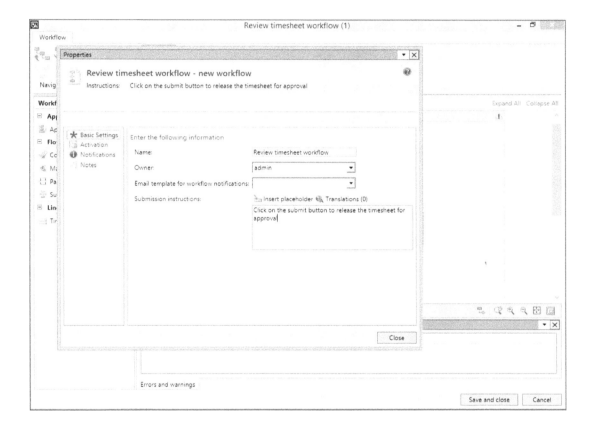

Within the **Submission Instructions** enter in a brief overview of why the workflow is going to be processed and then click on the **Close** button.

Creating A Timesheet Approval Workflow

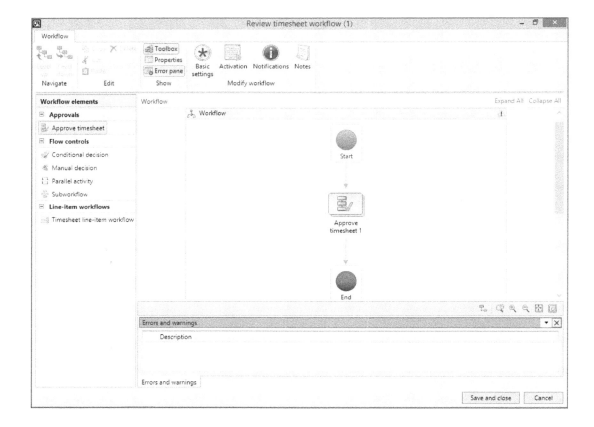

Now when you return to the canvas you will see that here are no errors or warnings and you can click on the **Save And Close** button.

Creating A Timesheet Approval Workflow

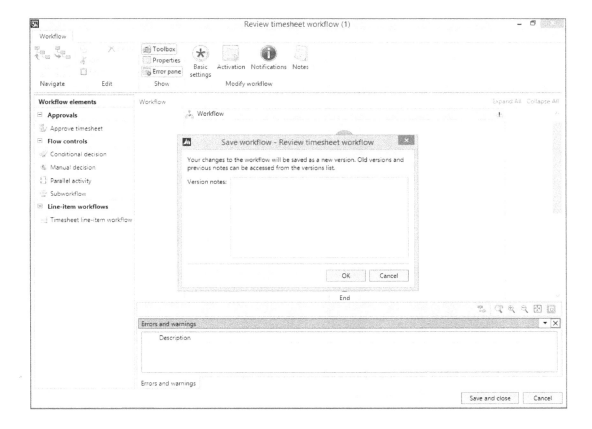

This will open up the **Save Workflow** dialog box.

Creating A Timesheet Approval Workflow

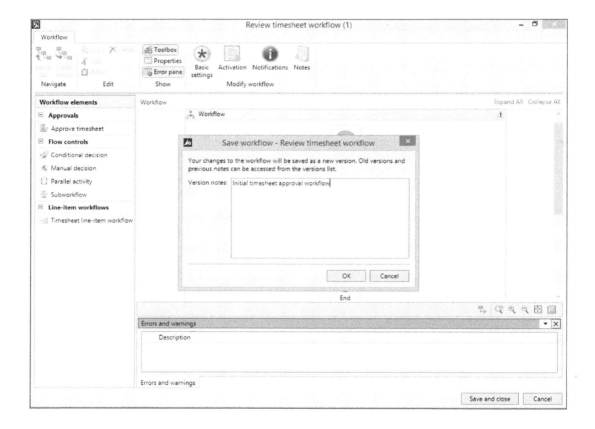

Enter in some **Version Notes** to describe the workflow and then click on the **OK** button.

Creating A Timesheet Approval Workflow

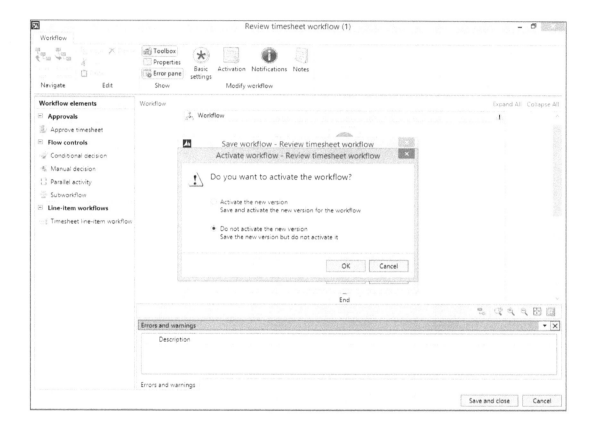

Then the system will ask you if you want to **Activate the Workflow**.

Creating A Timesheet Approval Workflow

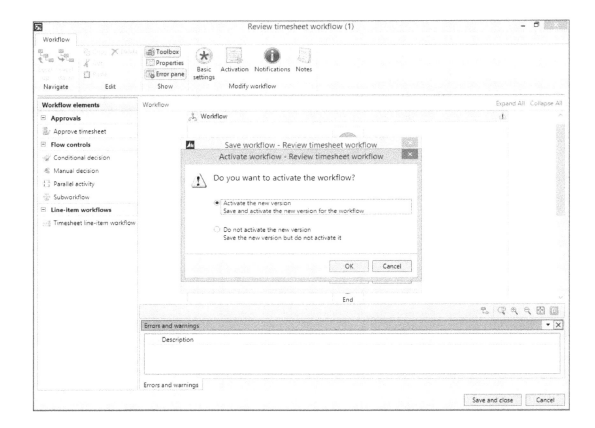

Of course you do. Click on the **Activate The New Version** radio button and click on the **OK** button.

Creating A Timesheet Approval Workflow

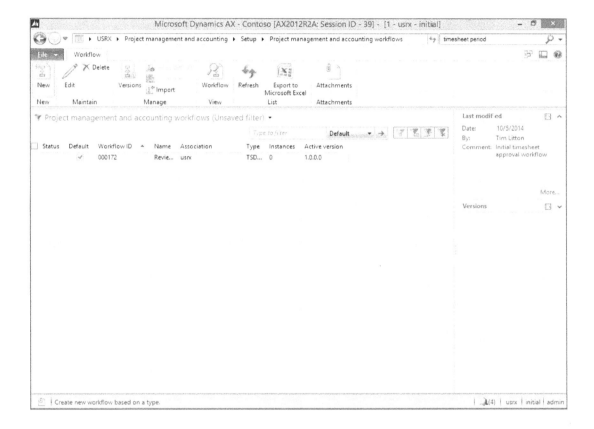

Now when you return to the **Workflow** list page you will see that you have a new workflow.

Submitting Timesheets For Approval Through Workflow

Now that you have a workflow assigned for the Timesheet Approval, you will notice that you can submit timesheets for approval.

Submitting Timesheets For Approval Through Workflow

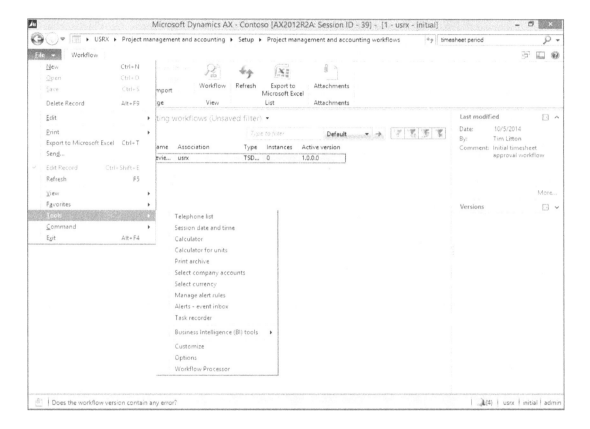

If you ware in a development environment then there is a little trick that you need to know before you move on to the next step an that it to run the background **Workflow Processor**. In a live environment this will be running in the background, but usually in development systems this needs to be kicked off manually.

All you need to do it click on the **Files** menu, then select the **Tools** submenu, and then select the **Workflow Processor** menu item.

Submitting Timesheets For Approval Through Workflow

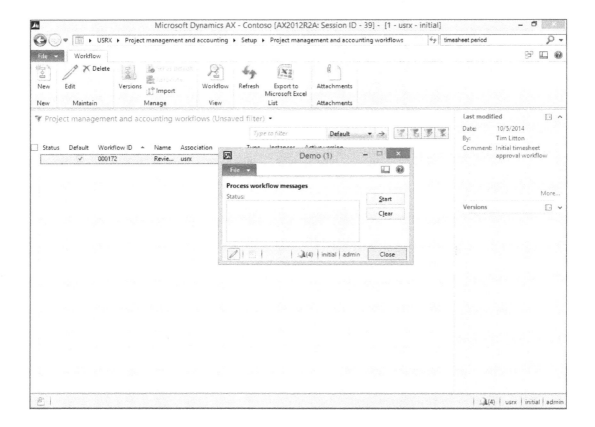

This will open up a small form for the **Workflow Processor**. Just click on the **Start** button.

Submitting Timesheets For Approval Through Workflow

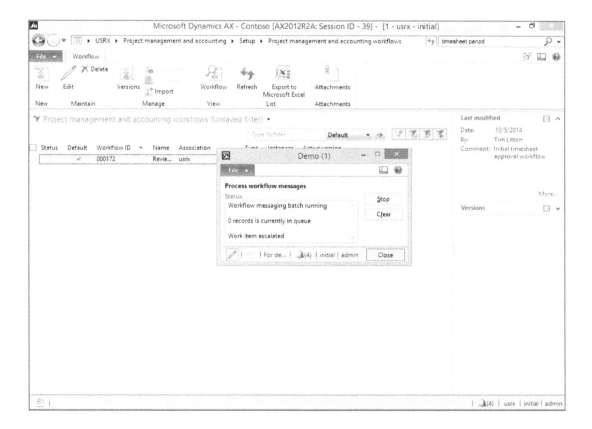

This will start showing you a status log of workflows that are running. Minimize the form now.

Submitting Timesheets For Approval Through Workflow

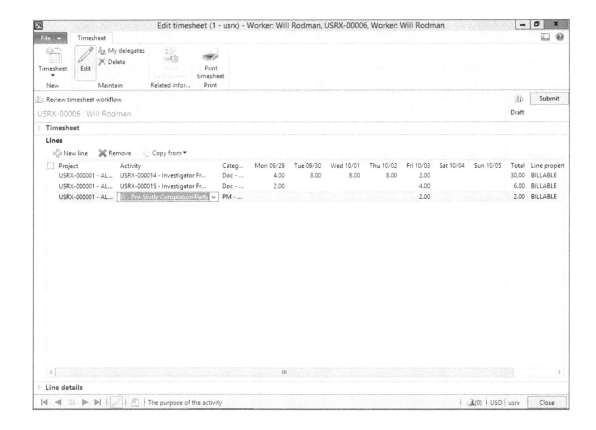

Now return to your Timesheet. You will notice now there is a **Submit** button in the top right hand corner of the form showing that there is a workflow associated with it. Click on the **Submit** button.

Submitting Timesheets For Approval Through Workflow

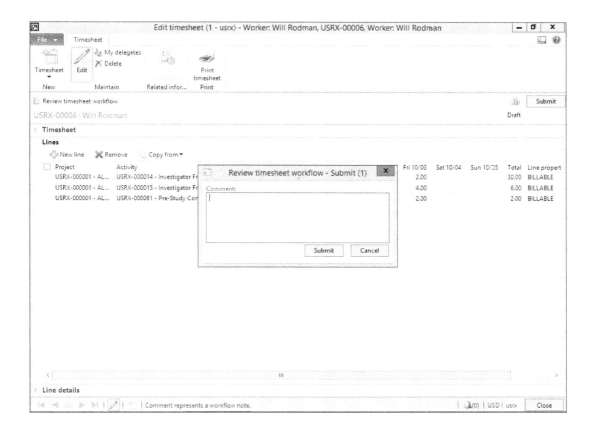

This will start off the workflow process for the approval by allowing you to enter comments.

Submitting Timesheets For Approval Through Workflow

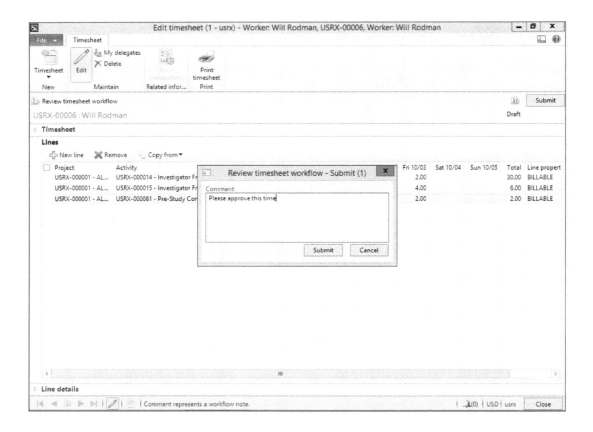

If you like, enter some **Comments** and then click on the **Submit** button.

Submitting Timesheets For Approval Through Workflow

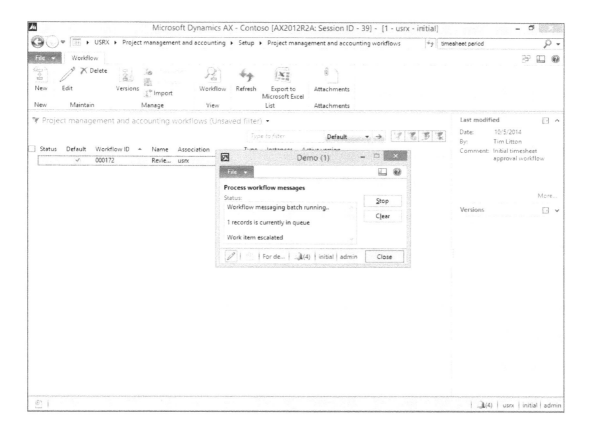

If you watch the **Workflow Processor** then you will see a blip on the radar that shows the workflow was picked up and processed.

Approving Timesheets Through Workflow

Now that the timesheets are being processed through the workflow you will need to approve them through the workflow processes as well.

Approving Timesheets Through Workflow

One way to do this is to click on the **Timesheets for my Review** menu item within the **Timesheets** folder of the **Common** group within the **Project Management And Accounting** area page.

Approving Timesheets Through Workflow

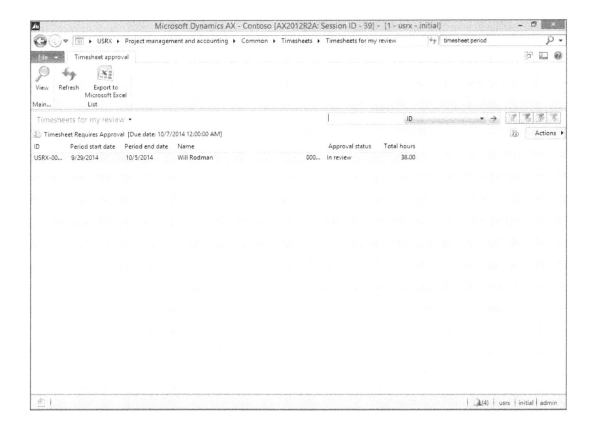

When the **Timesheets For My Review** list page is displayed you will see all of the new timesheets and also an **Action** button that is a workflow button in the top right hand corner of the form.

Approving Timesheets Through Workflow

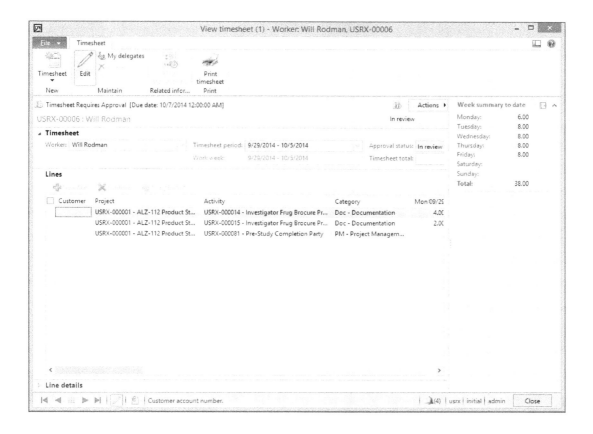

If you double click on the timesheet you will be able to see all of the detail associated with the timesheet as well.

Approving Timesheets Through Workflow

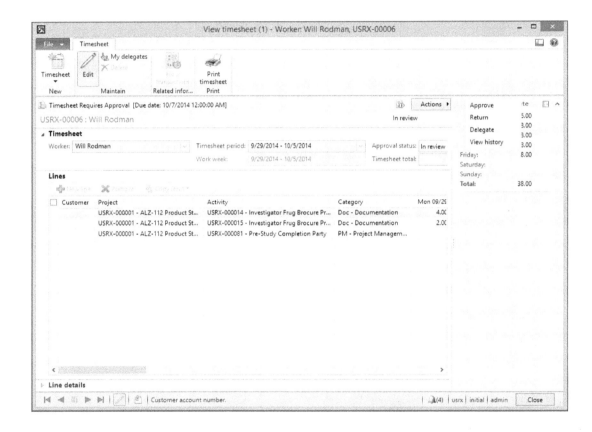

To approve the timesheet just click on the **Actions** button and then click on the **Approve** option.

Approving Timesheets Through Workflow

This will open up another **Comments** dialog box.

Approving Timesheets Through Workflow

Enter in any additional comments that you may want to have on record regarding the timesheet and then click the **Approve** button.

Approving Timesheets Through Workflow

Again, if you watch the **Workflow Processor** you will see the approval task be processed and then clear out.

Approving Timesheets Through Workflow

After that the timesheet will disappear from your **Timesheets For My Review** list.

Viewing Posted Time Within The Projects

Now we can see all of this time within the Project.

Viewing Posted Time Within The Projects

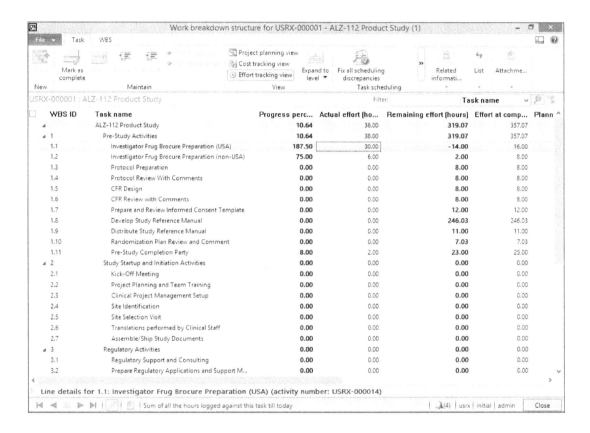

To do this, open up your Projects **Work Breakdown Structure** but this time switch to the **Effort Tracking View**. You will see that there is now time posted to the project.

Viewing Posted Time Within The Projects

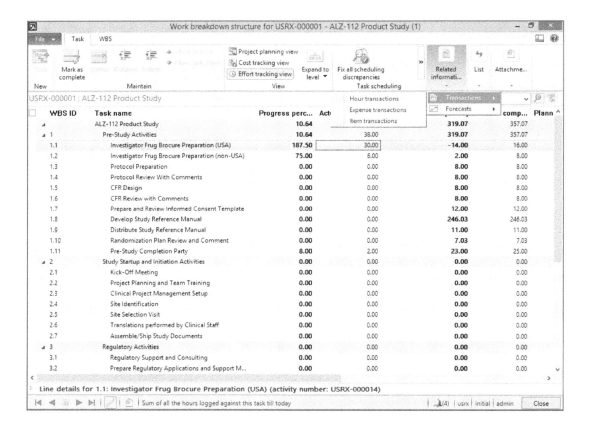

To see the detail, select the line within the Work Breakdown Structure and then click on the **Transactions** button within the **Related Information** group of the **Task** ribbon bar. From there click on the **Hour Transactions** menu item.

Viewing Posted Time Within The Projects

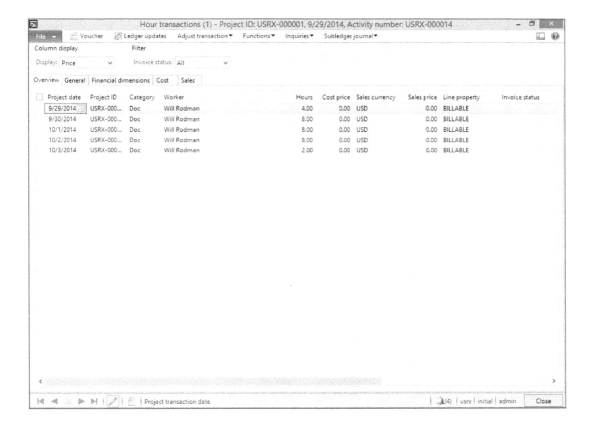

That will take you directly to the hour journals that were posted through the timesheets.

How easy is that!

CONFIGURING EXPENSE REPORTING FOR PROJECTS

Timesheet entry is only half of the benefits that you get from the **Employee Self Service Portal** when it comes to managing your project costs. You can also have your workers post their expense reports through the **Employee Self Service Portal** as well allowing them to use the web portal to post their expenses rather than having to access the project itself.

In this chapter we will show you how the Expense Reporting may be used in conjunction with Projects to make your life simpler.

Configuring Expense Payment Methods

If you have not used the **Expense Management** feature then there may be a little extra setup that you need to perform before you allow the users to start posting expenses. The first is to set up an **Expense Payment Method.**

Configuring Expense Payment Methods

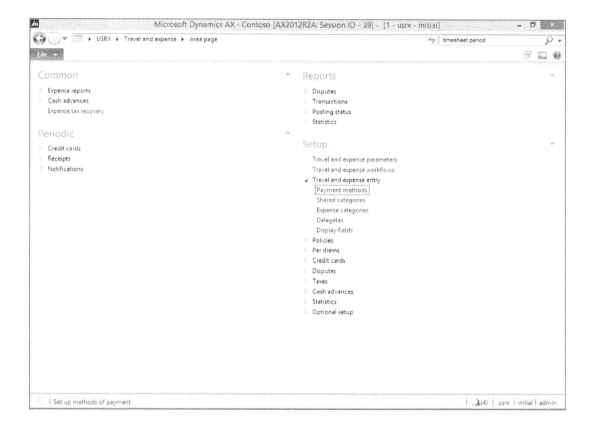

To do this click on the **Payment Methods** menu item within the **Travel And Expense Entry** folder of the **Setup** group within the **Travel And Expense** area page.

Configuring Expense Payment Methods

When the **Payment Methods** list page is displayed, click on the **New** button in the menu bar to create a new record.

Configuring Expense Payment Methods

Set the **Payment Method** to be **CREDITCARD** and the **Description** to be **Credit Card**.

Configuring Expense Payment Methods

Then from the **Offset Account Type** dropdown list select the **Bank** option to say that this will be paid from the bank.

Configuring Expense Payment Methods

Click on the **Offset Account** dropdown list and select the **Bank Account** that you want to pay the credit card from.

Configuring Expense Payment Methods

After you have done that, click on the **Close** button to exit from the form.

Configuring Expense Categories

Next we want to configure a set of **Expense Categories** that we will track our expenses against.

Configuring Expense Categories

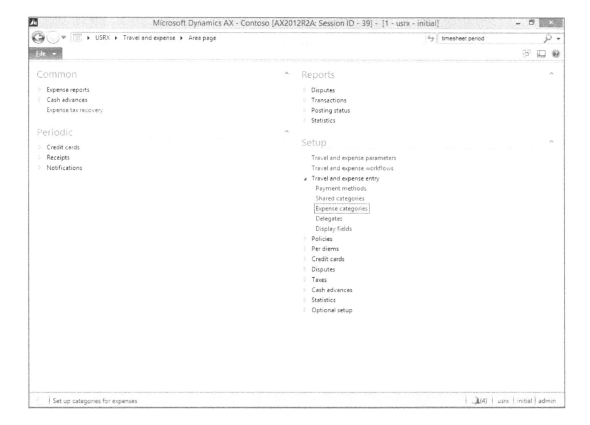

To do this, click on the **Expense Categories** menu item within the **Travel And Expense Entry** folder of the **Setup** group within the **Travel And Expenses** area page.

Configuring Expense Categories

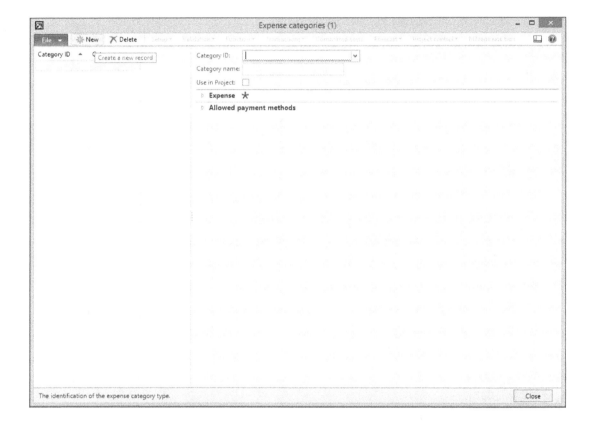

When the **Expense Categories** form is displayed, click on the **New** button to create a new record.

Configuring Expense Categories

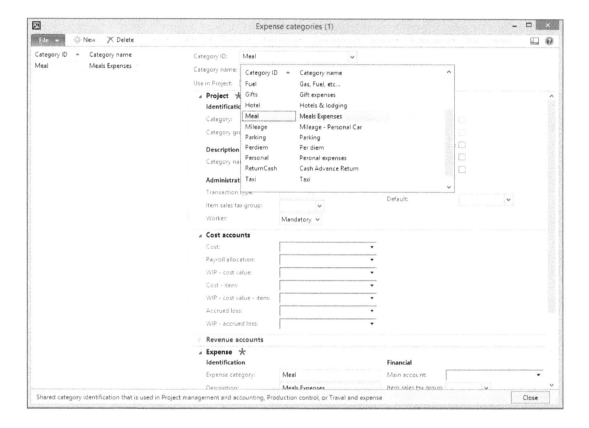

From the **Category ID** dropdown list, select the **Meal** option.

Configuring Expense Categories

Set the **Category Group** to be **ProjectExp.**

Configuring Expense Categories

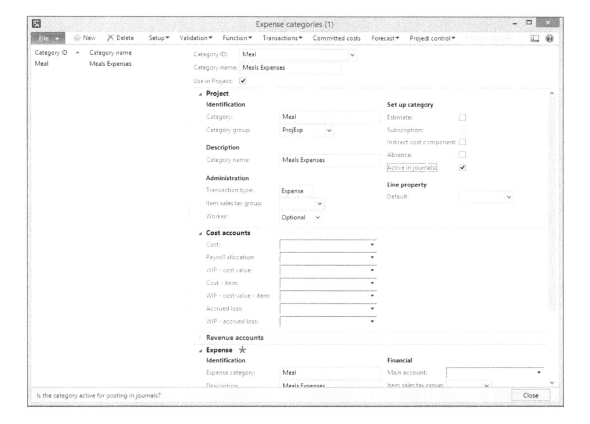

And then check the **Active In Journals** so that you can post these expenses to the project.

Configuring Expense Categories

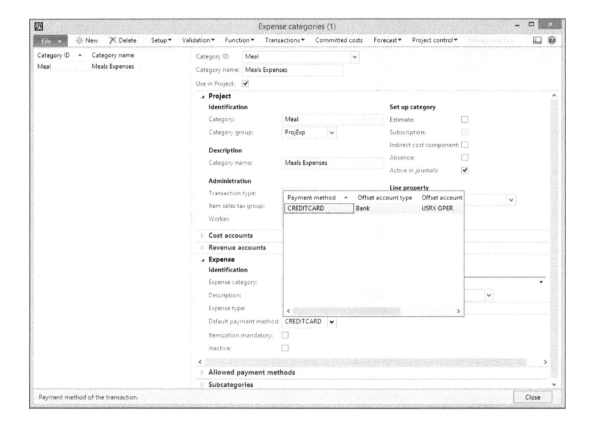

Also, set the **Default Payment Method** on the Expense Category to be **CREDITCARD.**

Configuring Expense Categories

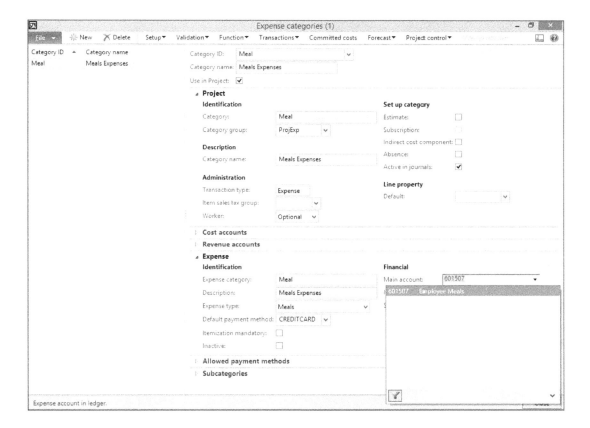

Finally, assign your expense item a **Main Account** to post to.

Configuring Expense Categories

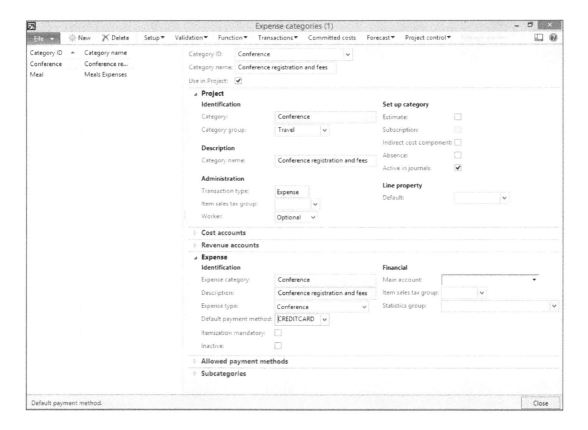

Next click on the **Add** button in the menu bar to create a new record. Set the **Category ID** to **Conference,** the **Category Group** to **Travel**, check the **Active In Journals**, and set the **Default Payment Method** to **CREDITCARD.**

Configuring Expense Categories

Click on the **Add** button again in the menu bar to create a new record. Set the
Category ID to **Flight,** the **Category Group** to **Travel**, check the **Active In Journals**, and
set the **Default Payment Method** to **CREDITCARD.**

Configuring Expense Categories

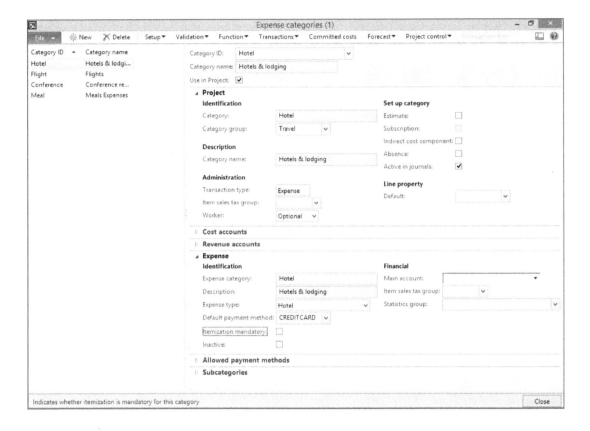

Click on the **Add** button again in the menu bar to create a new record. Set the **Category ID** to **Hotel,** the **Category Group** to **Travel**, check the **Active In Journals**, and set the **Default Payment Method** to **CREDITCARD.**

Configuring Expense Categories

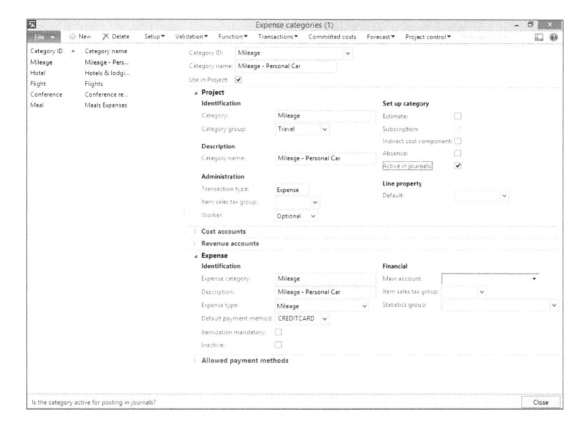

Click on the **Add** button again in the menu bar to create a new record. Set the **Category ID** to **Mileage,** the **Category Group** to **Travel**, check the **Active In Journals**, and set the **Default Payment Method** to **CREDITCARD.**

Configuring Expense Categories

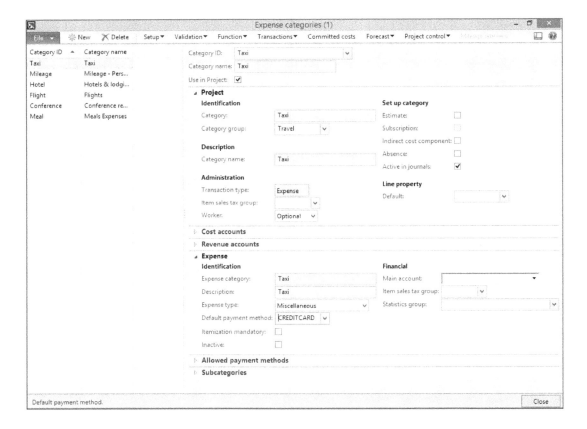

And finally Click on the **Add** button one last time in the menu bar to create a new record. Set the **Category ID** to **Taxi,** the **Category Group** to **Travel**, check the **Active In Journals**, and set the **Default Payment Method** to **CREDITCARD.**

After you have done that, just click on the **Close** button to exit from the form.

Entering In Expense Reports For Projects Within The Employee Self Service Portal

Now that we have all the codes set up for our expense reports we can start entering them in through the **Employee Self Service Portal**.

Entering In Expense Reports For Projects Within The Employee Self Service Portal

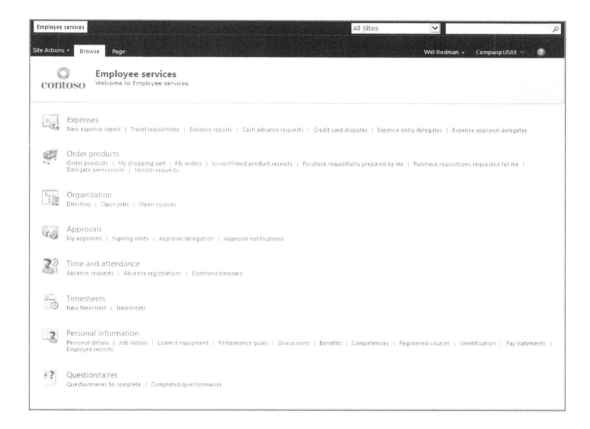

To do that, open up the **Employee Self Service Portal** and click on the **New Expense Report** link within the **Expenses** menu item group.

Entering In Expense Reports For Projects Within The Employee Self Service Portal

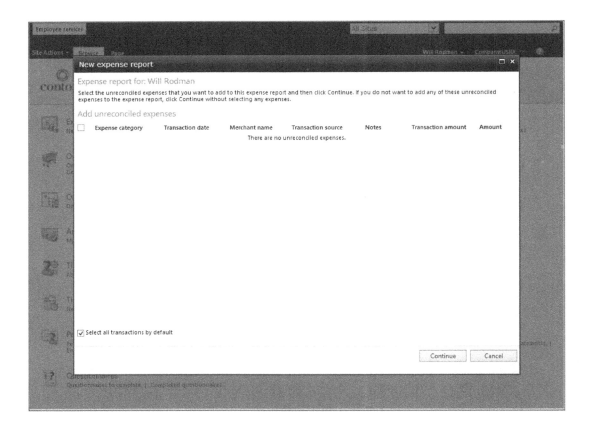

That will start up the **New Expense Report** dialog and ask you if you want to import any credit card transactions. We don't have that configured yet so we can just click on the **Continue** button.

Entering In Expense Reports For Projects Within The Employee Self Service Portal

This will take us directly into the **Expense Report** form.

Entering In Expense Reports For Projects Within The Employee Self Service Portal

Start off by entering in an **Expense Purpose**.

Then click on the **New Expense Report Line** button within the **Expense Lines** tab group.

Entering In Expense Reports For Projects Within The Employee Self Service Portal

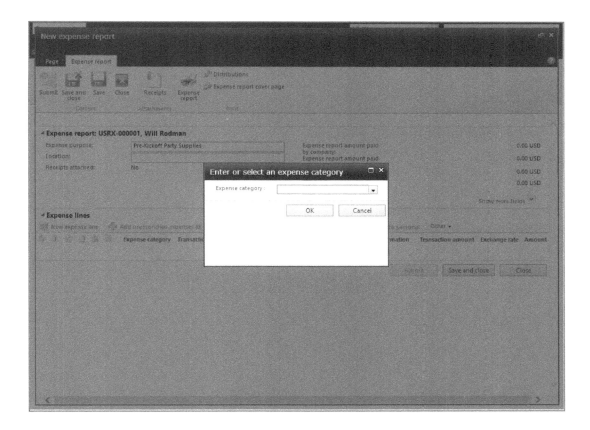

This will open up a dialog box asking for the **Expense Category**.

Entering In Expense Reports For Projects Within The Employee Self Service Portal

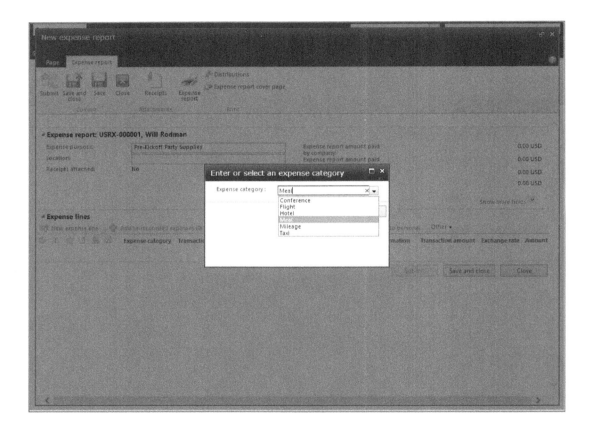

Select an **Expense Category** from the list that we just configured.

Entering In Expense Reports For Projects Within The Employee Self Service Portal

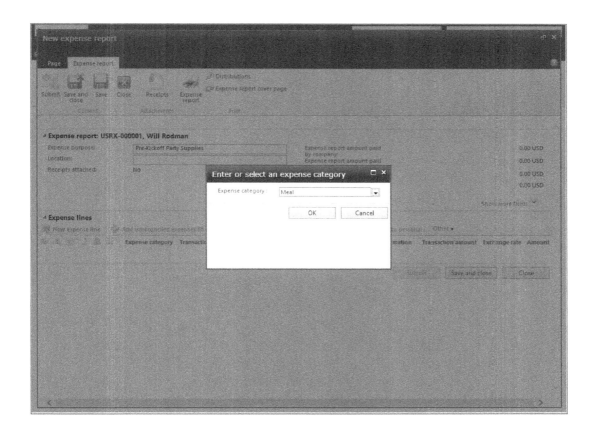

And then click on the **OK** button.

Entering In Expense Reports For Projects Within The Employee Self Service Portal

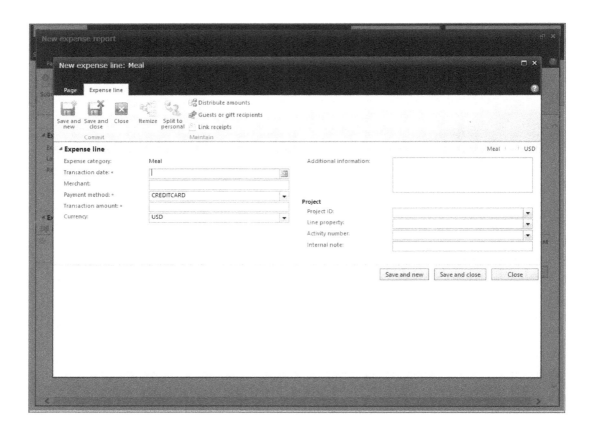

We will then be taken into a more detailed expense line entry form just for that **Expense Category Type.**

Entering In Expense Reports For Projects Within The Employee Self Service Portal

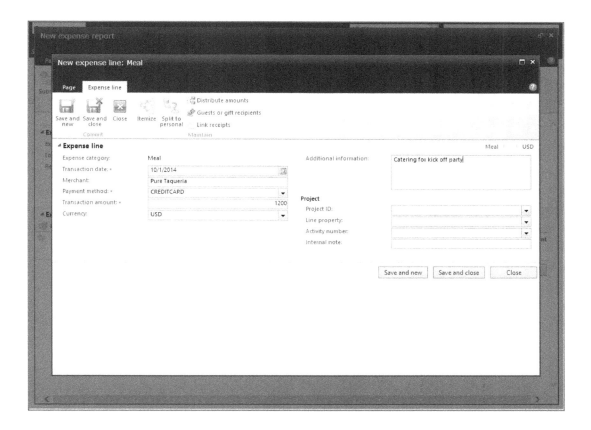

Enter in the **Transaction Date, Transaction Amount**, and any additional information that you may need such as the Merchant and Additional comments.

Entering In Expense Reports For Projects Within The Employee Self Service Portal

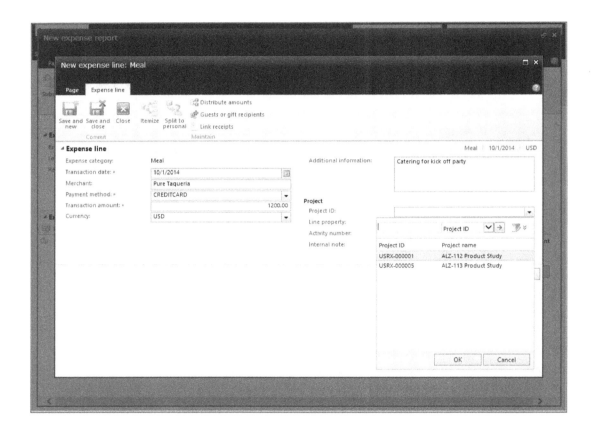

Then click on the **Project ID** dropdown list and you will be able to select the project that this expense was associated with.

Entering In Expense Reports For Projects Within The Employee Self Service Portal

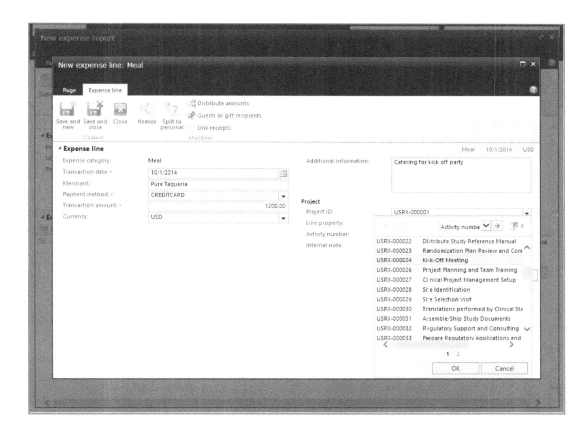

You can also click on the **Activity Number** and select the activity that this expense was associated with.

Entering In Expense Reports For Projects Within The Employee Self Service Portal

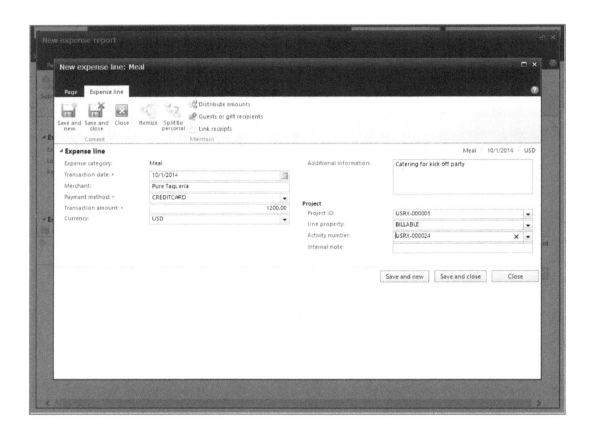

When you are done, just click the **Save And Close** button.

Entering In Expense Reports For Projects Within The Employee Self Service Portal

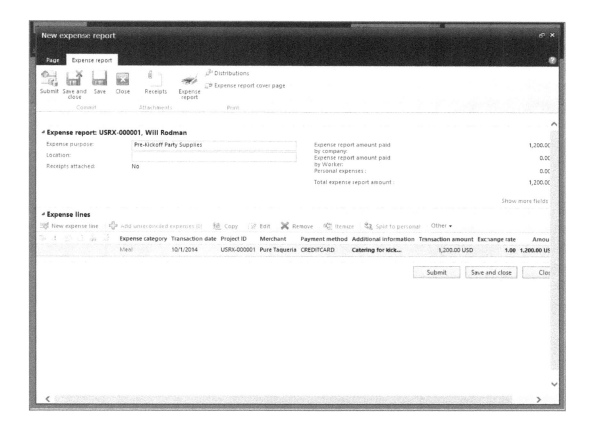

You can keep on adding expense lines this way, and when you are finished, just click on the **Submit** button.

Entering In Expense Reports For Projects Within The Employee Self Service Portal

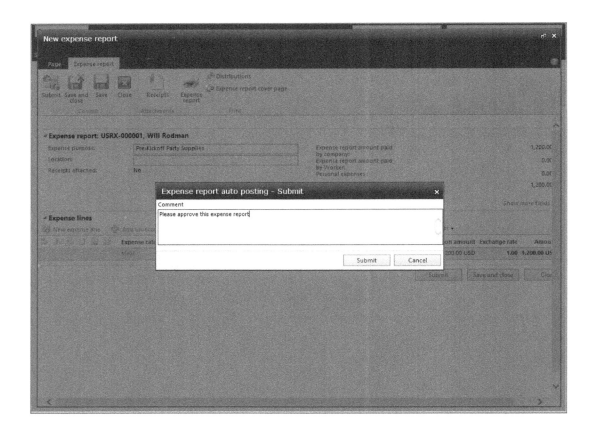

You will then be asked to enter in any additional comments about the expense report and when you have done that, click on the **Submit** button.

Entering In Expense Reports For Projects Within The Employee Self Service Portal

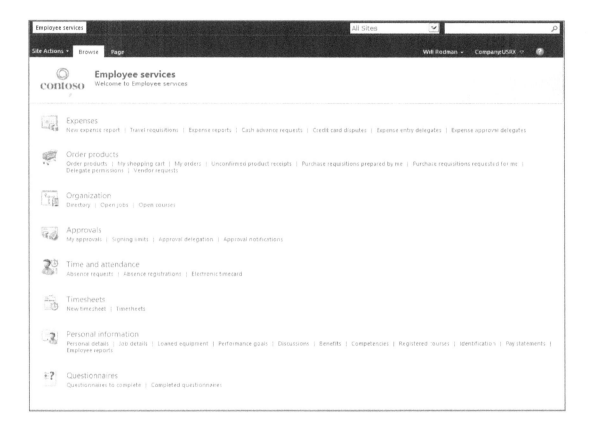

You will then be returned back to the **Employee Self Services** portal.

Configuring An Expense Approval Workflow

Just as with the Timesheets you can also have an approval workflow associated with your expense reports. These are just as easy to set up and add so much control around your Expense Report process.

Configuring An Expense Approval Workflow

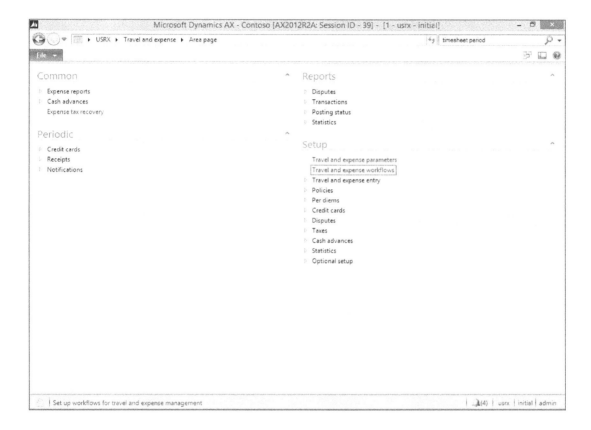

To do this, click on the **Travel And Expense Workflows** menu item within the **Setup** group of the **Travel And Expenses** area page.

Configuring An Expense Approval Workflow

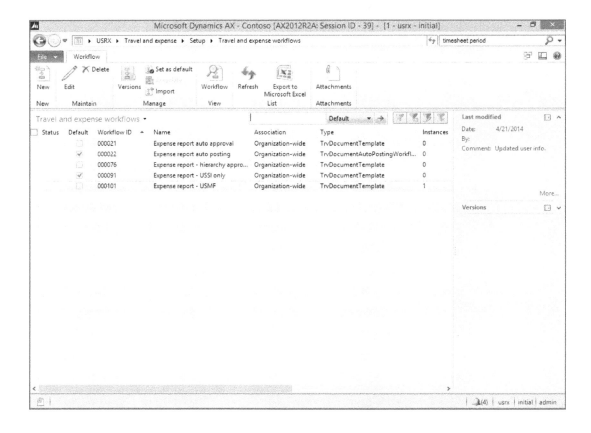

When the **Travel And Expenses Workflow** list page is displayed, click on the **New** button within the **New** group of the **Workflow** ribbon bar.

Configuring An Expense Approval Workflow

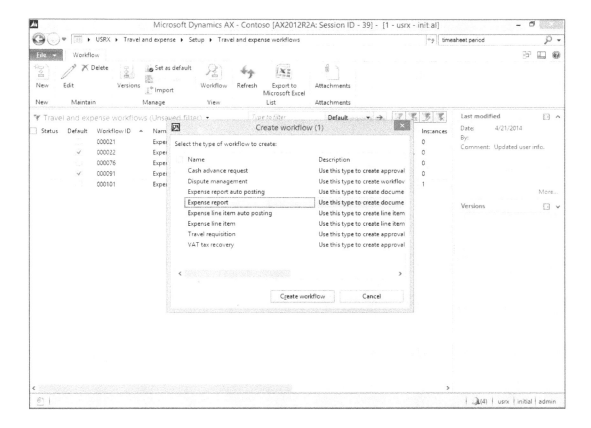

When the **Create Workflow** dialog box is displayed, you will see all of the workflow types that you can create. Select the **Expense Report** workflow template and then click on the **Create Workflow** button.

Configuring An Expense Approval Workflow

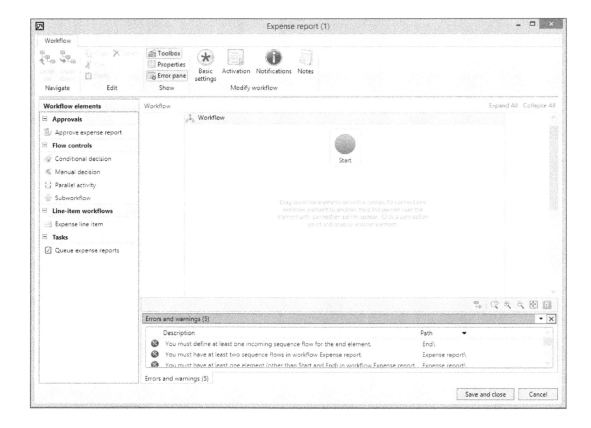

This will take you straight to the workflow designer canvas.

Configuring An Expense Approval Workflow

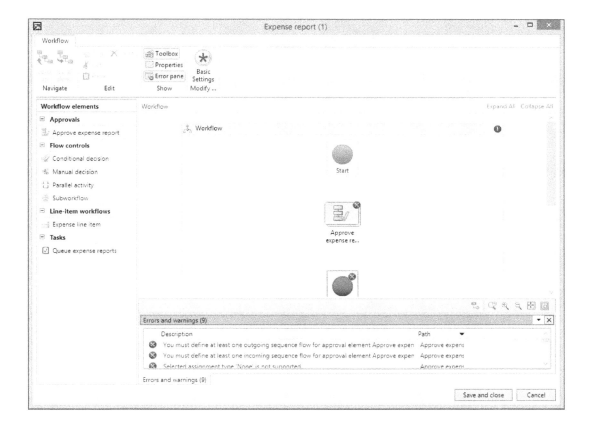

From the palette on the left, drag the **Approve Expense Report** element onto the canvas.

Configuring An Expense Approval Workflow

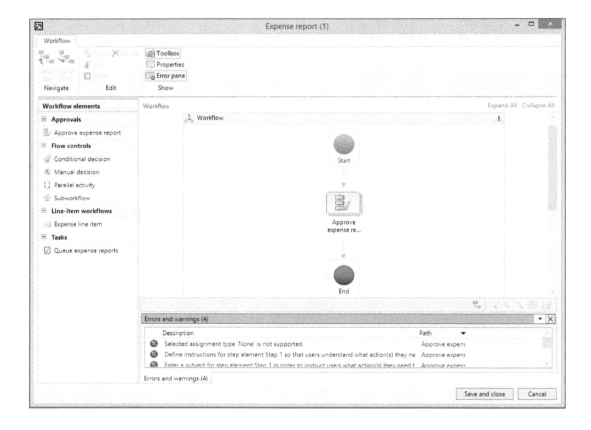

Then link the **Start** and **End** elements to the workflow to create a connected workflow.

Notice that within the bottom section of the Workflow designer is a list of loose ends that you need to tidy up. Double click on the first one.

Configuring An Expense Approval Workflow

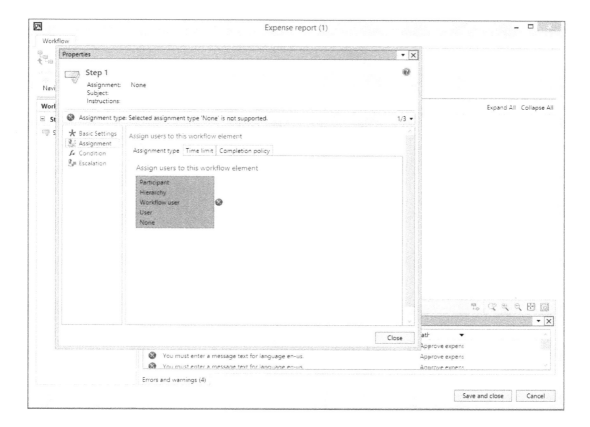

That will take you into a **Properties** page where you need to assign the person that will approve the timesheet.

Configuring An Expense Approval Workflow

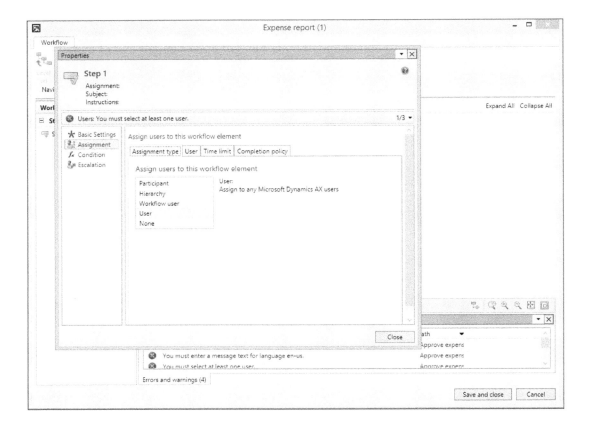

Within the **Assignment Type** list, click on the **User** option to assign the timesheet approval just to one person.

Configuring An Expense Approval Workflow

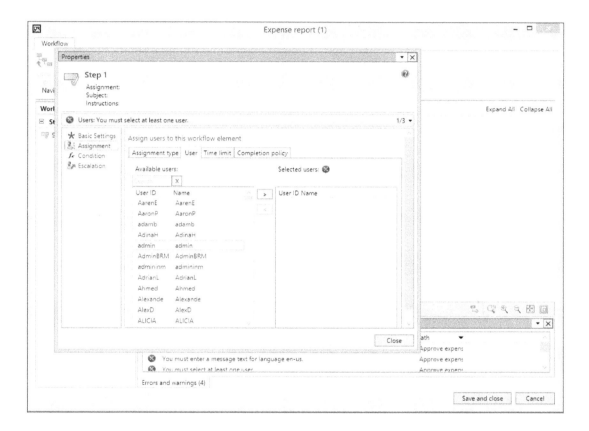

Now switch to the **User** tab.

Configuring An Expense Approval Workflow

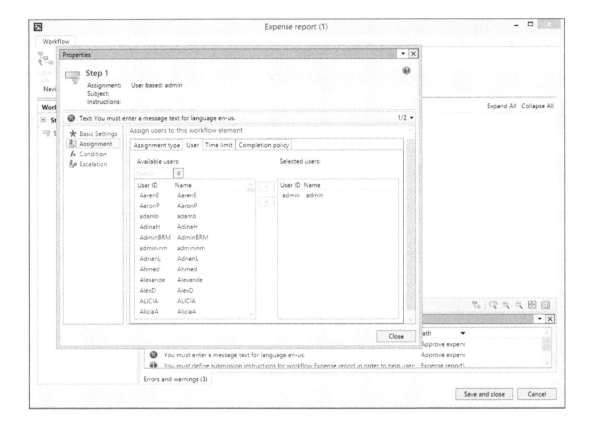

Select the user that you want to approve the timesheet from the list of **Available Users** and then click on the **>** button to assign them to the **Selected Users.**

Configuring An Expense Approval Workflow

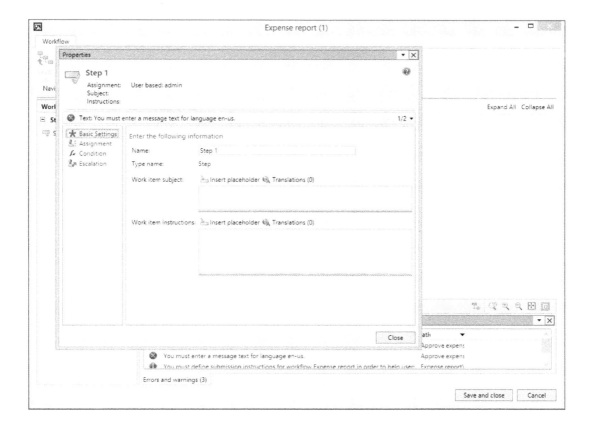

Now click on the **Basic Settings** on the left hand side of the dialog box, and you will see that there are a few more fields that need to be updated.

Configuring An Expense Approval Workflow

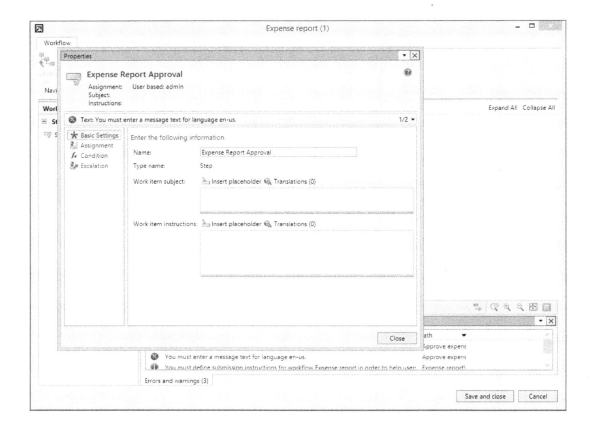

Give your step a more descriptive **Name**.

Configuring An Expense Approval Workflow

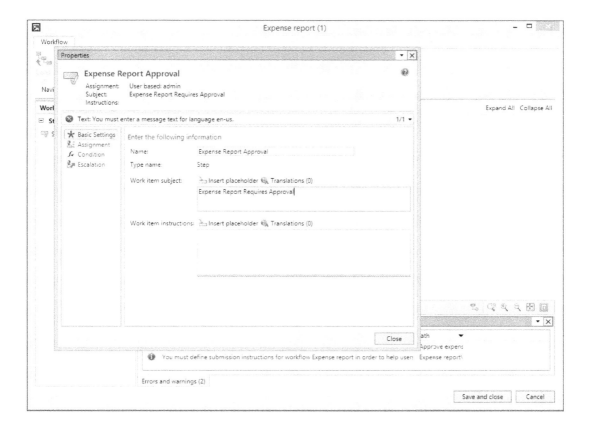

Then within the **Work Item Subject** enter in a quick description of the task which will show in the alerts and subjects of emails.

Configuring An Expense Approval Workflow

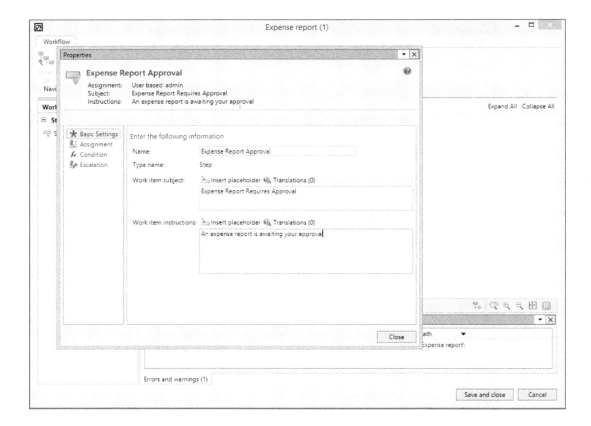

Finally, add some **Work Item Instructions** for a more detailed explanation of what the user needs to do in order to complete the workflow.

After you have done that, click on the **Close** button to exit from the form.

Configuring An Expense Approval Workflow

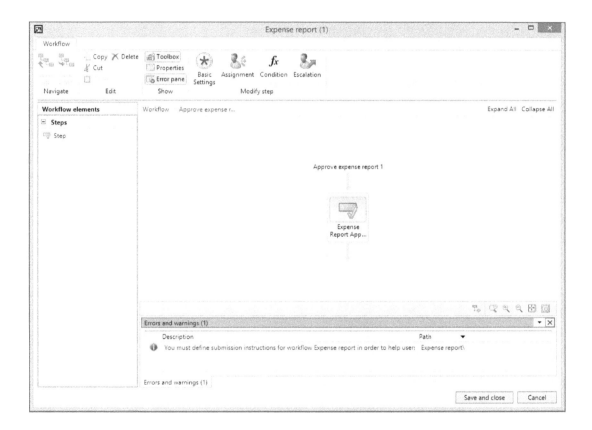

When you return to the canvas you will see that there is still one more warning in the **Errors And Warnings** panel. Just double click on it.

Configuring An Expense Approval Workflow

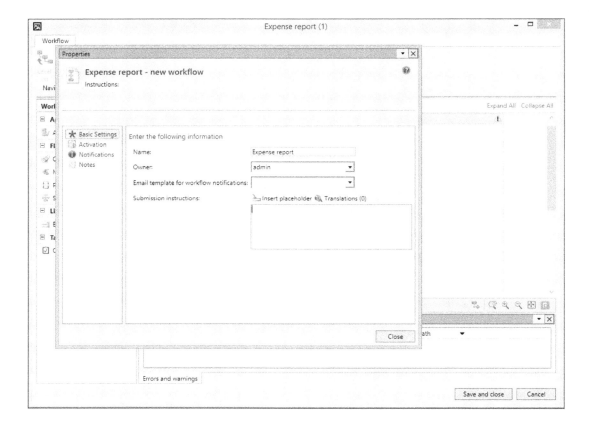

This will take you to a properties page for the workflow where the **Submission Instructions** are required.

Configuring An Expense Approval Workflow

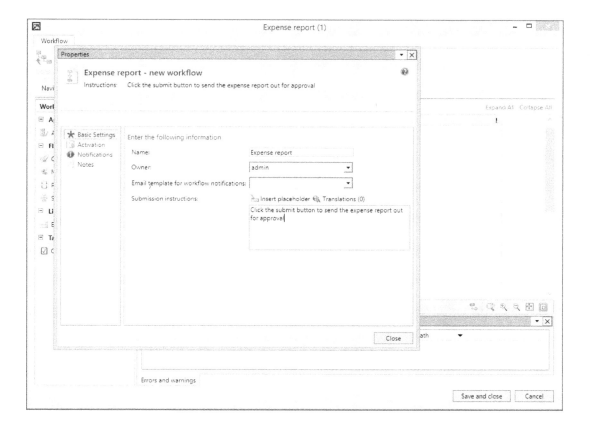

Within the **Submission Instructions** enter in a brief overview of why the workflow is going to be processed and then click on the **Close** button.

Configuring An Expense Approval Workflow

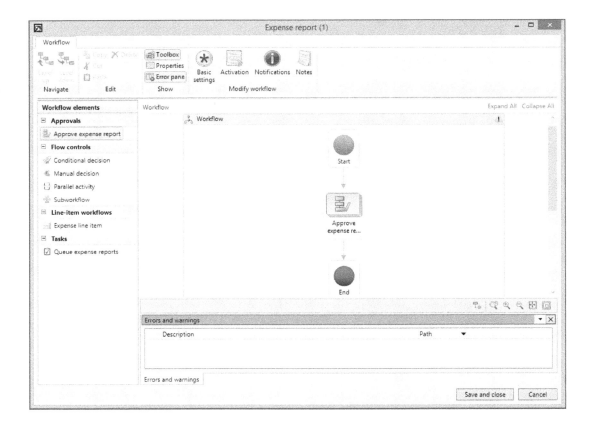

Now when you return to the canvas you will see that here are no errors or warnings and you can click on the **Save And Close** button.

Configuring An Expense Approval Workflow

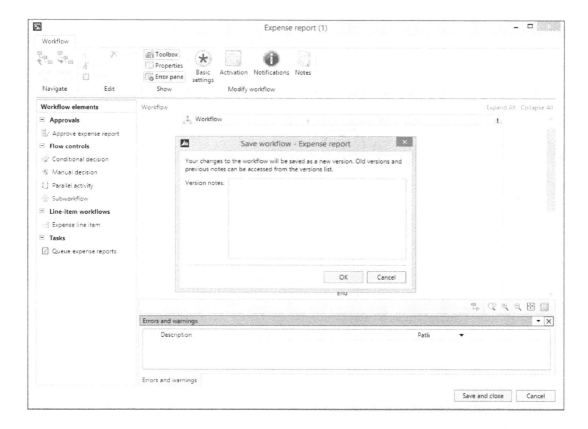

This will open up the **Save Workflow** dialog box.

Configuring An Expense Approval Workflow

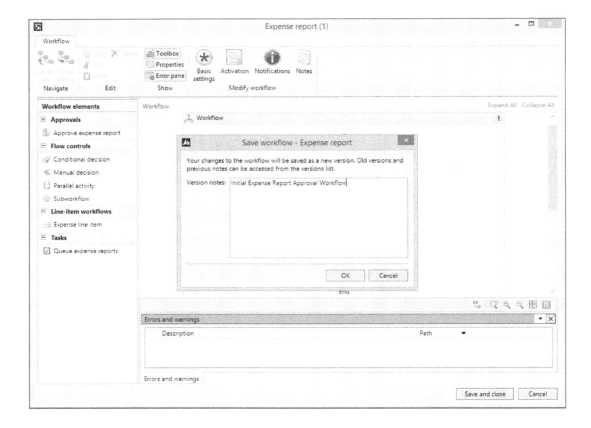

Enter in some **Version Notes** to describe the workflow and then click on the **OK** button.

Configuring An Expense Approval Workflow

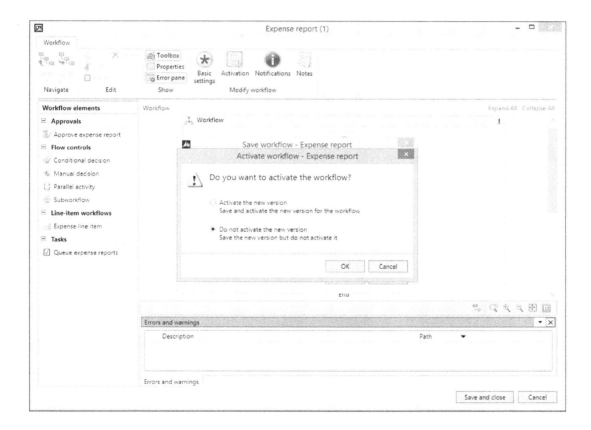

Then the system will ask you if you want to **Activate the Workflow**.

Configuring An Expense Approval Workflow

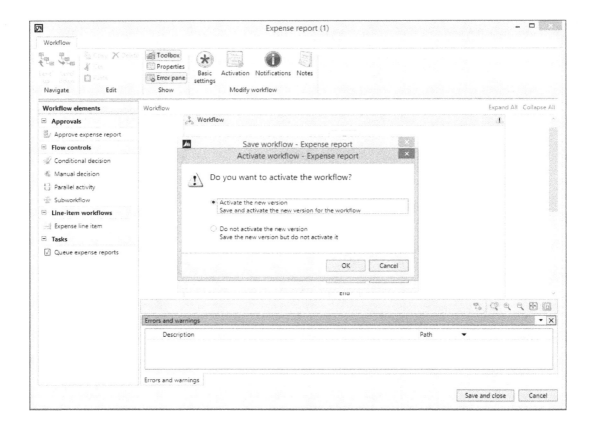

Of course you do. Click on the **Activate The New Version** radio button and click on the
OK button.

Configuring An Expense Approval Workflow

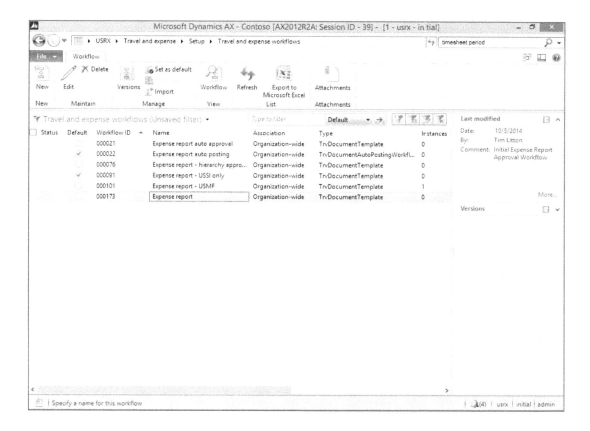

And then you will return back to the **Time And Expense Workflows** list page and you are done.

Submitting Expense Reports Through Workflow Approval

Now that we have a workflow we can start approving our Expense Reports electronically.

Submitting Expense Reports Through Workflow Approval

Now you will notice that there is a **Submit** button in the top right corner of our Expense Reports. To submit them for approval just click the **Submit** button.

Submitting Expense Reports Through Workflow Approval

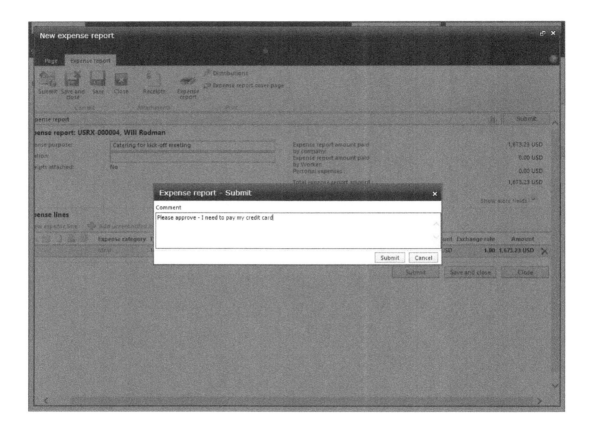

You will be asked if you have any additional comments that you want to add to the expense report before sending it off for approval. If you want to add any notes you can and when you are finished, just click on the **Submit** button.

Submitting Expense Reports Through Workflow Approval

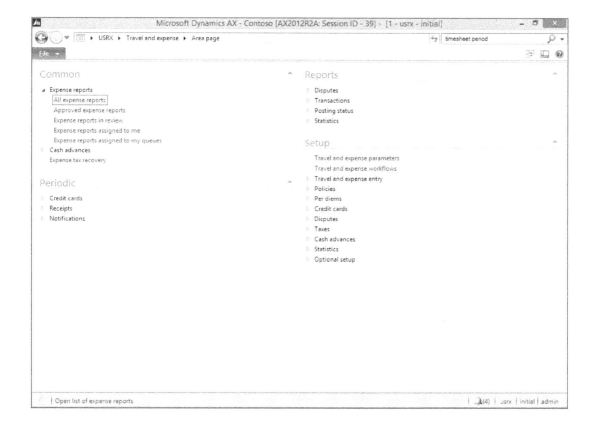

If you want to view your expense reports within the Rich Client then just click on the **All Expense Reports** menu item within the **Expense Reports** folder of the **Common** group within the **Travel And Expenses** area page.

Submitting Expense Reports Through Workflow Approval

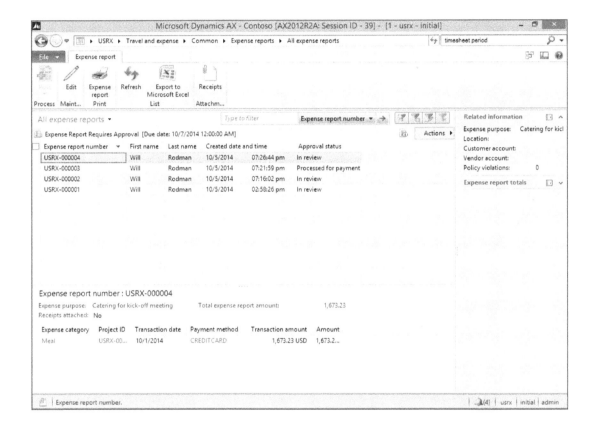

That will take you to a list of all the expense reports and also their status.

Approving Expense Reports Through Workflow

Now that we have submitted our Expense Reports for review through Workflow we can see the approval process in action.

Approving Expense Reports Through Workflow

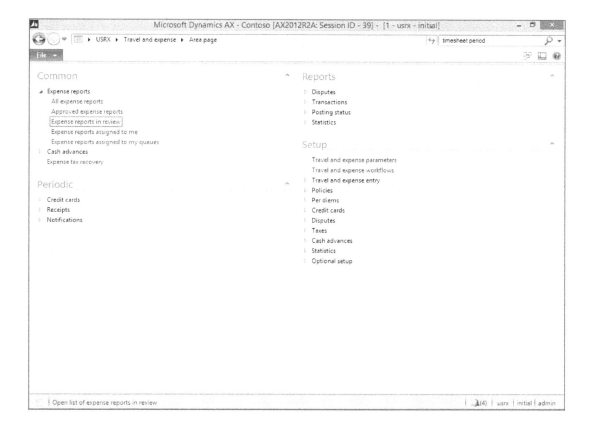

To see all the **Expense Reports** that you need to approve, click on the **Expense Reports In Review** menu item within the **Expense Reports** folder of the **Common** group within the **Travel And Expenses** area page.

Approving Expense Reports Through Workflow

When the **Expense Reports In Review** list page is displayed you will see all o fthe expense reports that are waiting for you to approve.

Approving Expense Reports Through Workflow

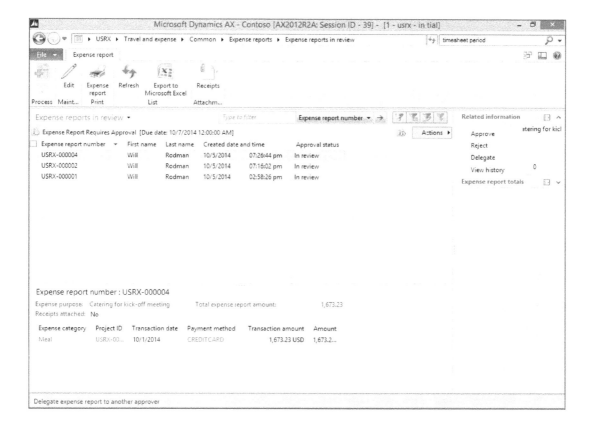

To approve an expense report, just select is and then click on the **Actions** workflow button and select the **Approve** option.

Approving Expense Reports Through Workflow

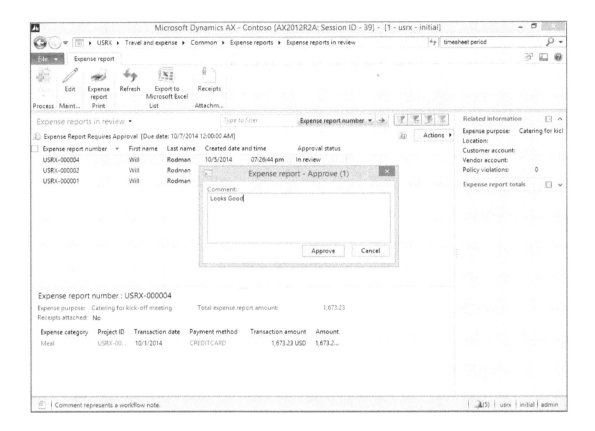

This will open up a **Comments** dialog box and you can enter any additional notes that you may want to associate with the expense report and then click on the **Approve** button.

Approving Expense Reports Through Workflow

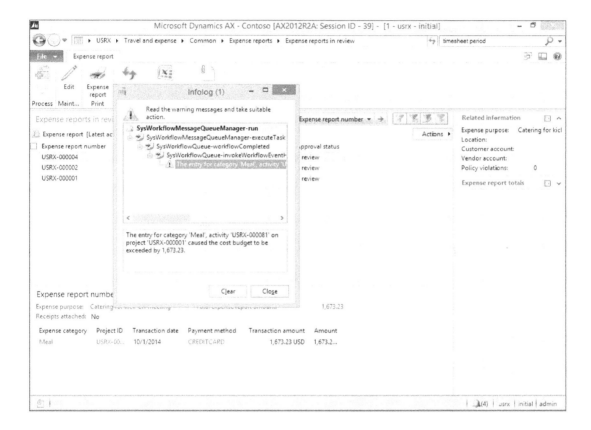

Note: If you have budget management in place then you will also be notified of any budget issues that may have arisen by posting this expense report.

Posting Approved Expense Reports

Once the Expense Reports have been approved by the managers then they can be posted and as a result, posted against the project.

Posting Approved Expense Reports

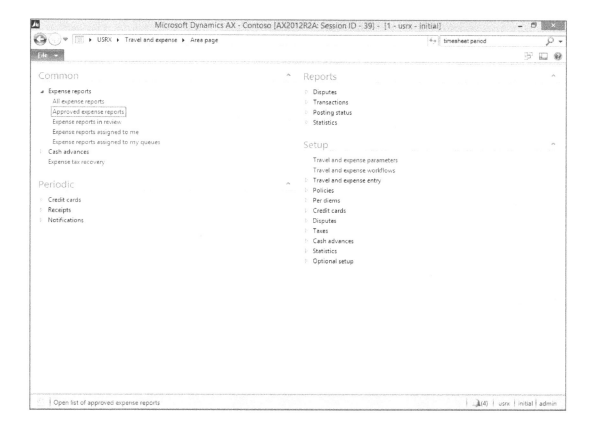

To do this, click on the **Approved Expense Reports** menu item within the **Expense Reports** folder of the **Common** group within the **Travel And Expenses** area page.

Posting Approved Expense Reports

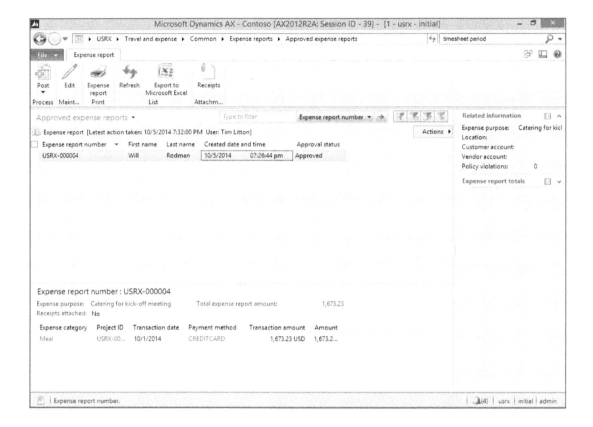

When the **Approved Expense Reports** list page is displayed you will wee all of the approved expense reports that are waiting to be ported.

Posting Approved Expense Reports

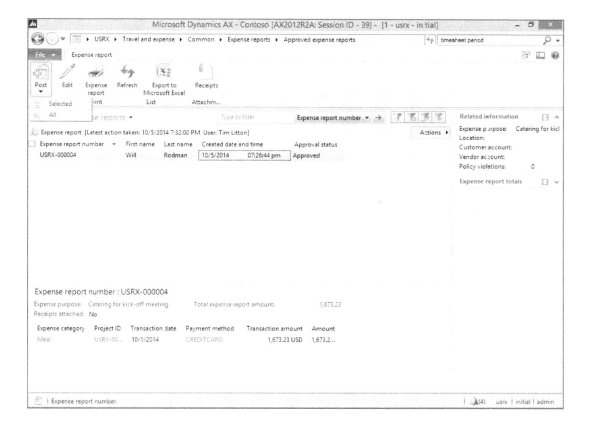

All you need to do is select the Expense Report to be posted and then click on the **Post** button within the **Process** group of the **Expense Report** ribbon bar, and then either select the **Selected** menu item to post just that one Expense Report, or the **All** option to post all approved Expense Reports.

Posting Approved Expense Reports

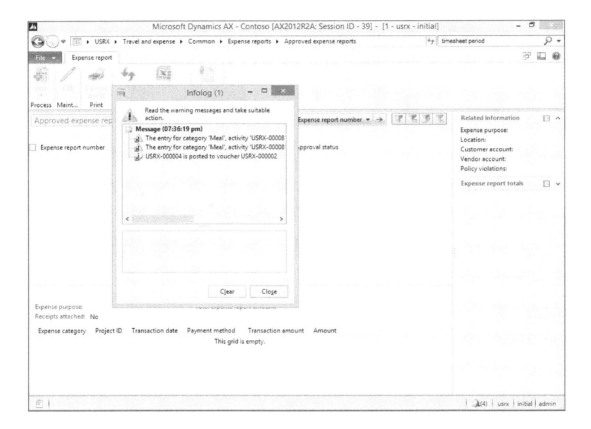

If everything works out fine you will be notified that the expense reports have been posted.

Viewing Expense Transactions On Projects

After doing that we can now see all of the expense report transactions against our projects.

Viewing Expense Transactions On Projects

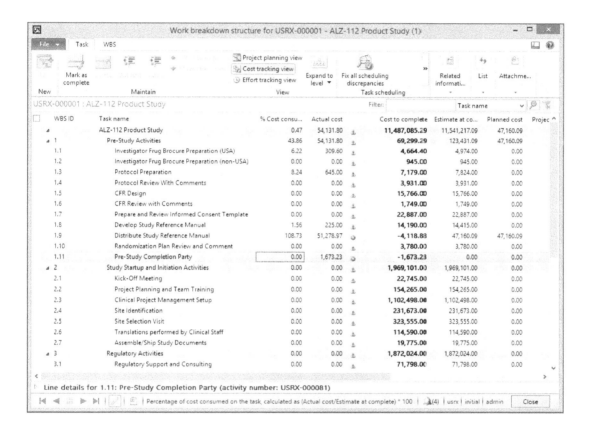

To do this, just open up your Project Work Breakdown Structure and then switch to the **Cost Tracking View**.

Viewing Expense Transactions On Projects

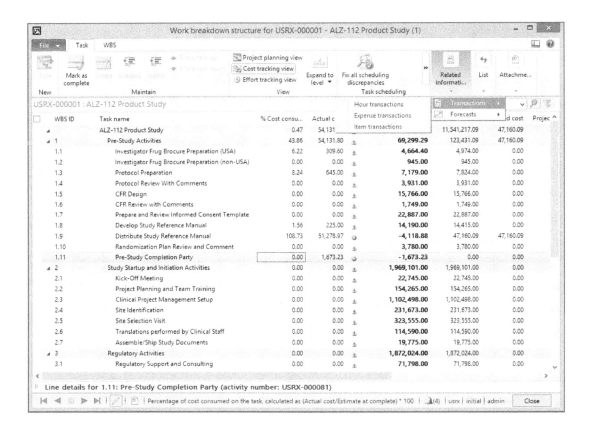

Select the line that you want to see all of the posted expenses against and then click on the **Transactions** button within the **Related Information** group of the **Task** ribbon bar and select the **Expense Transactions** option.

Viewing Expense Transactions On Projects

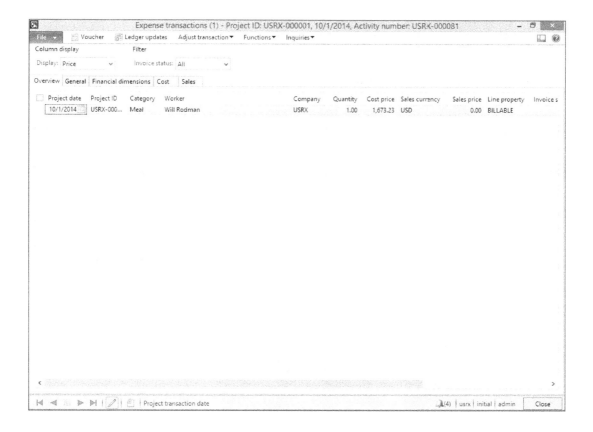

This will take you right into the expense report detail that made up that project expense line.

How cool is that!

SUMMARY

I this book we have shown you a lot of the features within Dynamics AX within the **Project Management And Accounting** module that should give you a foundation to then start exploring all of the other features. There is so much more that you can take advantage of within this module, so don't think that this is all that's available.

Have fun tracking your projects.

Want More Tips & Tricks For Dynamics AX?

The Tips & Tricks series is a compilation of all the cool things that I have found that you can do within Dynamics AX, and are also the basis for my Tips & Tricks presentations that I have been giving for the AXUG, and online. Unfortunately book page size restrictions mean that I can only fit 50 tips & tricks per book, but I will create new volumes every time I reach the 50 Tip mark.

To get all of the details on this series, then here is the link:

http://dynamicsaxcompanions.com/tipsandtricks

Need More Help With Dynamics AX?

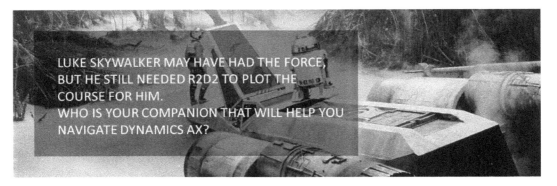

LUKE SKYWALKER MAY HAVE HAD THE FORCE,
BUT HE STILL NEEDED R2D2 TO PLOT THE
COURSE FOR HIM.
WHO IS YOUR COMPANION THAT WILL HELP YOU
NAVIGATE DYNAMICS AX?

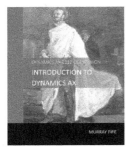

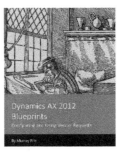

After creating a number of my walkthroughs on SlideShare showing how to configure the different areas within Dynamics AX, I had a lot of requests for the original documents so that people could get a better view of many of the screen shots and also have a easy reference as they worked through the same process within their own systems. To make them easier to access, I am in the process of moving all of the content to the Dynamics AX Companions website to easier access. If you are looking for details on how to configure and use Dynamics AX, then this is a great place for you to start.

Here is the link for the site:

http://dynamicsaxcompanions.com/

About Me

I am an author - I'm no Dan Brown but my books do contain a lot of secret codes and symbols that help guide you through the mysteries of Dynamics AX.

I am a curator - gathering all of the information that I can about Dynamics AX and filing it away within the Dynamics AX Companions archives.

I am a pitchman - I am forever extolling the virtues of Dynamics AX to the unwashed masses convincing them that it is the best ERP system in the world.

I am a Microsoft MVP - this is a big deal, there are less than 10 Dynamics AX MVP's in the US, and less than 30 worldwide.

I am a programmer - I know enough to get around within code, although I leave the hard stuff to the experts so save you all from my uncommented style.

WEB	**www.**murrayfife.me
EMAIL	murray@dynamicsaxcompanions.com
TWITTER	@murrayfife
SKYPE	murrayfife
AMAZON	www.amazon.com/author/murrayfife
WEB	www.dynamicsaxcompanions.com